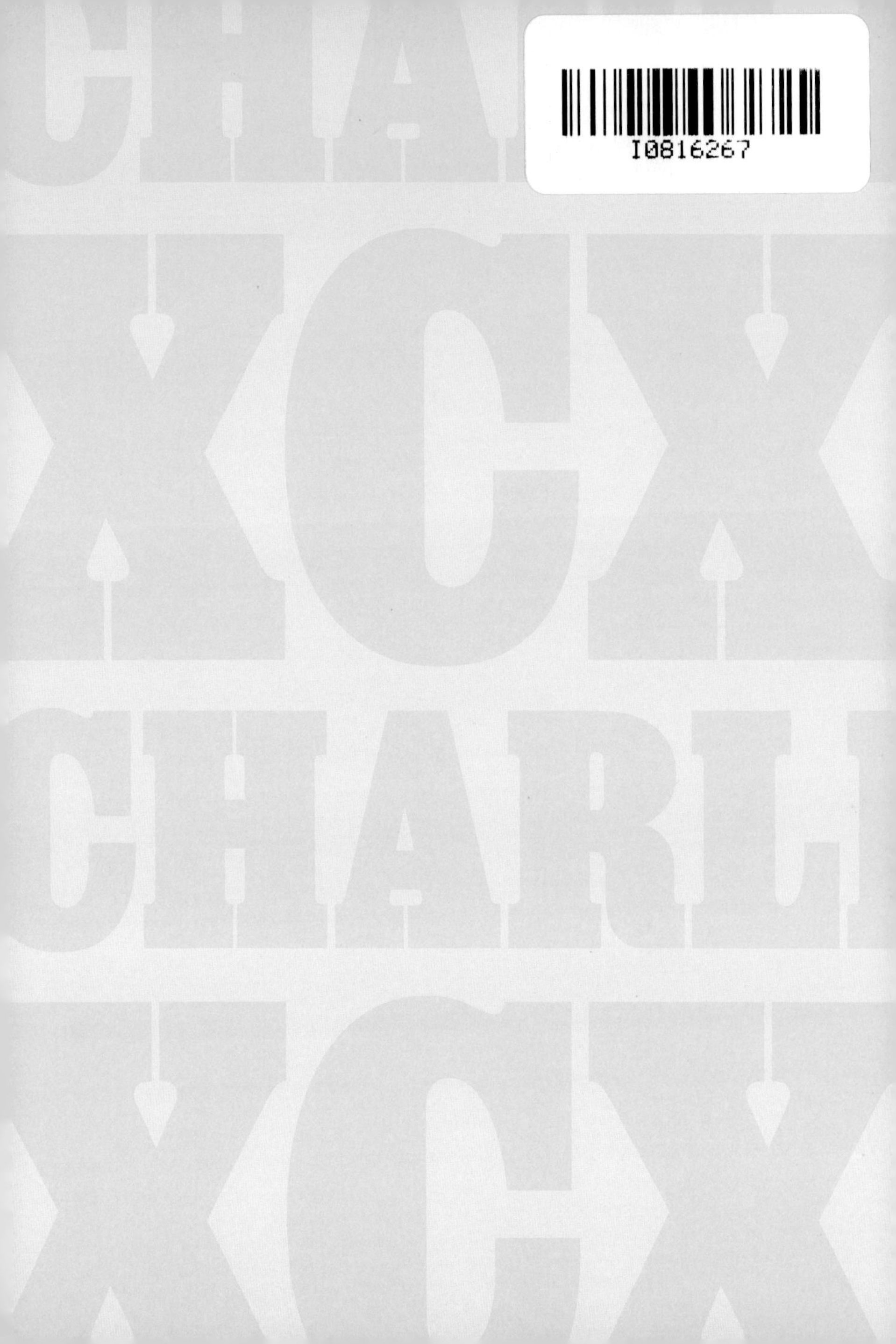
I0816267

THE LIFE, STYLE AND MUSIC OF

CHARLI XCX

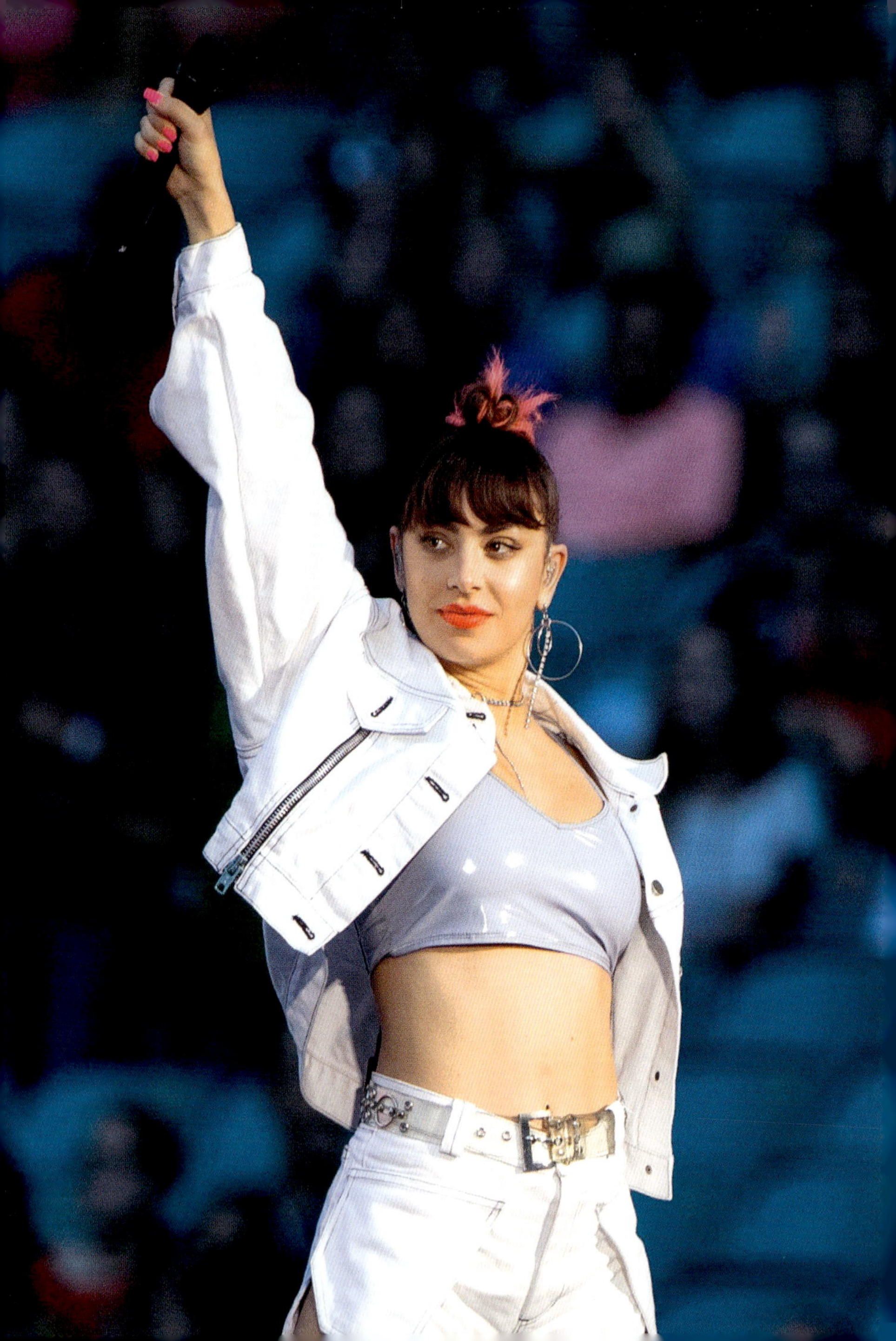

THE LIFE, STYLE AND MUSIC OF

CHARLI XCX

UNOFFICIAL AND UNAUTHORIZED

BY CHARLOTTE GUNN

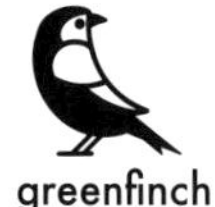

CONTENTS

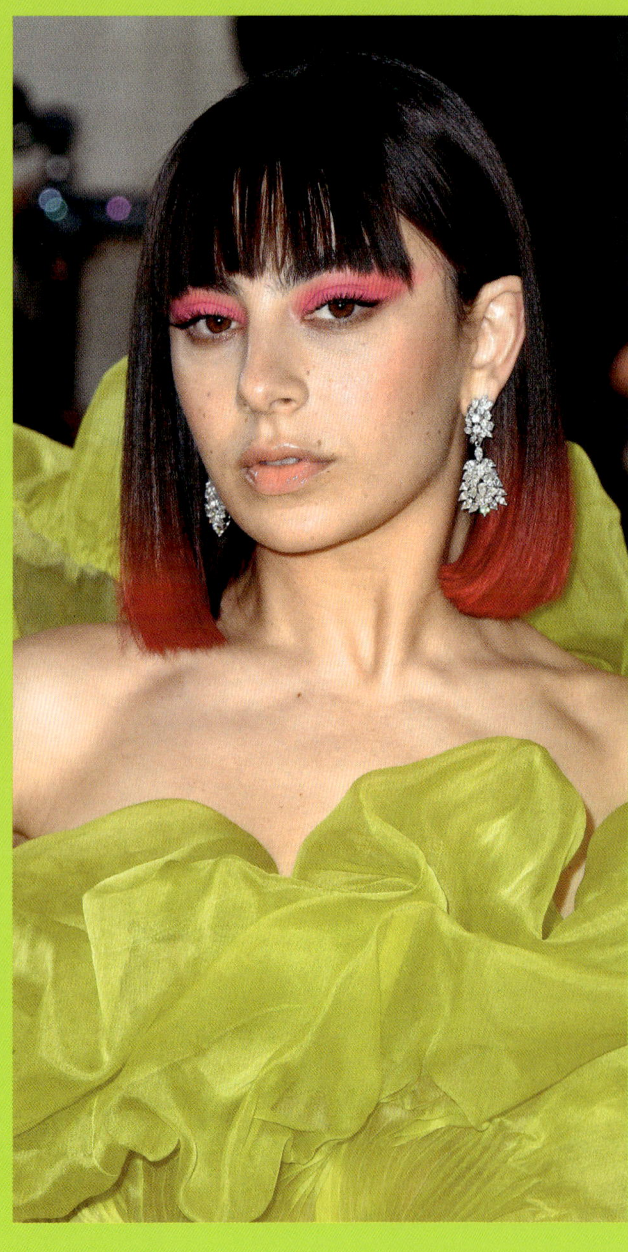

THE RISE *of* CHARLI XCX

An Introduction

Pop music has always thrived on innovation. From Madonna to Lady Gaga, Prince to David Bowie, the most celebrated artists don't just follow trends, they define them. Charli XCX is one of those special few. A shape-shifting talent able to knock out a number 1 before her morning cig, but happiest in an underground rave, bumpin' the best beats of your life.

For Charli, the road to pop superstardom has been a wiggly one. From bloghouse teen to 365 party girl, pop-punk troublemaker to hyperpop trailblazer, she's never stopped experimenting, darting between the mainstream and the underground like they're rooms at a party.

Her legacy is undebated. From the massive pop hits she's penned for Icona Pop and Camila Cabello to the pioneering avant-pop she forged with SOPHIE and A.G. Cook, she has constantly evolved.

Her live shows are euphoric, transcendiary experiences; her music videos, high-art provocations. In 2024 she turned an album title into Collins Dictionary's Word of the Year and single-handedly sent sales of strappy white tops stratospheric.

But Charli's story is about more than just the music. It's a tale about authenticity and standing up for yourself. It's about perseverance and dreaming big. And it's a story about friendship – and how life-affirming it feels when you finally find your people.

So, whether you're reading this book as a day-one Angel or a recent inductee into the church of Charli, buckle up, because you're about to embark on a wild ride with a woman who, at every turn, has torn up the rulebook, redefined the face of pop and proved that real artists don't just play the game – they *unlock* it.

p.2: Performing on Taylor Swift's Reputation tour, Miami, August 2018
p.4: Attending the Met Gala 'Celebrating Camp: Notes on Fashion', New York, May 2019
Overleaf: Performing at the 67th Annual Grammy Awards, Los Angeles, February 2025

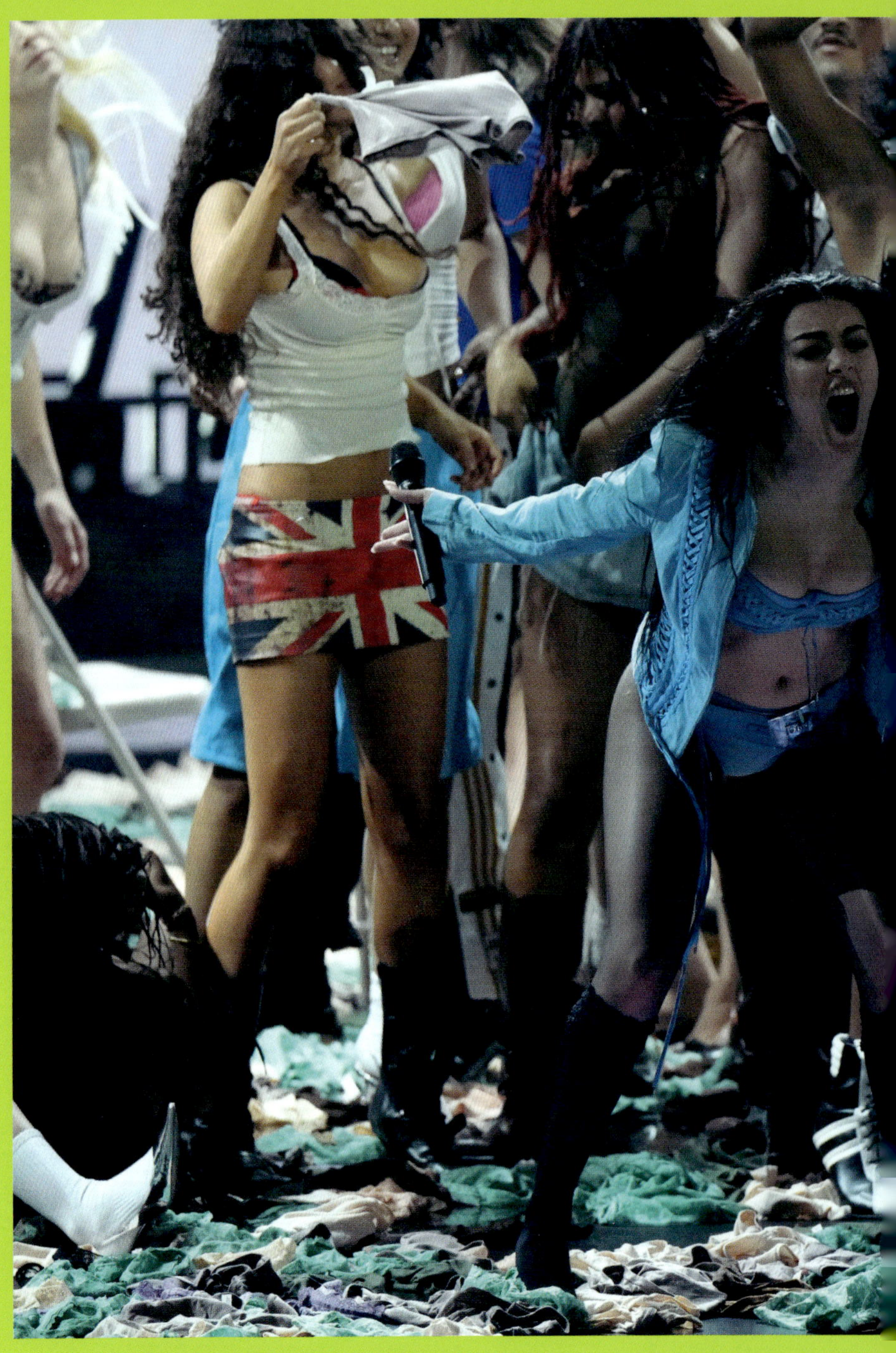

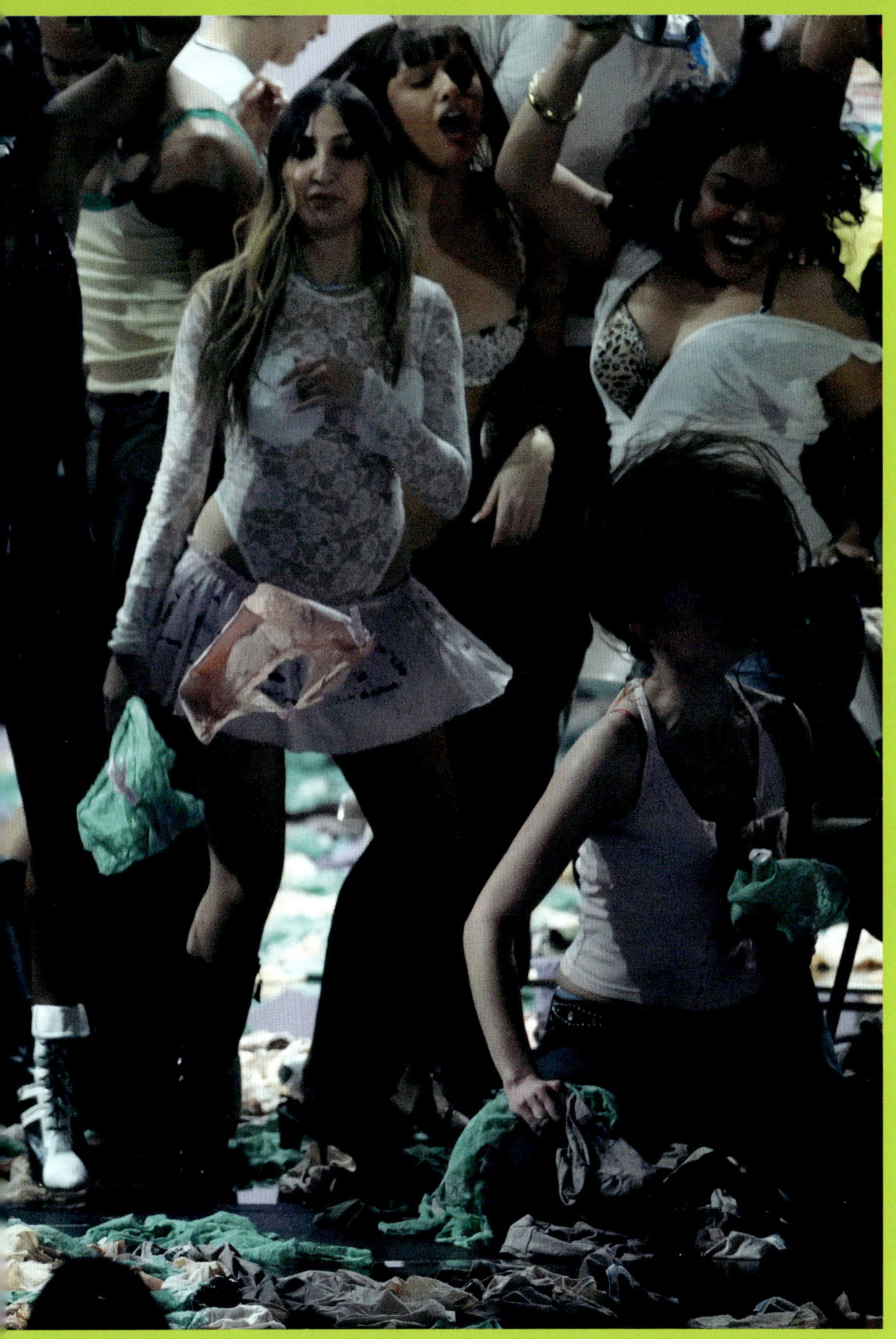

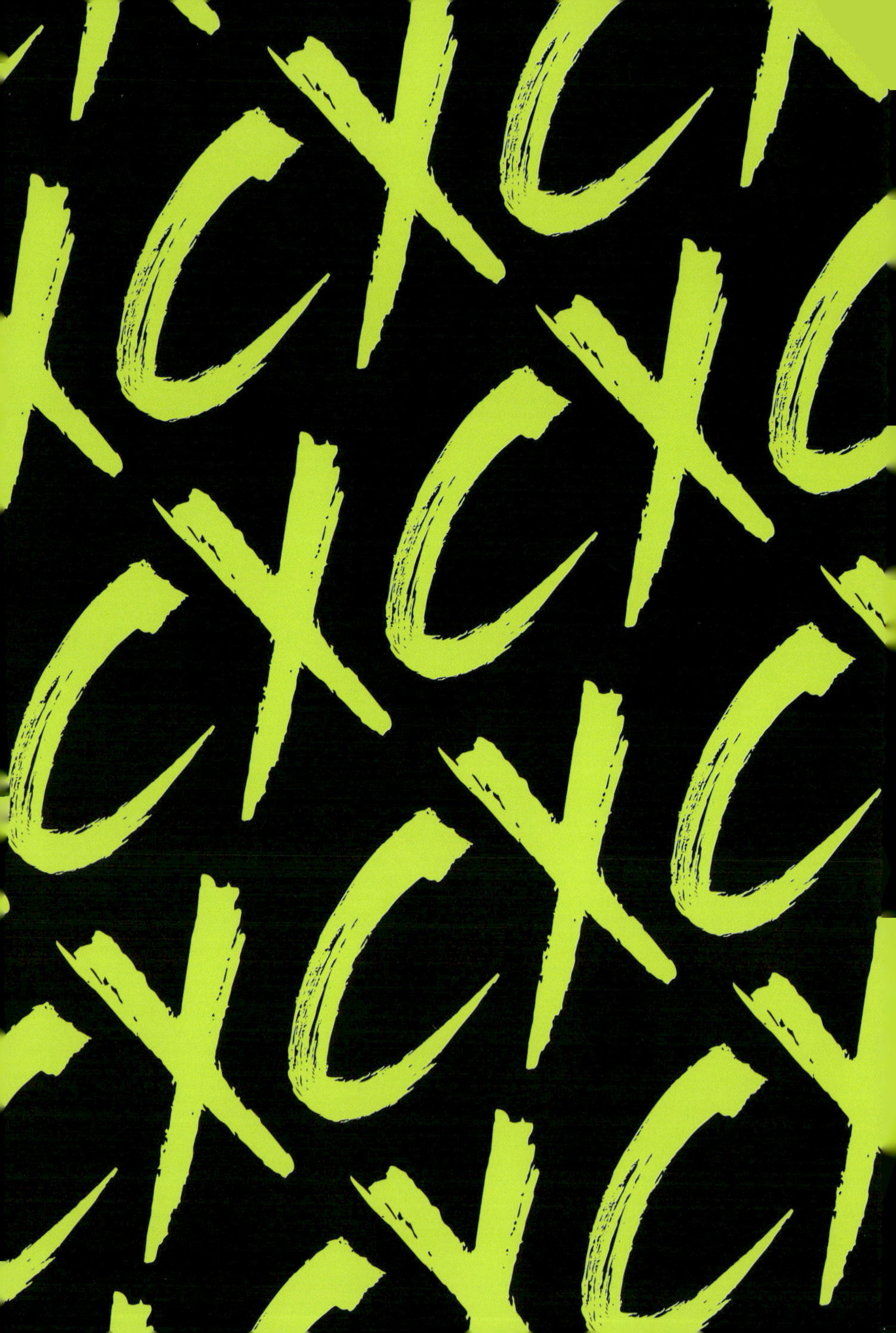

A YOUNG GIRL *from* ESSEX

The Early Years

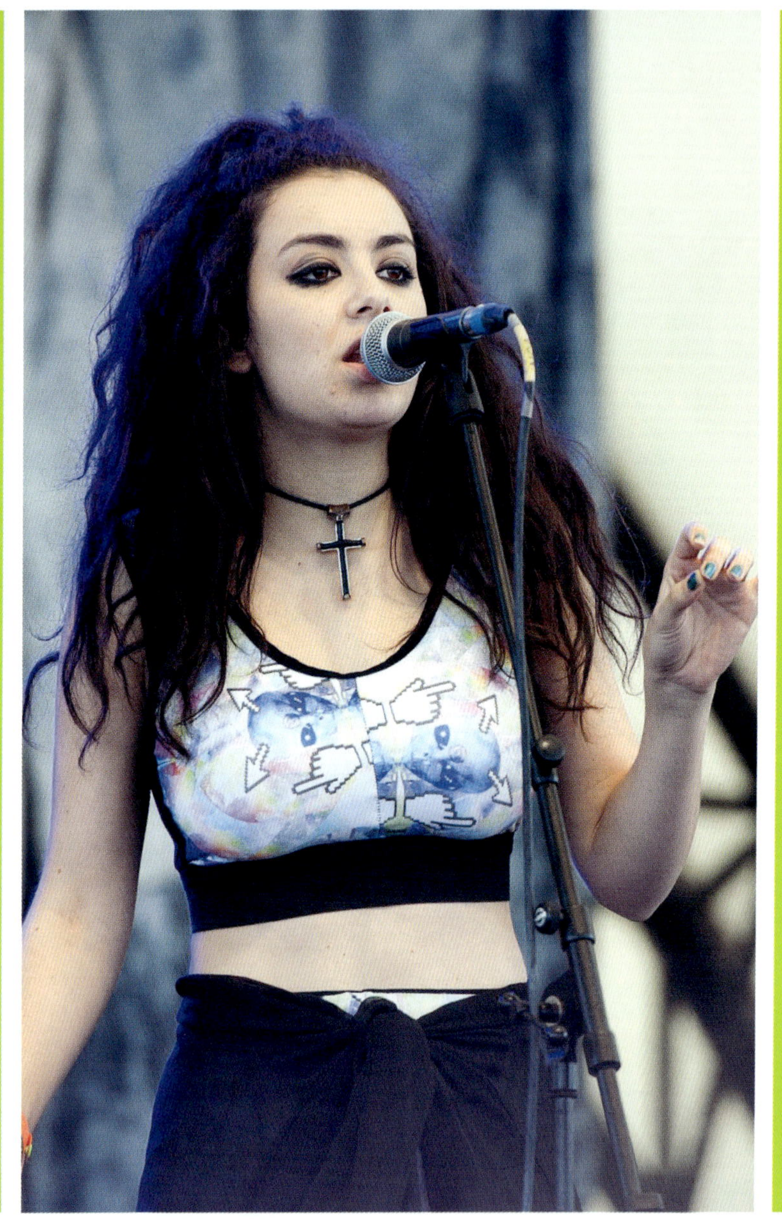

'I was this half-Indian girl with frizzy hair and different interests.'

On 2 August 1992, in a hospital in Cambridge, as Snap!'s 'Rhythm Is a Dancer' topped the charts and the Conservative Party were gearing up to secure their fourth-term general election victory, Charlotte Emma Aitchison was born.

The first and only child of a Scottish father and Gujarati mother, this tiny, dark-haired newborn would one day grow up to know pop superstardom, bridging the gap between the underground and the mainstream and soaring to global chart-topping fame.

Charli's mother, Shameera, wasn't exactly the partying type. She was raised in Uganda in a Muslim family, but in the 1970s, as Idi Amin's brutal regime escalated, was forced to flee to Britain. Her family arrived at Stansted Airport, just north of London, in the dead of winter, with no coats and little money.

Fate intervened one New Year's Eve, when Shameera met Jon – a Scottish club promoter with a wild streak. He was eccentric, a former punk-booker-turned-disco-club-owner, and that night, dressed as *Saturday Night Fever*-era John Travolta, he was midway through changing a keg when their eyes locked. The rest is history.

BETWEEN TWO WORLDS

You could say that Charli is a perfect blend of both her parents – Shameera's groundedness the counter to her dad's spontaneous energy. Before long, Shameera had given up nursing to become a flight attendant; Jon packed in the clubs and became a businessman. Together, they built a comfortable life for their daughter.

For Shameera, adapting to life in Britain hadn't been easy. As a brown-skinned woman growing up in a predominantly white neighbourhood, she'd tried hard to assimilate. Charli, too, felt the tension of living between two worlds. Weekends were spent with her maternal grandparents, Nana and Bappa, in Crawley, West Sussex, watching Bollywood films. Back home, things felt very different. 'When I would go and visit my mum's

Live on stage at Bestival, Isle of Wight, 2012

family, I felt very Indian. But then I'd go home to this other world which was largely white,' she told *Vogue Singapore* in April 2024. 'It was almost like I would experience the Indian part of my identity only on the weekends. I never quite felt like I fit into either world, which I think commonly happens with mixed-race kids.'

WANNABE

When Charli was young, the family moved to rural Start Hill in Essex, where she spent most of her youth. Her mother raised Charli to be well-balanced and to treat people as she wished to be treated. Jon was the one encouraging her to be bold and express herself.

Charli's pop obsession started early, her first taste of stardom arriving at age five, when she won a talent contest on a family cruise holiday. Her song of choice? Aqua's 'Barbie Girl'. 'My parents really didn't want me to do it because they were worried I'd cry on stage and they'd have to come up and get me,' she recalls. 'But I was OK. I sang the whole thing a cappella with no music. Which must have been pretty awkward.'

Like most little girls growing up in the '90s, Charli was obsessed with the Spice Girls. Charli would prance around the house, pretending to be Baby Spice (though she was often made to be Scary, on account of her thick, curly hair). When *Spice World: The Movie* was released in 1997, she begged her parents for it on VHS and watched it on repeat for three years straight. Her favourite scene involved an alien touching Geri Halliwell's boob.

Even as a kid, there was something about the band's rebellious pop and fearless fashion that resonated with Charli, and the Spice Girls would continue to be an influence throughout her career, with Charli even reworking 'Wannabe' with Diplo and Herve Pagez in 2019 to create new track 'Spicy'.

The Spice Girls at the Cannes Film Festival, 1997

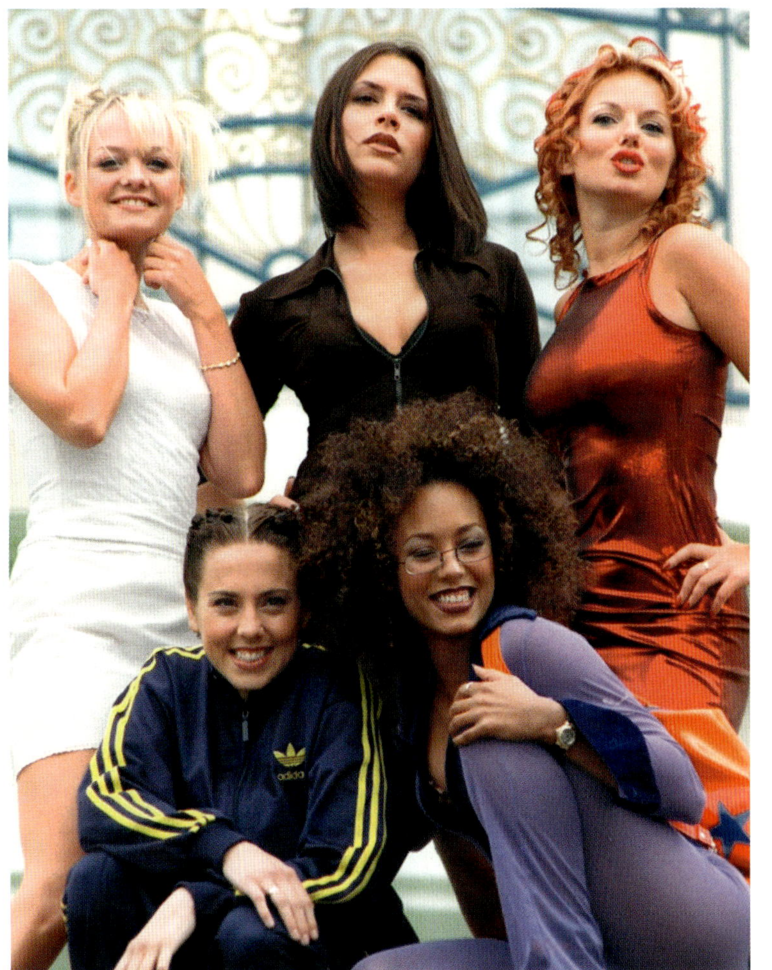

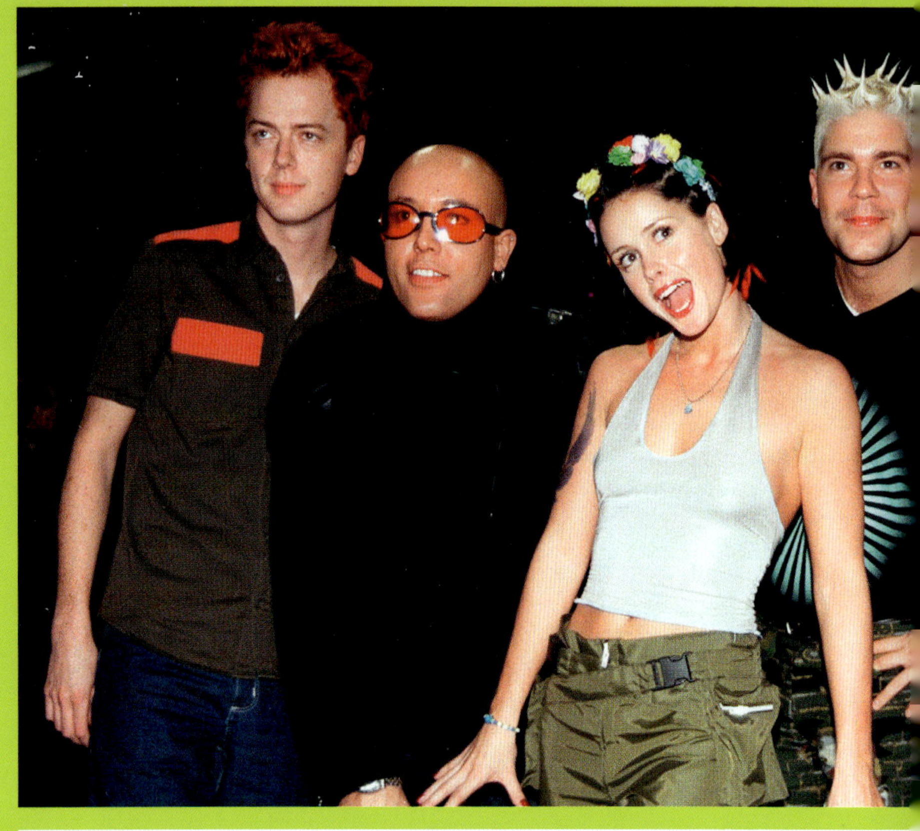

*Seeing **Britney**, in her school uniform, dancing through the corridors was the first time **Charli** knew: she wanted to be a **pop star**.*

Clockwise from top left: Danish pop group Aqua, November 1997; UK pop group Five, 1998; Britney Spears, 2004

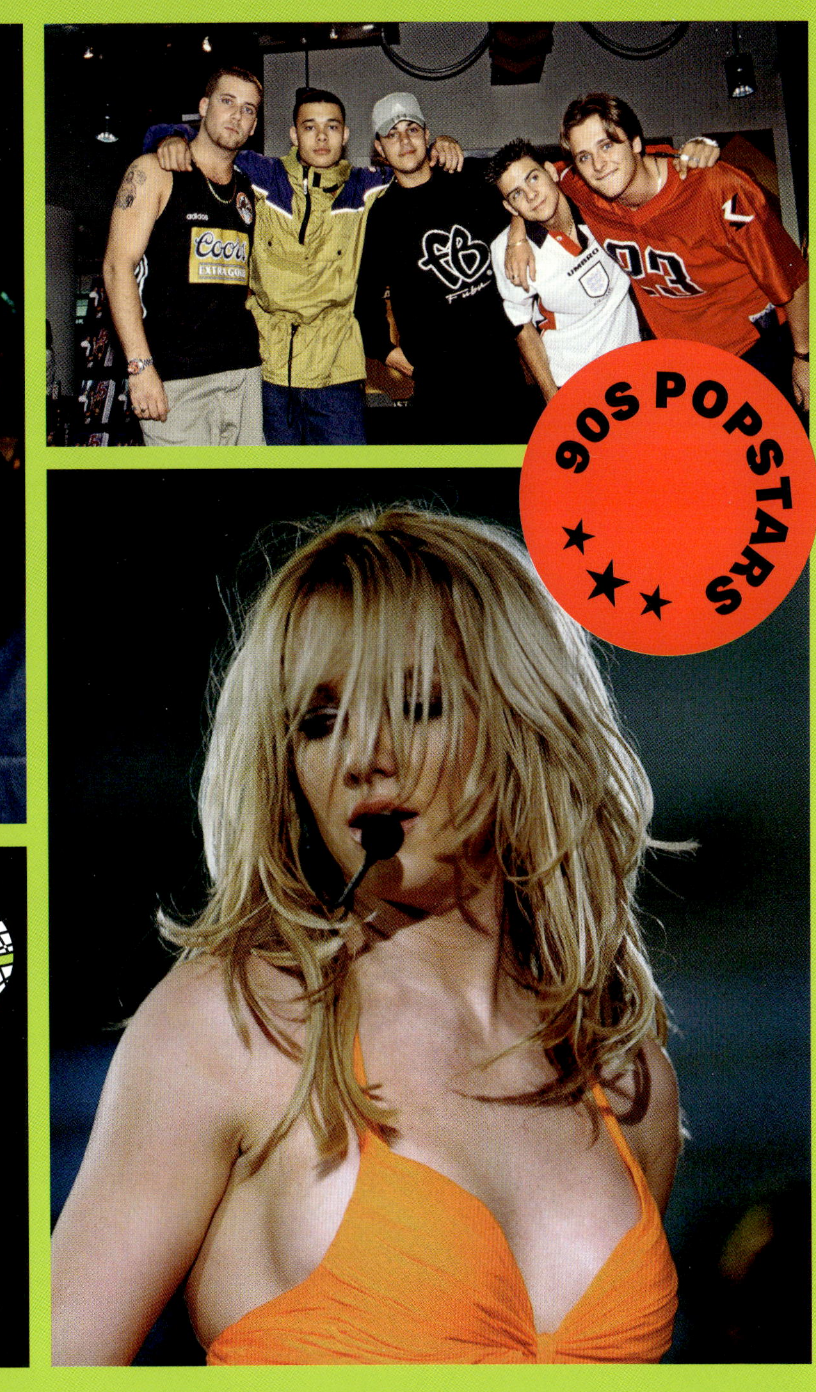

90S POPSTARS

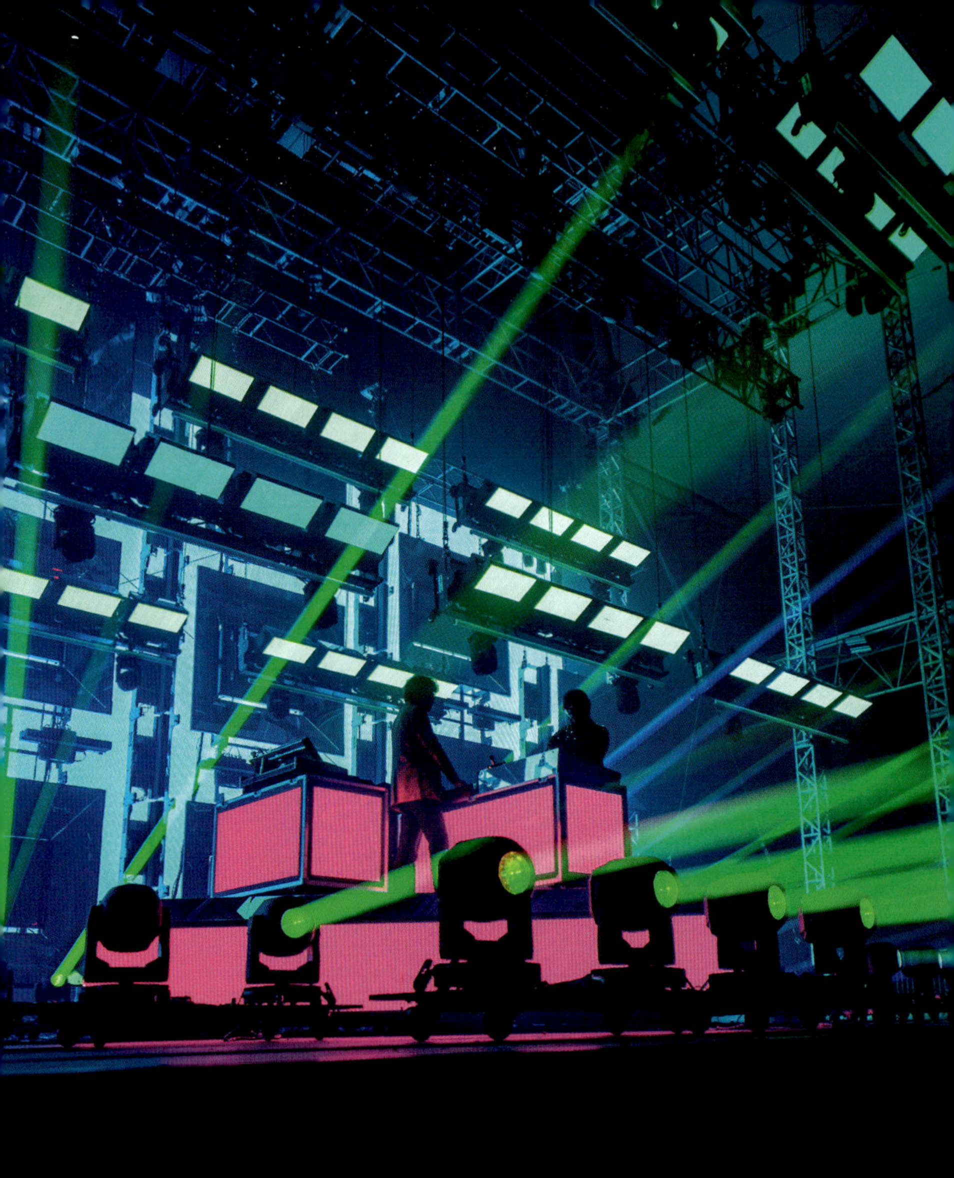

By the late '90s and early '00s, the charts were dominated by sugary pop acts like Five, Aqua and Britney Spears – and the rise of European electro. Taking her pocket money to high-street record store HMV, Charli bought her first CD single: The Tamperer ft. Maya's 'Feel It', with the love-it-or-loathe-it chorus ('What's she gonna look like with a chimney on her?'). The same year, a young girl with big pop ambitions released her debut single, 'Baby One More Time', and young Charli was captivated. Seeing Britney in her school uniform dancing through the corridors was the first time Charli knew: she wanted to be a pop star.

Still, a life in music would have to wait. Her parents believed in the importance of good grades and working hard. And Charli toed the line, describing herself as 'geeky' and 'kind of a nerd' at school.

A FEAR OF BEING BORING

On her first day of high school, something happened that changed the course of the next 20 years. Watching a girl getting pushed into a bush, Charli jumped in – not to offer a helping hand but to point and yell 'TWIGGY', as the dishevelled student emerged with bits of foliage sticking out of her blonde hair. Somewhat surprisingly, the pair would go on to become best friends, 'Twiggy' being Twiggy Rowley, one half of Charli's management team to this day.

Throughout high school, Charli, Twiggy and Sam Pringle – another of Charli's long-serving managers – were a firm unit; not exactly the cool kids, but not unpopular either. 'I always felt like a loser,' she told British *GQ* in 2024. 'My school was full of blonde white girls and I was this half-Indian girl with frizzy hair and different interests. That always made me feel a little bit rejected. I thought if I made music, people would think I was interesting ... Deep down, one of my biggest fears was being boring.'

In her early teens, Charli discovered Ed Banger Records, the French electro label home to the likes of Justice, Cassius and Uffie. 'Whenever I would listen to their music, I felt like I was in a movie, and it made me feel alive,' she revealed in 2020. 'Even still, to this day, apart from SOPHIE and A.G. [Cook], [there's] not a lot of music makes me feel truly alive like that French electro stuff did.'

Finding music awoke a new side to Charli, as she developed interests outside of her friends and schoolwork for the first time – music made her feel like she was in her own secret world.

Justice perform at Alexandra Palace, London, February 2025

At age 14, Charli was taken by her dad to see the Sex Pistols reunion show. Watching a bunch of old men thrash about the stage, Charli was less than impressed. But something about their punk spirit must have seeped in, the genre's DIY sensibility and attitude of rebellion laying the foundations for Charli's creative path.

All those hours singing Spice Girls songs had paid off – Charli earned her Grade 8 in singing and started to take an interest in making her own music. Inspired by Uffie and her Ed Banger labelmates, and armed with a guitar, a Yamaha keyboard and a loan from her parents, she set out to make an album. In need of a stage name, she settled on Charli XCX, her MSN screen name at the time (the 'XCX' standing for kiss Charli kiss).

THE MYSPACE DEBUT

Charli's early songs were mostly about her mates: floppy-haired boys, irritating girls and teenage ne'er-do-wells. In 2007, indie sleaze was rife, nu-rave was on the up and UK artists like The Streets, Kate Nash and The Kooks were selling out venues with their straight-talking, diaristic approach to songwriting.

Charli's debut album *14* – the title referencing her age at the time – drew from the same reference pool: overlaying no-filter outpourings from her teenage brain with acoustic guitar and piano. She sang and played every instrument, roping in the help of producer Dan Bazzini to finesse the album before self-releasing it on ORGY Music, her own DIY label. It was only the album opener, '!Francheskaaar!', that showed hints of the electro-pop sound she would go on to adopt.

Seeing the likes of Lily Allen and Arctic Monkeys blow up after uploading songs on a then-nascent social media platform called MySpace, Charli wanted in. In 2007, aged 15, she made her first account, listing her influences as Uffie, M.I.A., Larrikin Love, Test Icicles, Lady Sovereign and 'of course ... The Spice Girls'. MySpace was a game-changer for Charli: a place to express herself creatively, vlog and share her music publicly for the first time.

'!Francheskaaar!' became an early single. 'It's about typical posh girls from Cambridge who slouch about in their Jack Wills with all their clingy friends just being generally boring,' she wrote on the platform. 'I hate people like that, with no life in them! Everyone seems to think it's a big jealous rant about some girl I went to school with, but that's not really the angle I take on "!Francheskaaar!". It's more about this girl who has it all and just doesn't know what to do with it, so instead carries on with her typical posh girl status.'

More singles came in 2008, more closely aligned to '!Francheskaar!'s electro sound. 'Art Bitch' and 'Emelline' had propulsive beats, made for the raves that Charli was still too young to play.

Before long, her music caught the attention of Chas Cool, an east London promoter who, with her parents' consent, introduced her to a world of underground parties. Her first rave was at the Peanut Factory in Hackney when she'd just turned 16. 'My parents refused to let me go alone,' Charli recalled. 'I played at 3am. It felt like *Skins*, that was my only reference because I was so young and living in the countryside.'

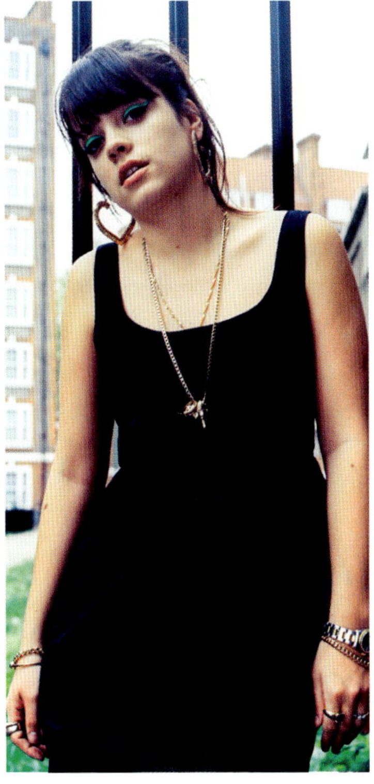

Lily Allen in London, 2016

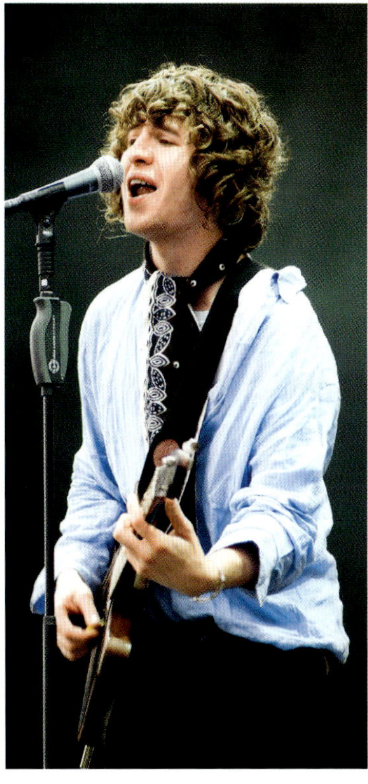

Luke Pritchard, lead singer of The Kooks, at T in the Park, 2008

THE RAVE YEARS

Charli was captivated by the whole scene – the music, the lifestyle, the fashion – and started to book more and more shows. Armed with her trusty iPod, she began to make a name for herself on the warehouse scene, becoming the teen queen of parties that involved bubbles, glitter and head-to-toe neon. 'I like to really involve myself with the audience and jump around and get off the stage and roll around,' she told *Dazed* at the time. 'I like to be like a big firework – I just want to erupt!'

Playing raves at night and still turning up for college classes to get her A-levels – a deal struck with her parents – Charli was living an oddly double life, becoming a fixture on the 'bloghouse' fashion and music scene that was bubbling up. But her plan was working – she was inching closer towards a career in music, and eventually got spotted by Atlantic Records A&R Ed Howard. At 16, she chose to sign with Asylum Records, part of Atlantic, largely because of her connection with Howard and his wife, Miranda Cooper, one of the songwriting forces behind UK girl bands Girls Aloud and Sugababes.

*'I didn't know what I **sounded** like yet.'*

But despite her admiration for their work, she struggled with being pulled into the traditional pop system. 'When you're 16 and you sign and you go through rounds with producers, that kind of factory way where you go in and you meet someone and you do a song and you leave – you don't really know who you are,' she told *The Fader* in 2016. 'Even though I think I wrote some really fucking good songs in that time, it sounded like everybody else. I didn't know what I sounded like yet.'

Still, Charli started playing the game, doing press and promoting herself as an artist. By chance, her first-ever photoshoot was with Rankin. But a detour on her musical journey came via a stint at top-tier London fine art school the Slade School of Fine Art (where she once staged a performance piece involving a bikini stuffed with hamburgers). But art school wasn't a fit: 'I left because I'm not good at analyzing things,' she admitted. 'I wasn't good at talking about my work and explaining it.' Dropping out allowed her the time to focus on the ultimate goal: becoming the pop star she always wanted to be.

Supporting Peaches at the Royal Festival Hall, London, April 2009

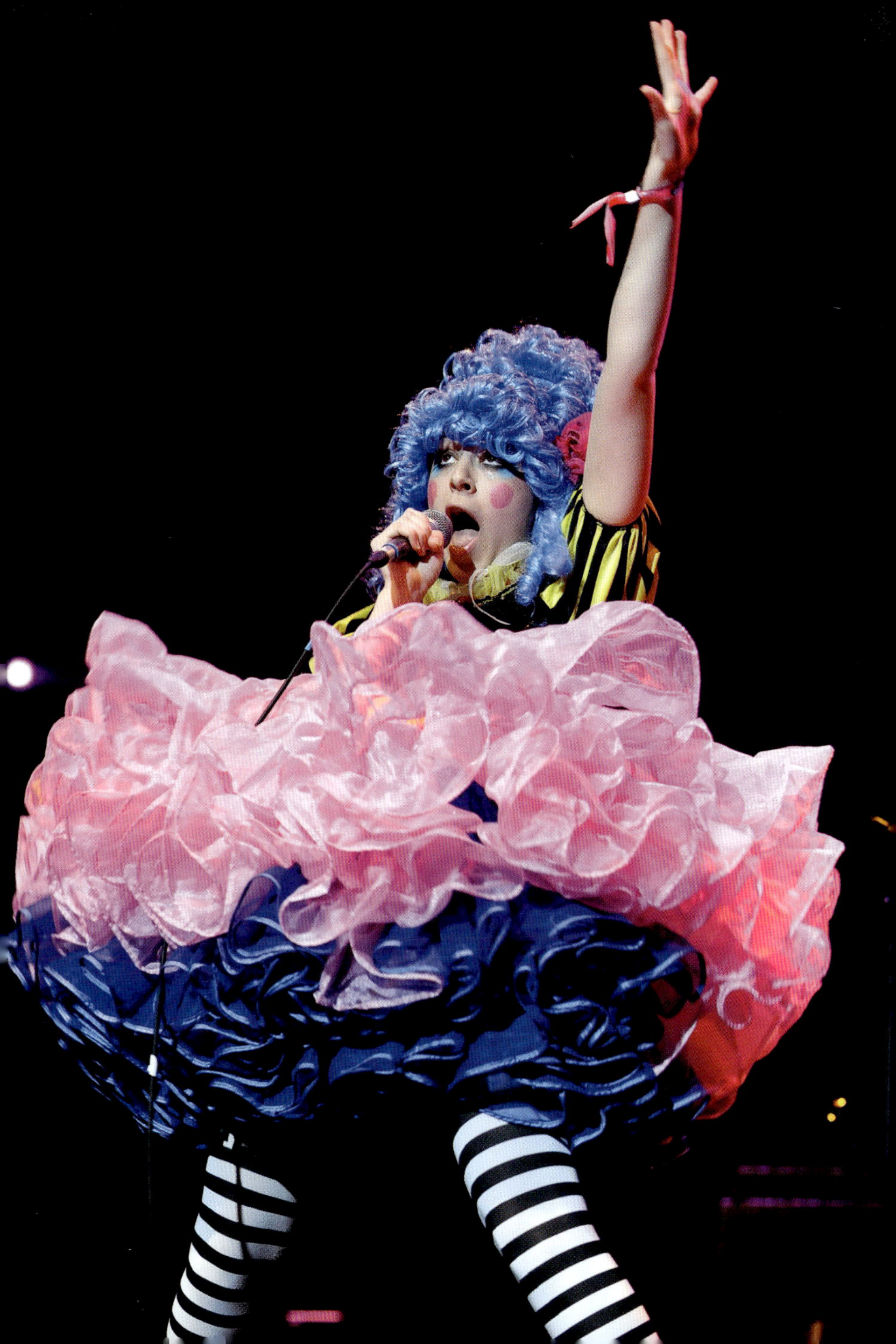

In June 2012, aged 20, Charli XCX released her first mixtape, *Heartbreaks and Earthquakes*, which was available on YouTube and Soundcloud for free. The eight tracks featured remixes and samples of tracks by Jai Paul, Blood Orange (also known as Dev Hynes), Rudimental and Drake, and were themed around some of Charli's favourite movies: a very '00s list that included *Beyond the Black Rainbow* (2010), *The Craft* (1996), *Kill Bill* (2003), *Cruel Intentions* (1999) and *American Beauty* (1999). The standout track was 'Spoons', for its house-ier sound.

The same month, Charli joined buzzy microblogging platform Tumblr and discovered a new way to share visual references and connect with her fans online. Posting glitchy photos of herself, and gifs of her favourite movies, her internet-based world-building continued. This was savvy; Charli recognized the benefit of building an online fandom long before follower counts were a barometer of success.

SUPER ULTRA

The mixtape made enough noise that when Frank Ocean dropped out of Coldplay's *Mylo Xyloto* tour, Charli was booked as the replacement. The buzz around her live show had been building, with Charli earning frequent write-ups in the music blogs due to her energetic on-stage antics and penchant for keeping things weird (Echo & The Bunnymen covers? Enya's 'Orinoco Flow' as walk-on music?) But despite easily packing out the back rooms of London pubs and warehouse raves, the Coldplay tour would be a stratospheric jump, giving Charli her first taste of performing to stadium-sized crowds and a glimpse of superstardom.

Written on the road, while on tour with Coldplay, Charli's next release was *Super Ultra*, another mixtape that took all the internet references she was consuming and spat them out across eight tracks. 'I feel like the mixtapes are really when I found myself as an artist,' she explained to the *Guardian* in 2013. 'They're sort of like a collage of myself.'

Dropped in late 2012, with little fanfare but maximum intent, it was the sound of a pop outsider fully immersing herself in the digital underground. A neon-drenched fever dream of vaporous synths, skittering beats and reverberating heartbreak, *Super Ultra* captured Charli in flux – still enamoured with the gauzy haze of Tumblr-era electro-pop, yet already flirting with a more commercial future. *Consequence* called it 'a candy-coated hit of molly, a pupil-dilating emotional explosion'. It was shadowy and self-assured, melding sultry R&B with pop. There was some

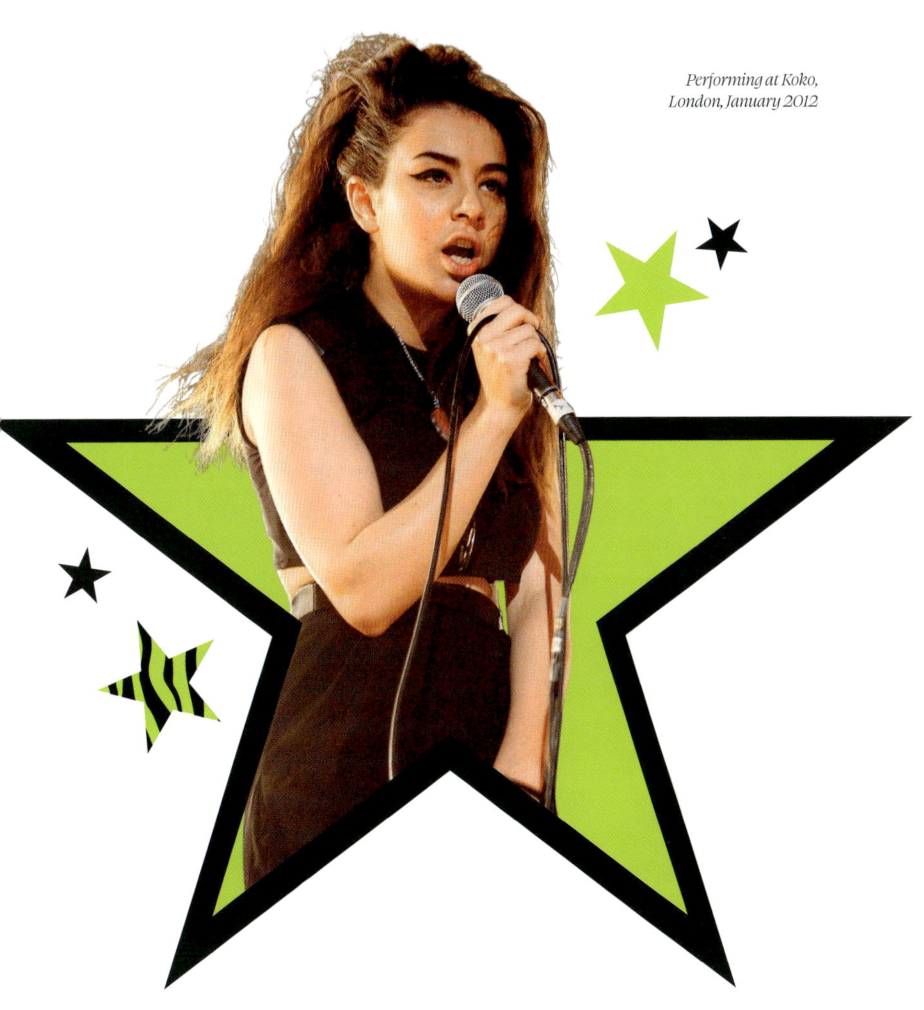

Performing at Koko, London, January 2012

head-scratching at the choice to feature Brooke Candy – a then-obscure rapper better known for her Tumblr notoriety and a cameo in Grimes's 'Genesis' video than for any chart impact. But Charli was already ahead of the curve, attuned to the disruptive power of internet fame before the industry had fully caught on.

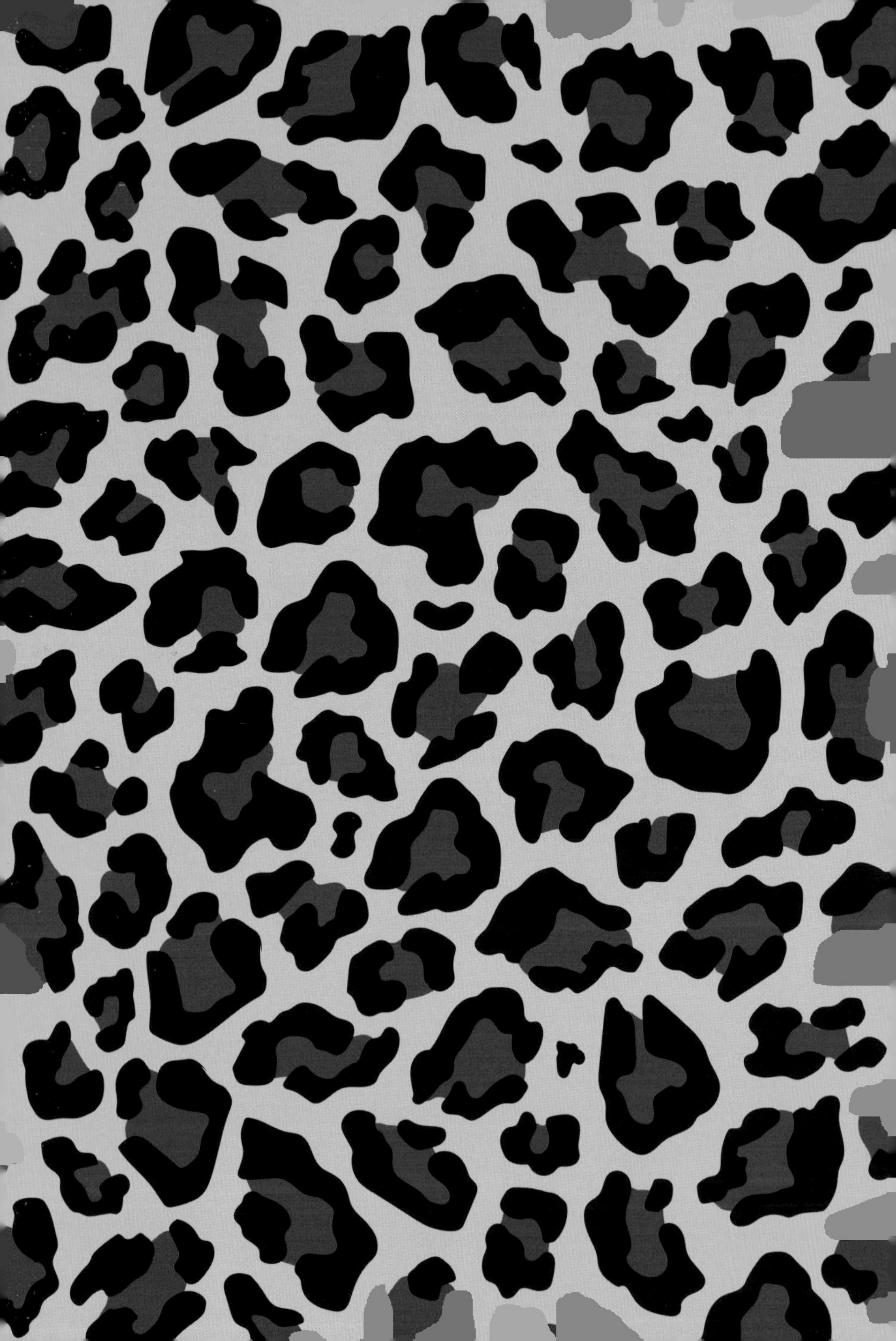

The POP DEBUT

Hits and Heartbreak

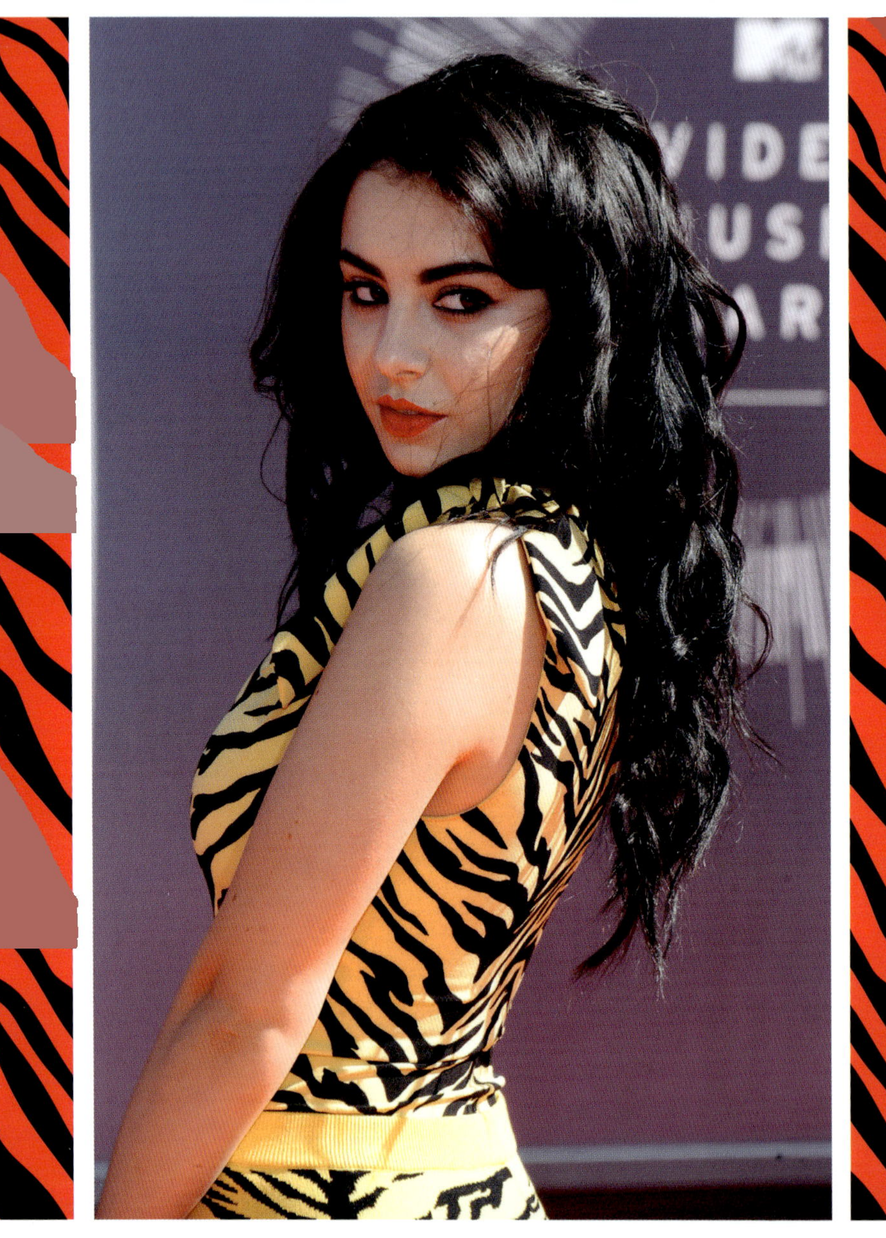

It's 2012 and Charli XCX is a pop outlier with big ambitions. She's already an artist of dualities: the Tumblr-adored goth-pop icon with an instinct for crafting stadium-sized hooks. *Super Ultra* had helped her carve out a niche, but it was a niche nonetheless.

By the tail-end of 2012, Charli was knee-deep in crafting her debut album proper – a process that was worlds apart from the scrappy DIY releases of her teens – but nailing down a definitive sound was proving tricky. She ricocheted between rap, pop and electro, unsure where she truly belonged. Her label, sensing the creative tug-of-war, flew her between LA and Europe, pairing her with a carousel of producers in search of the right fit. It wasn't until she linked up with Ariel Rechtshaid – already a go-to name for work with Sky Ferreira, Haim and Solange Knowles – that things finally clicked. 'We only had two hours together and in that time we wrote "Stay Away",' she recalled. 'I was freaking out: I had found a piece of myself in this crazy world where people are trying to drag you apart and make you into something. That's when things started to come together.'

But it was in Sweden, during a 30-minute writing session with producer Patrik Berger, that something happened that would supercharge Charli's career. The pair wrote 'I Love It', a brash, explosive anthem that Charli initially deemed too abrasive for her own project. She gave the track to the Swedish duo Icona Pop, and the song became an international sensation in 2013, hitting number 7 on the Billboard Hot 100 and landing Charli in rooms she hadn't imagined entering just a year before. Suddenly the world was asking, who is the 20-year-old behind this mammoth hit? Surely not the day-glo rave princess they saw tumbling out of clubs with Marina Diamandis and Rita Ora?

'When "I Love It" happened, people were like, "Did you ...?" and I was like, "Yeah, I fucking wrote it, why are you so shocked? Oh, it's because I've got a vagina?",' she snapped sassily at the time, already becoming attuned to the industry's gender bias.

Attending the MTV Video Music Awards, Los Angeles, California, August 2014

Despite the song's success, Charli wasn't sure how to navigate the reaction. She didn't want to be a faceless songwriter, she wanted to be Britney Spears. In April 2013, her debut album, *True Romance*, finally arrived. Named after the cult '90s movie starring Christian Slater and Patricia Arquette, it was a fusion of shimmering synth-pop, moody electronica and bratty lyricism, and the sum of her early years as a MySpace-bred pop renegade. The album received critical acclaim: 'emotionally direct, bubblegum-catchy, off-kilter songs,' said *Pitchfork*, while the *Guardian* praised its 'surprisingly oddball' nature.

At its core, *True Romance* was a record about falling in and out of love. Hedonism was the order of the day, with Charli reinforcing her party-starter creds on tracks such as 'Take My Hand'. Smart sampling of Gold Panda on the deliciously bitter 'You (Ha Ha Ha)' showed off her production smarts and wide pool of references.

'I never wanted to be cool, or make a *hipster* record,' she told *Complex* ahead of its release. 'I've wanted to write good pop music, beautiful pop music – not just throwaways. I've always wanted to make it sound luscious and cinematic. I feel like I've done that with this record. The way that I describe it is purple pop music, it's moody, emotional and rich.'

Despite *True Romance* being all of those things and more, commercially it underperformed, selling just 1,100 copies in its first week and failing to chart in the US or at home. Still, Charli saw it as a success in other ways. She'd made an album she felt truly proud of, and if people didn't get it, they just needed time.

AN ICONIC HIT

As 2013 bled into 2014, Charli was restless. The *True Romance* era, while enjoyed by critics, hadn't catapulted her into stardom. But another seismic shift was on the horizon – one that would push her into the mainstream, whether she was ready or not.

The shift was an Iggy Azalea song, 'Fancy', that would define the summer of 2014. Charli's hook – half-bubblegum pop, half-punk snarl – was instantly iconic, and the track spent seven weeks at number 1 on the Billboard Hot 100, helped along by its *Clueless*-referencing video. 'What was different about me and Iggy's collaboration was that there was no expectation,' Charli said of the linkup. 'At that point, people still saw me and Iggy as underdogs.'

Charli XCX, left, and Iggy Azalea perform at the Billboard Music Awards, Las Vegas, May 2014

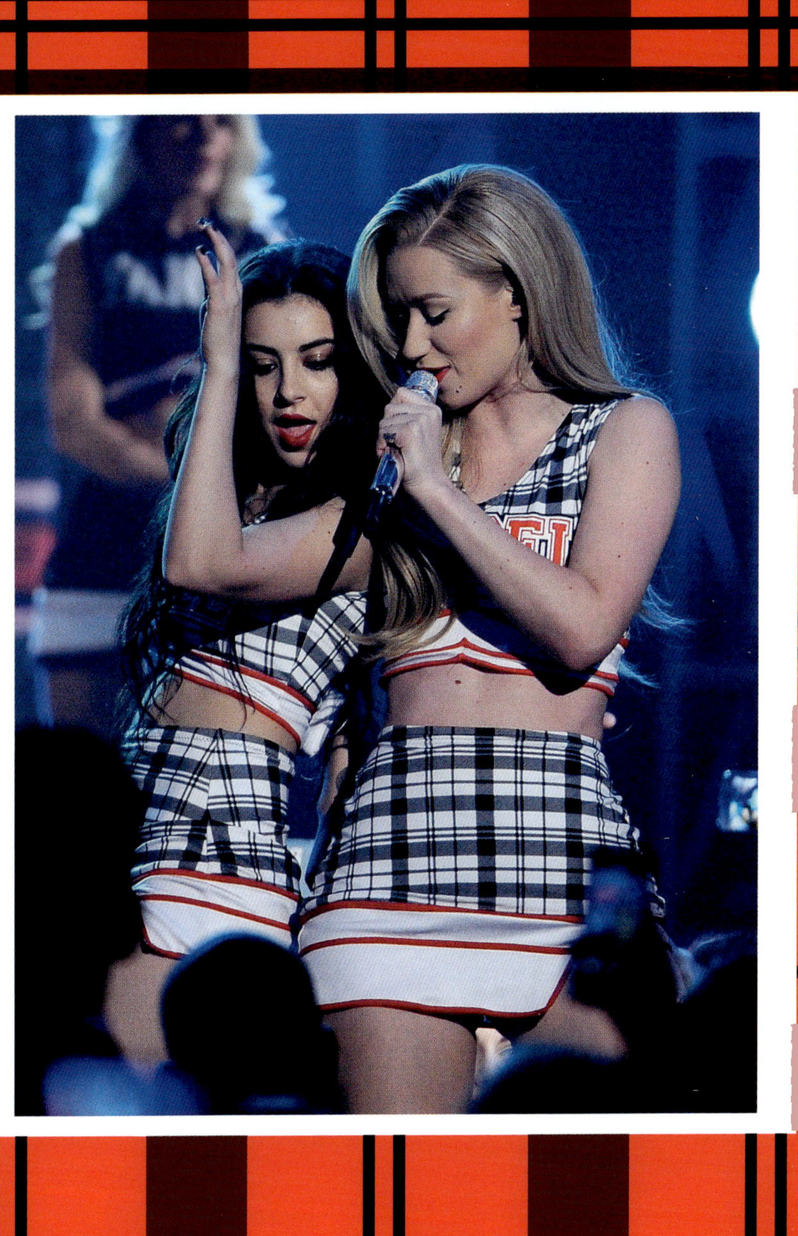

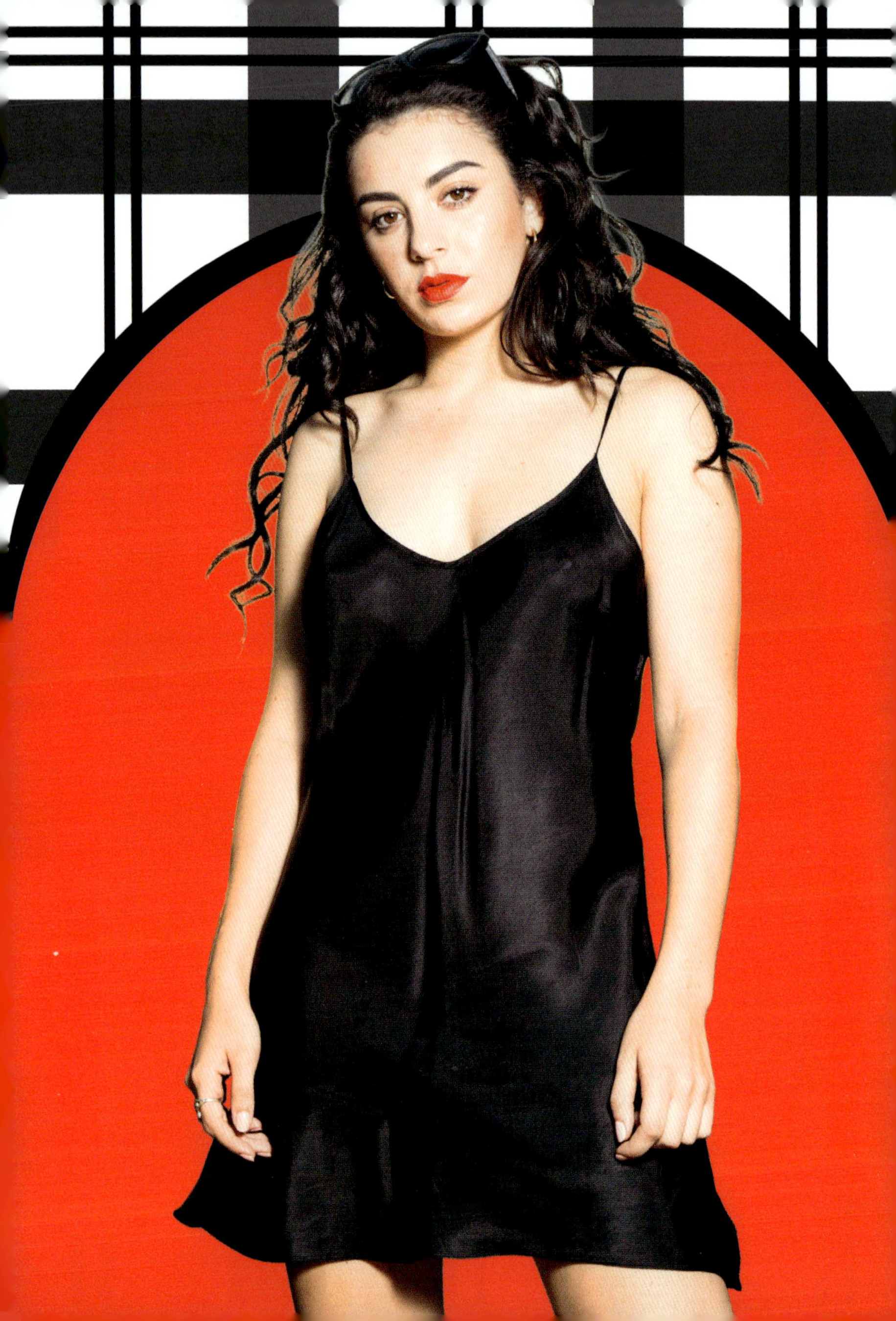

'Neither of us had real big shit popping off, we were just doing our thing. That's why "Fancy" worked so well: It was so genuine.'

'Fancy' was the global breakthrough Charli had been waiting for, but once again she found herself conflicted. Despite Iggy Azalea's insistence that the song was a shared success, Charli didn't want to be seen as a featured act or a songwriter – she wanted the limelight, and success of her own. As 'Fancy' dominated the charts, Charli was already sketching out her next move. The next album wouldn't be an extension of *True Romance*'s dreamy synths, it would be something louder, rawer and more aggressive.

The creative shift towards a ***punkier, Riot Grrl-influenced pop sound*** *had begun as far back as 2013.*

RIOT GIRL

Charli had a track called 'Boom Clap', written with Patrik Berger and his brother Fredrik, which had been kicking around for a while. It would end up on her third album, via a detour onto the soundtrack of the weepy teen romcom *The Fault in Our Stars* (2014). Patrik had wanted to create a track with an onomatopoeic chorus – cue the *booming* and *clapping* – and the track was an undeniable earworm. 'Catchier than the Clap,' said music TV channel 4Music. Initially, Charli, a lifelong *Lizzie McGuire* fan, had hoped to pass the song to Hilary Duff, but her team dismissed it as not quite cool enough. Their loss. Charli kept it for herself, and when 'Boom Clap' dropped in June 2014, it became her biggest solo hit to date, peaking at number 6 in the UK and breaking the Billboard Hot 100's Top 10 at number 8. After years of writing for others and flirting with the charts, this was a victory that was unequivocally hers.

The creative shift towards a punkier, Riot Grrl-influenced pop sound had begun as far back as 2013. Sessions with Rivers Cuomo of Weezer, Rostam Batmanglij of Vampire Weekend and Justin Raisen (Sky Ferreira, Ariel Pink) helped mould the jagged, bratty energy that would go on to define *Sucker*. Charli was embracing a more rebellious persona, drawing from her love of the Ramones, Bow Wow Wow and The Vibrations.

Posing for a portrait in Los Angeles, August 2014

Since 2012, Charli had been in a relationship with Welsh filmmaker Ryan Andrews, the man behind six of her music videos, including the gun-toting, grindhouse-inspired visuals for 'You (Ha Ha Ha)'. But as her career hit turbo mode in the lead-up to *Sucker*, the pair called it quits. 'I'd just had a break-up and I was in this angry, aggressive zone,' she recalls of the period leading up to the record. 'In the past I'd been so worried about pleasing everybody. And then I kind of realized, what's the point? It was the most liberating thing. I'm not afraid to be exactly who I am or say exactly what I want any more.' By 2014, she had crossed paths with Huck Kwong, a former music manager, kicking off an on-again, off-again long-distance relationship that would span the next seven years.

As her career skyrocketed, Charli became a fixture in the fashion and music party circuits of London, New York and Los Angeles. She was frequently spotted at after-parties with the likes of Sky Ferreira, Grimes and FKA twigs – fellow pop outsiders who were redefining the landscape in their own ways. She was focused on the whirlwind lifestyle that came with her rise – late nights in London's underground clubs, impromptu studio sessions in LA and DJ sets at some of the buzziest industry parties. It was around this time she met avant-pop producer SOPHIE, after Kwong played her the SOPHIE track 'Lemonade' on Soundcloud. Charli got in touch and they agreed to try and write together (more on that later).

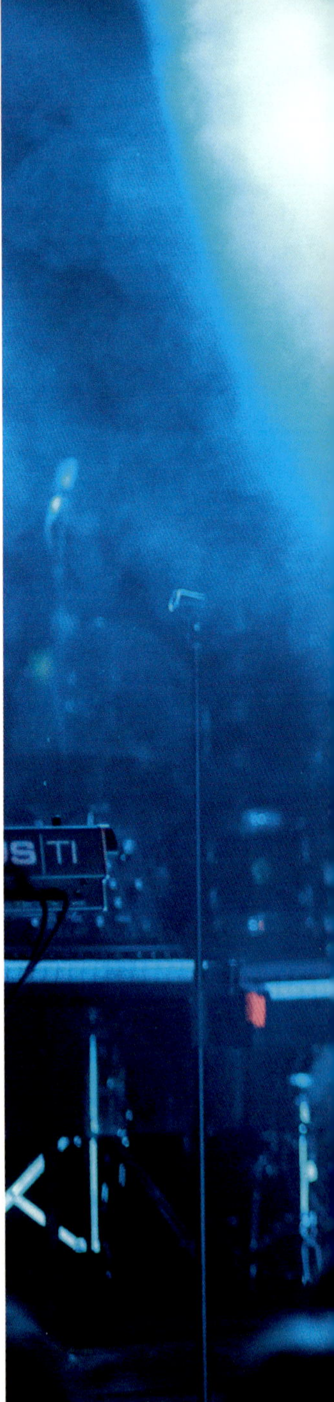

Performing live at Tavastia Club, Helsinki, April 2013

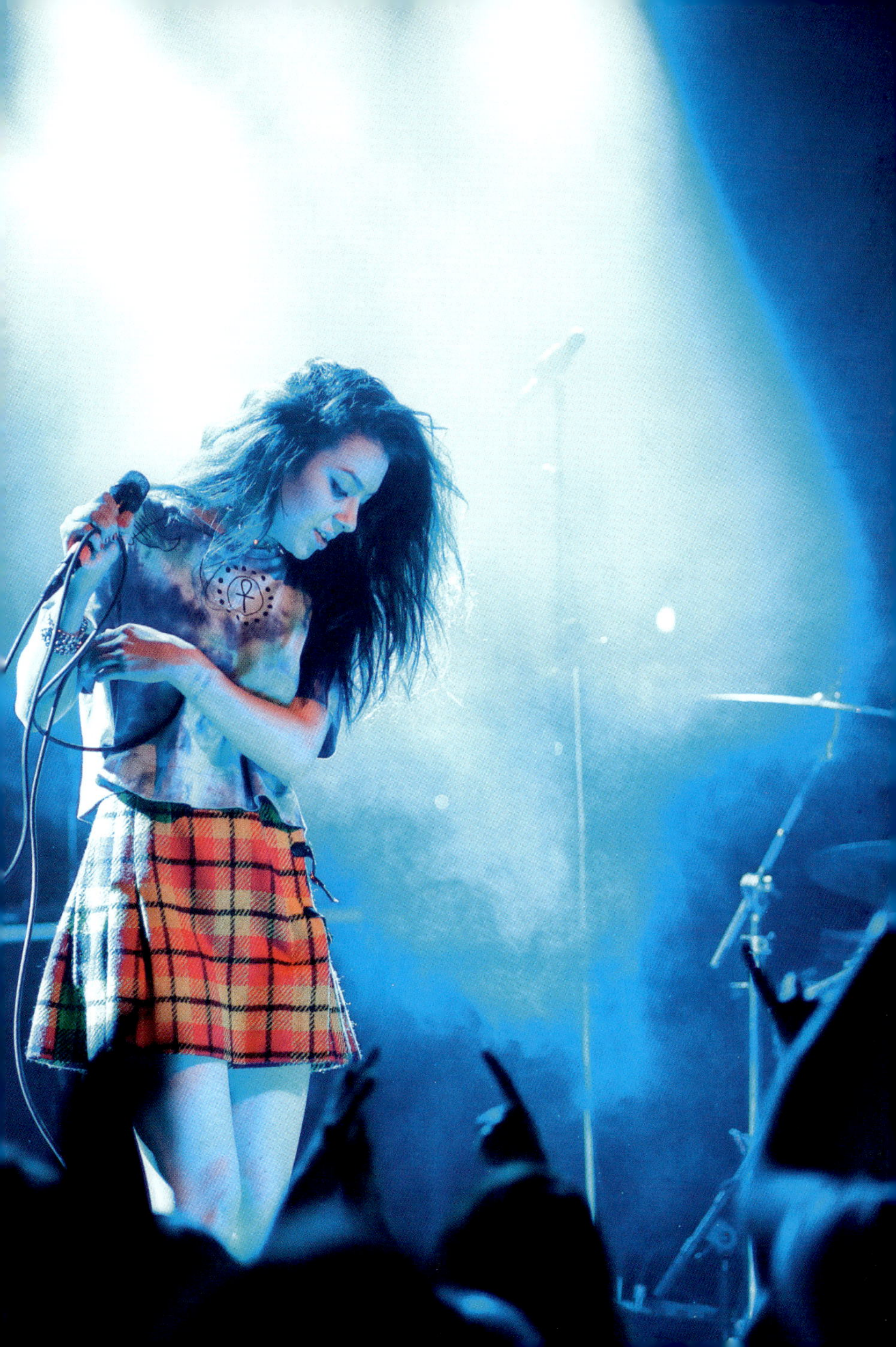

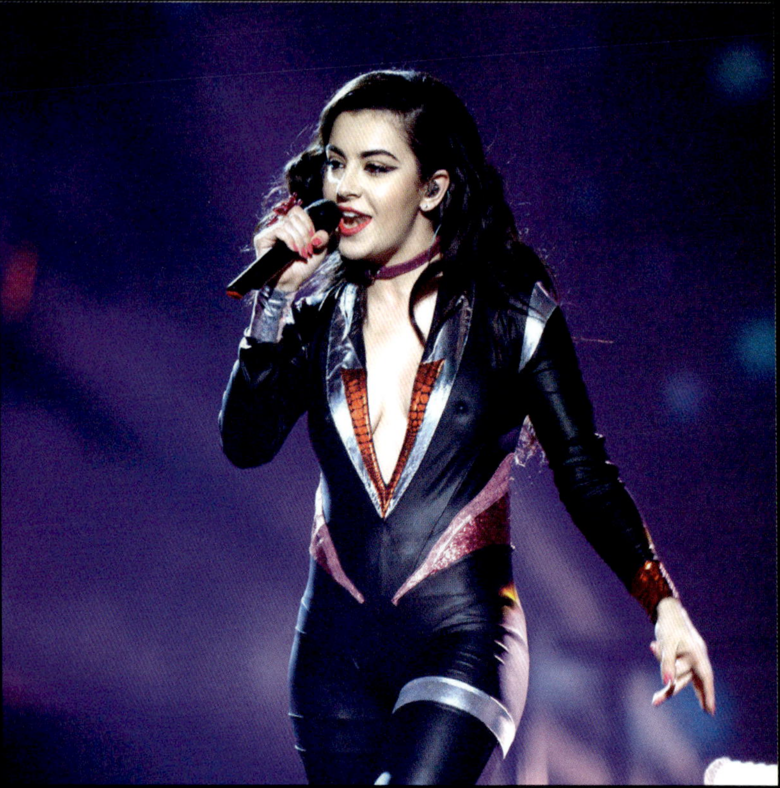

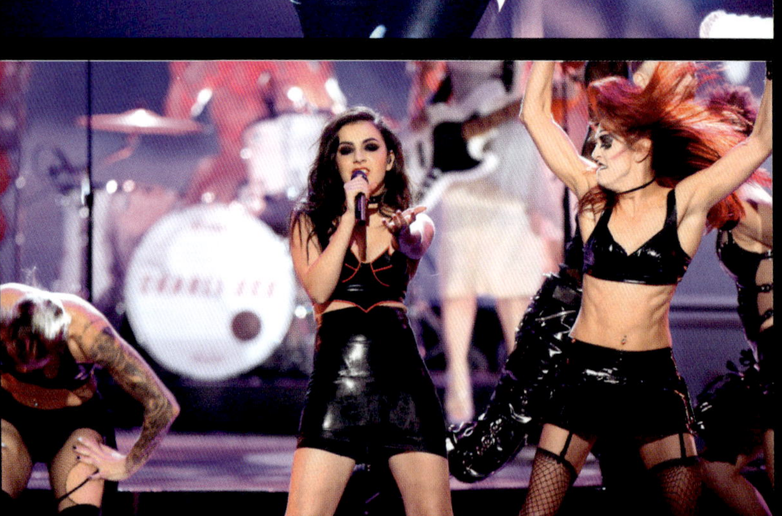

Clockwise from top: Performing at the 2014 MTV Europe Music Awards, Glasgow, November 2014; The Great Escape, Brighton, May 2014; American Music Awards, Los Angeles, November 2014

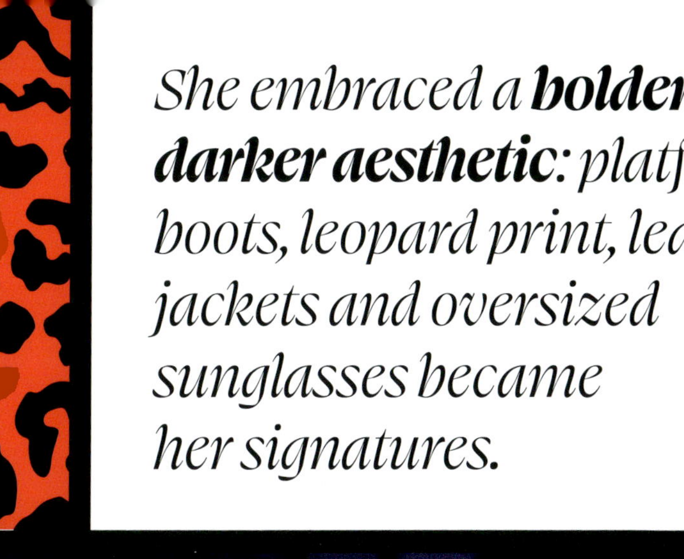

*She embraced a **bolder, darker aesthetic**: platform boots, leopard print, leather jackets and oversized sunglasses became her signatures.*

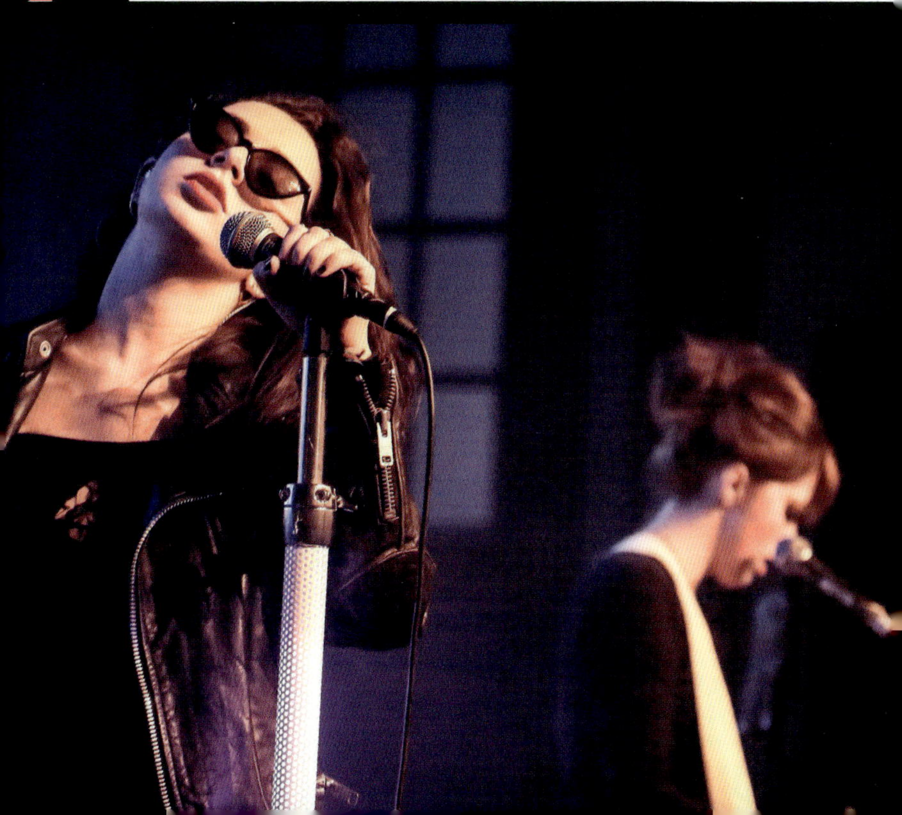

As 2014 drew to a close, she was climbing festival bills and playing larger venues. This was no longer the underground-leaning Charli XCX of *Super Ultra.* This was something bolder, brasher. The industry was finally paying attention – not just to her hooks, but to her as an artist.

Her look was evolving too. The day-glo rave clothes were kicked aside; instead, she embraced a bolder, darker aesthetic: platform boots, leopard print, leather jackets and oversized sunglasses became her signatures. It was sexier, edgier. She drew inspiration from punk icons like Joan Jett and Kathleen Hanna, meshing their rebellious edge with the pop glamour of Britney Spears and the Spice Girls.

Her wardrobe became the visual manifestation of her sonic shift – louder, more brash and completely unapologetic. She had transformed herself once again.

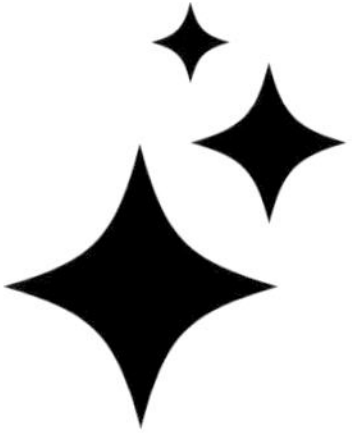

Ditch Fridays at the Palms Pool and Dayclub, Las Vegas, June 2014

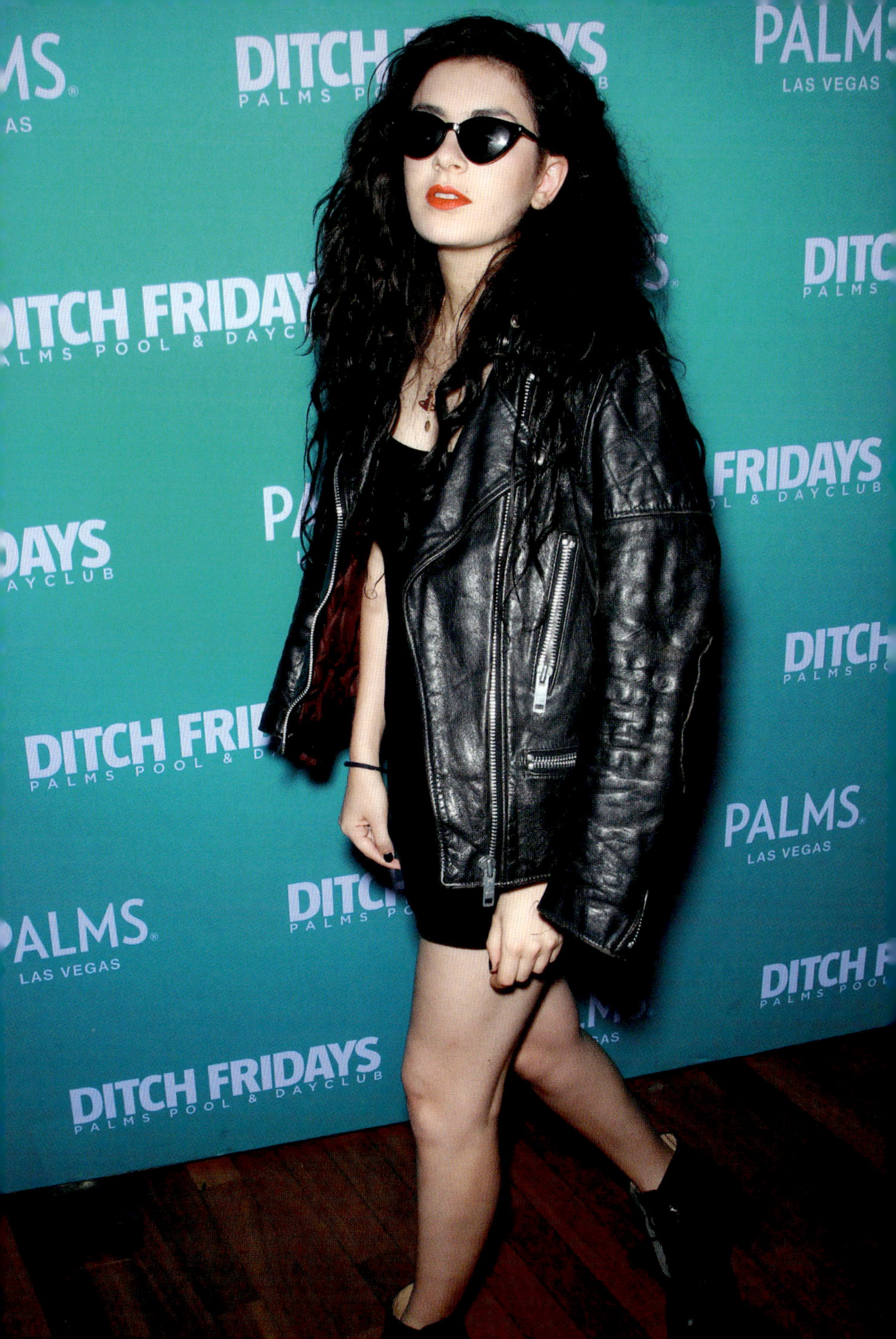
DITCH FRIDAYS
PALMS POOL & DAYCLUB
PALMS
LAS VEGAS

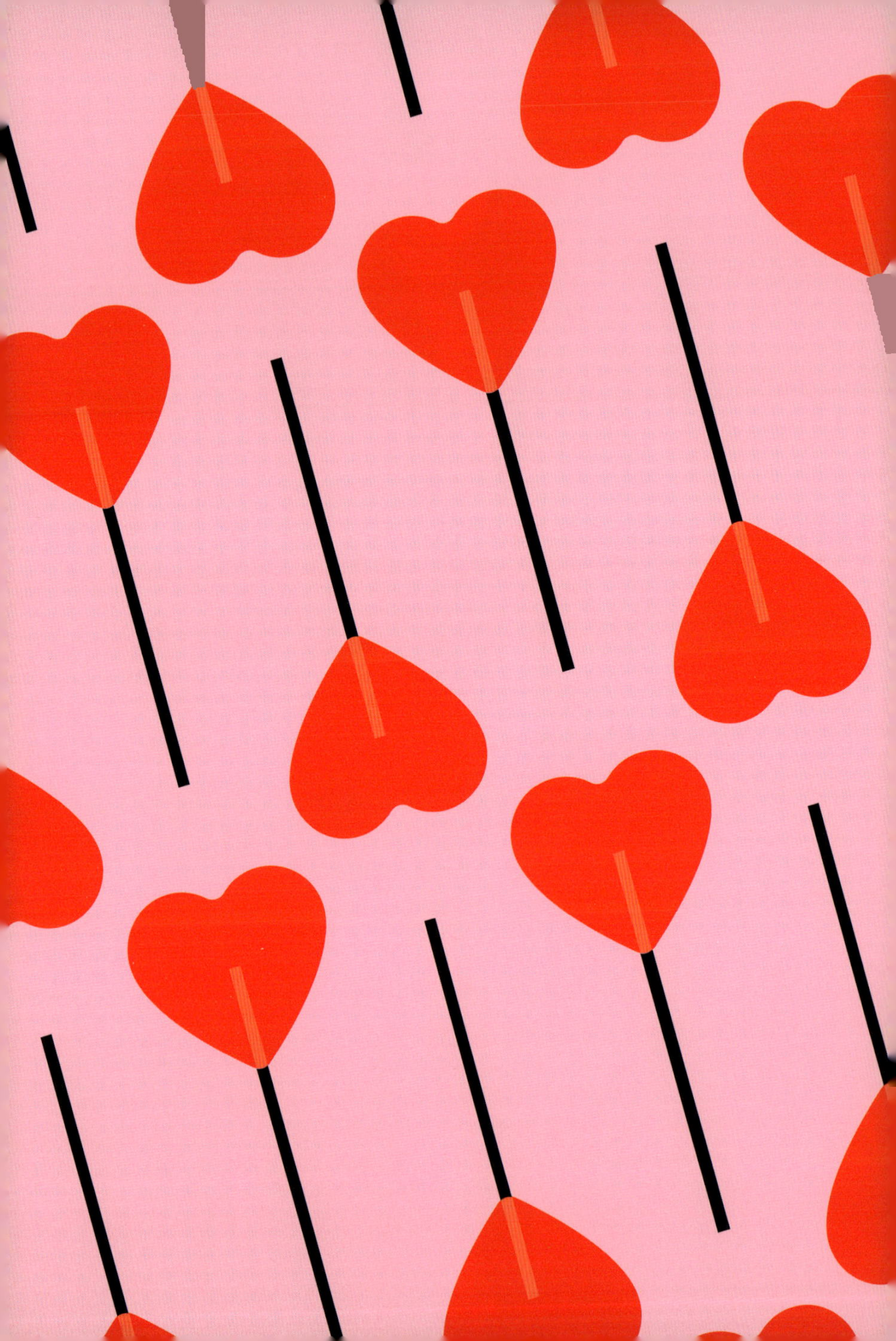

REBEL WITHOUT A *Pause*

Charli Goes Punk

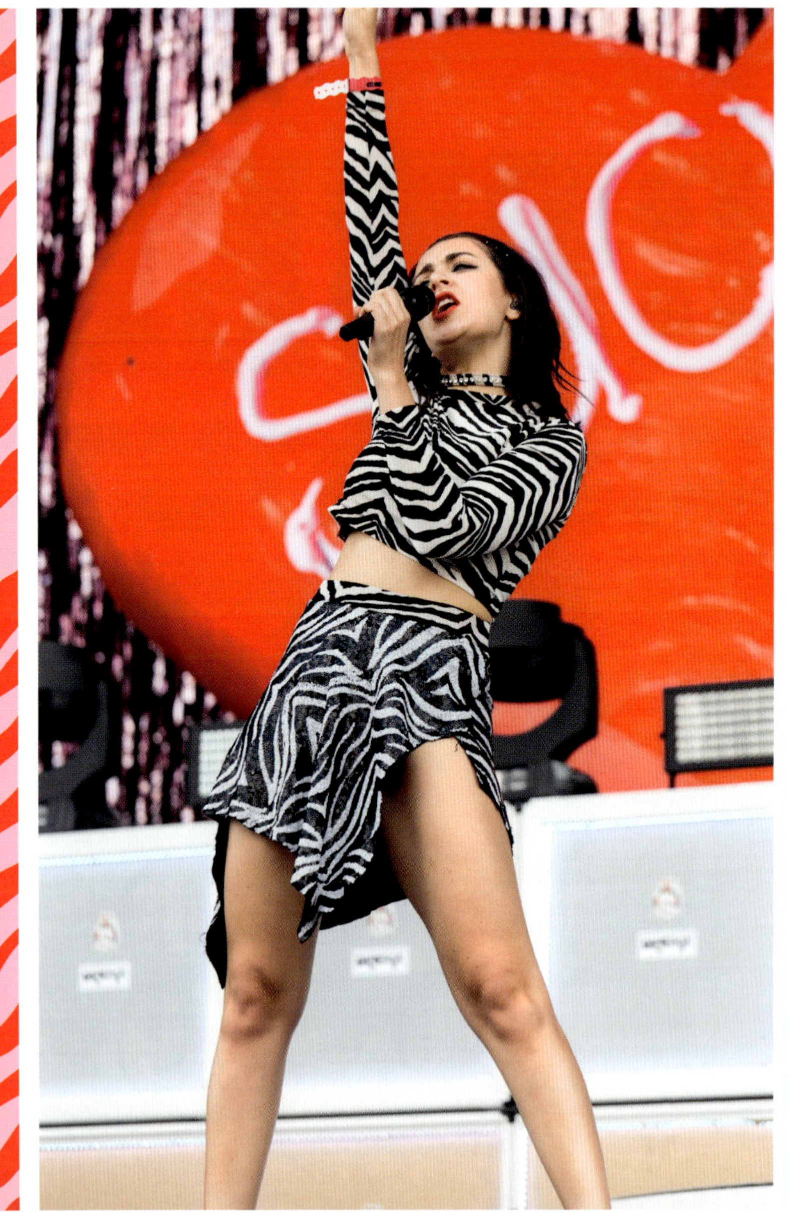

When *Sucker* arrived on 15 December 2014, there was a lot at stake. Charli XCX had proved herself as a songwriter, but could she become a successful album artist?

If it hadn't been for the success of 'Boom Clap', her label might have lost faith, but they knew she could write a hit – *Sucker* would be the make-or-break moment.

Charli was feeling the pressure. But rather than adopt the pop-by-numbers approach that would have kept the fat cats happy, she refused to chase the charts. *Sucker* was a direct response to the powers that be. 'It's not a synth-pop record. I don't wanna just make a new version of the record I already made. I want to make something completely different,' she told *NME* in May 2014. At just 22 years old, she was already developing a deep cynicism regarding the music industry, but was resolute – remaining authentic was the best way forward.

'After "I Love It", I was just being asked to repeat myself,' she explained. 'I built up a lot of anger, so I started listening to punk bands and infusing it into my music.'

Punk encapsulates more than just the mohawked oiks of the '70s, and throughout the writing process, Charli immersed herself in the music of Weezer, Bow Wow Wow, The Hives and Snuffed by the Yakuza (Patrik Berger's punk side project). Though *Sucker* is still a pop record at its core, it shares the genre's defiant, stick-it-to-the-man energy. 'Do you get me now?', Charli asks provocatively on the album's titular opening track, following up with 'Fuck you, Sucker!'

Though starting strong, by dint of Charli working with multiple songwriters and producers, the record was a little schizophrenic. For every banger, there was something close to a misstep.

'Break the Rules' was the album's second single and Charli's 'Baby One More Time' moment. Filmed in a high school, the video saw Charli don a preppy school get-up to party on the school bus and trash prom with her girl gang. In an iconic move, it starred actress Rose McGowan, loved by Charli for her appearance in *The Doom Generation* (1995).

Performing at New Look Wireless Festival, London, July 2015

On the flipside, the Rita Ora-featuring 'Doing It' – ironically, the highest charting of *Sucker*'s tracks – lost some of Charli's alt-pop charm in favour of something more radio-friendly. Where 'Body of My Own' soared to synth-pop heights, 'Die Tonight' sounded like a One Direction B-side.

The critics were mostly kind, sensing the album was the work of a young artist being pulled in multiple directions. The resounding feeling was that she wasn't quite there yet, but she would be. '*Sucker* isn't an endpoint for Charli ... and it's not her finest work, but it's plenty good enough to rope a cohort of new fans into what's promising to be one hell of a creative ride,' said *Pitchfork*. The *Guardian* echoed that sentiment: 'For all its failings, and for all that it falls short of the more hysterical hype, it does enough to convince you that her long-delayed moment in the sun won't be fleeting.' Sonically, there was a lot going on. Back in 2015, being a genre-bending artist wasn't something to aspire to. Record labels liked boxes and *Sucker* was hard to pigeonhole. Sugary sweet, 'Need Ur Luv', written with Vampire Weekend's Rostam Batmanglij, was another left turn. Influenced by Sylvie Vartan and Brigitte Bardot – the French girls of yé-yé pop – it was completely at odds with *Sucker*'s more rebellious anthems.

Weezer's Rivers Cuomo also had a hand in the record, writing with Charli on the foot-stomping 'Hanging Around'. 'It was so interesting working with him because we're from such different worlds but he has such an interest in the formulas and structures of pop music, which is something I have no interest in at all,' Charli said of the pairing. 'And he's just a cool, nice guy. He's the kinda guy I wanna go bowling with because I feel like he'll let me cheat and win.'

Commercially, *Sucker* did OK, charting at number 15 in the UK and number 28 on the Billboard 200. *Rolling Stone* voted it number six in their top albums of 2014 list. But it wasn't the chart stormer everyone had hoped for. Charli was a bit fed up. A couple of months earlier, Taylor Swift had dropped *1989*, the record that would take her from country music darling to pop megastar. It sold 1.2 million copies in the first week, topping the US charts for over 11 weeks. Deep down, Charli knew she and Swift were worlds apart, but as a woman in an industry that still loves to pit women against each other, the comparisons were hard to shake.

KISS FM's Jingle Ball, Los Angeles, December 2014

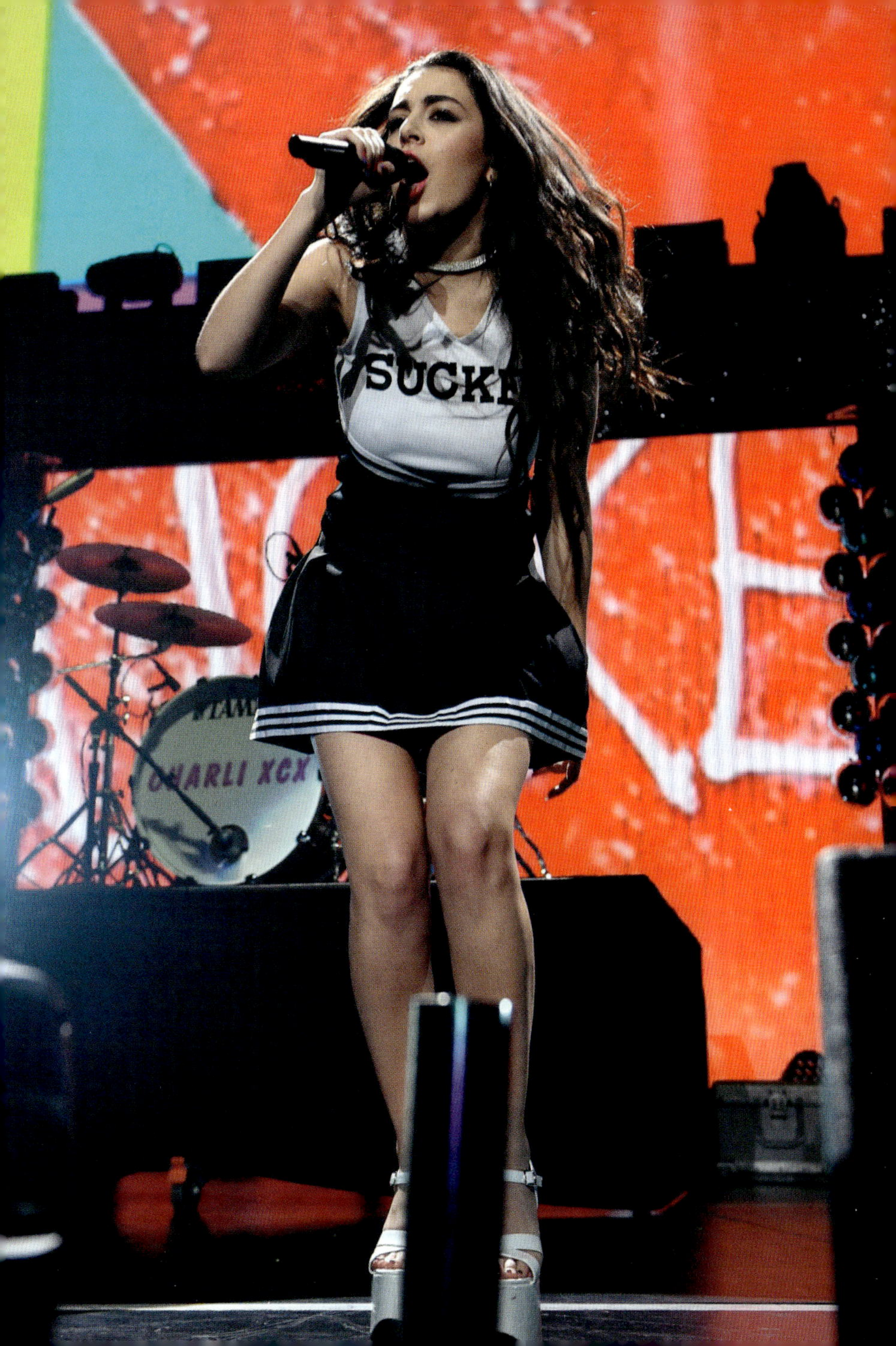
SUCKE
CHARLI XCX

'I still struggle with my place in the pop sphere because in my brain I'm not competing with Taylor Swift and Rihanna,' she told *The Line of Best Fit*. 'Not because I'm not good enough, because I am, but because my music's very different. I always feel like I have like one foot in the leftfield.' Charli was conflicted. Was she trying to be a pop star or an underground artist? Did she want chart success or was she happy outside the mainstream? It was something she'd spend the next few years figuring out.

> *'I **always feel** like I have like **one foot** in the **leftfield.**'*

In February 2015 she jumped on another feature: bouncy hip-hop chart pleaser 'Drop That Kitty' with Ty Dolla $ign and Tinashe. The three performers complemented each other and the track was a bona fide earworm, which they would go on to perform at the MTV Video Music Awards that year. But once again, Charli was a side note.

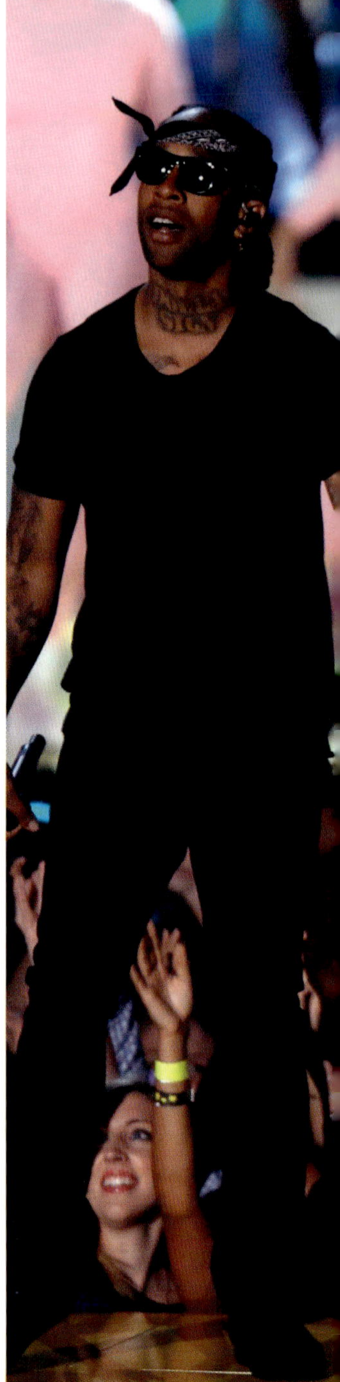

Performing with Ty Dolla $ign (left) and Tinashe (centre) at the MTV Video Music Awards, Los Angeles, April 2015

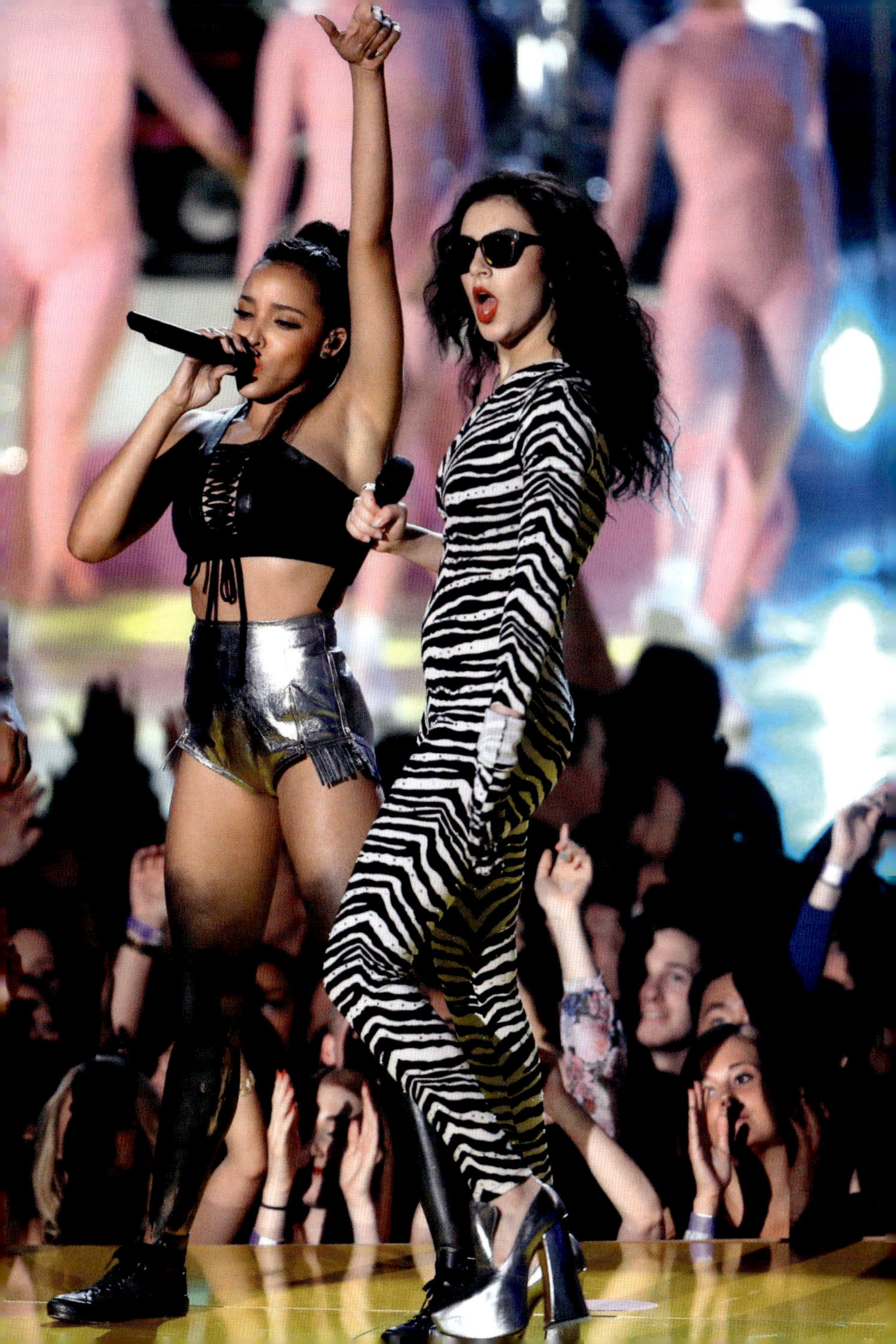

Soon after *Sucker*'s release, Charli was booked on another huge tour, this time supporting Katy Perry. This was a support slot Charli could really get excited about. Perry had cracked pop superstardom by being bold, brash and uncompromising. 'I've never opened for a superpop-tastic artist before,' Charli told *Teen Vogue.* 'It's amazing to see the props and the amount of production she has. She's in the air, then on a horse, and then she's dancing, and the whole thing is mental.'

Like every pop star worth her salt, Charli needed a name for her growing fandom. Katy had the Kitty Cats and Charli settled on Angels. For the Prismatic tour, Charli performed with a three-piece all-female band. It was a rock show with a pop edge – the guitarists wore celestial wings atop their baby-doll dresses.

Charli's stage outfits flitted between zebra-print miniskirts and sequinned playsuits. 'It really depends on how I'm feeling. I like leather. I like going out in slip dresses and dressing gowns. Always a red lip,' she said at the time. 'I feel like I've had the same eye makeup on since the day I started putting kohl on my eyes – and the more smudged it gets, the better.'

As the Prismatic tour came to a close, Charli was far from done with life on the road. Long before the 2024–25 SWEAT tour with Troye Sivan, Charli got her first taste of a co-headline show, teaming up with Jack Antonoff in the summer of 2015 for the Charli & Jack Do America tour. Jack and his band Bleachers had just dropped their debut album, *Strange Desire*, but Jack was already known for his Fun mega-hit 'We Are Young'. Charli was the hitmaker trying to make it on her own. They were a perfect pair; both knew what it was like to top the charts while still trying to build their own fanbases. The promo for the tour involved multiple interviews where the pair talked about their rider selects – Charli's vodka, gin and champagne at odds with Jack's health-conscious snacks. It's perhaps no surprise, then, that after a first run of dates – shows that saw Charli's stage production elevated to include huge inflatable guitars and lollipops – she pulled out of the tour.

Arriving at the 57th Annual Grammy Awards, Los Angeles, February 2015

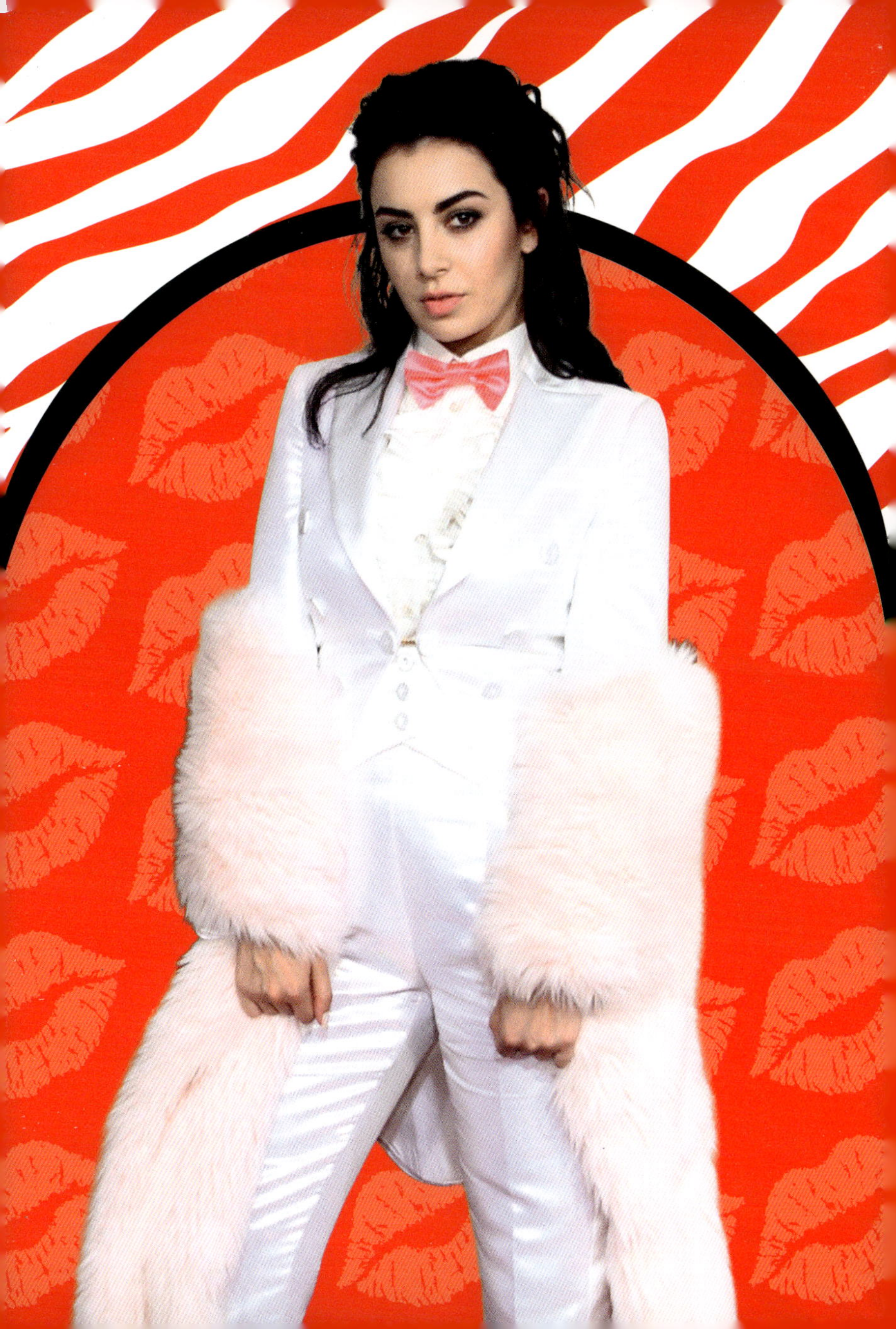

Charli's stage outfits flitted between ***zebra-print miniskirts*** *and* ***sequinned playsuits.***

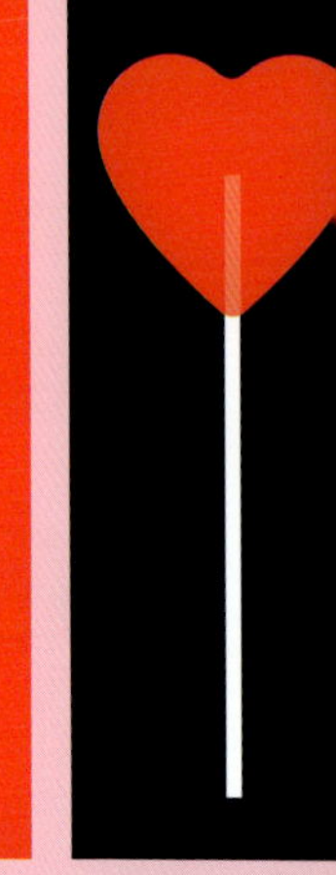

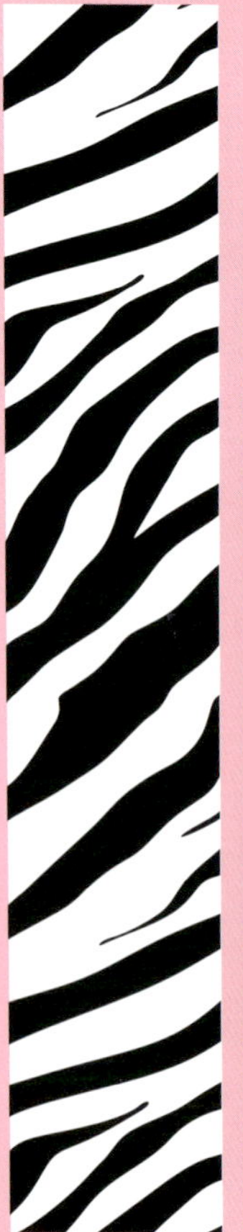

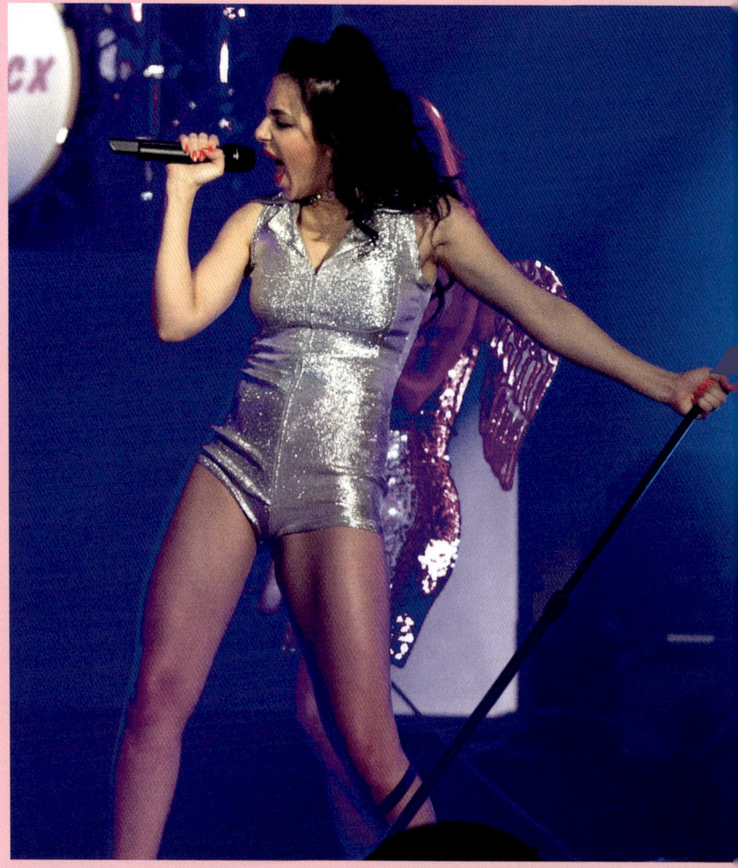

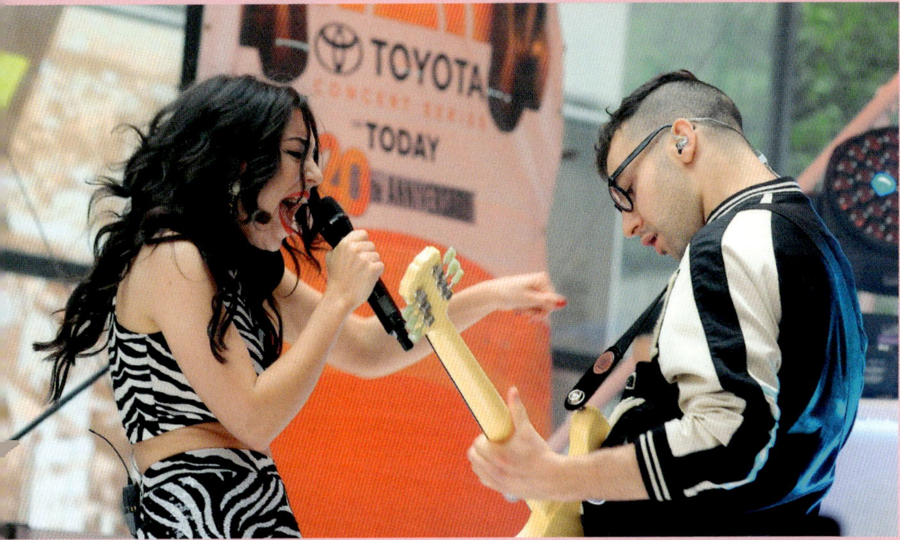

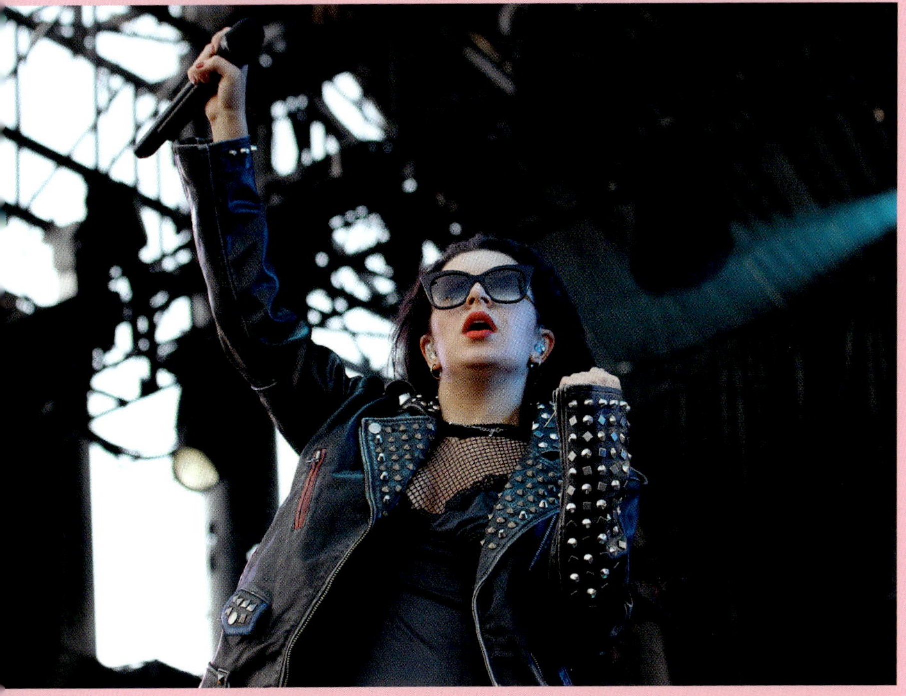

Clockwise from left: Supporting Katy Perry during her Prismatic tour, Amsterdam, March 2015; performing on NBC's Today *show with Jack Antonoff, New York, June 2015; performing at Rock in Rio music festival, Las Vegas, May 2015*

TOUR FATIGUE

Behind the scenes, having been on the road for the best part of two years, Charli was spiralling. The inside of a tour bus wasn't stimulating her creativity and she was frustrated – the bubblegum world of the stage shows was getting repetitive and she needed a break. 'I'm a creative person and I need to write music to be alright,' she told *NME* at Reading and Leeds festival later that summer. 'I'm just hungry to make new music. I started in January and it's been difficult to get in the studio. I just had to be selfish for once.'

By the end of 2015, Charli was ready for something new – to feel inspired again. And little did she know, she was about to meet someone who would change her life.

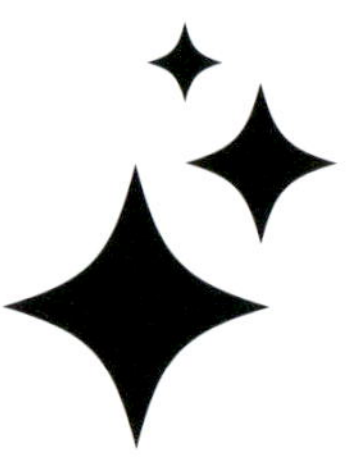

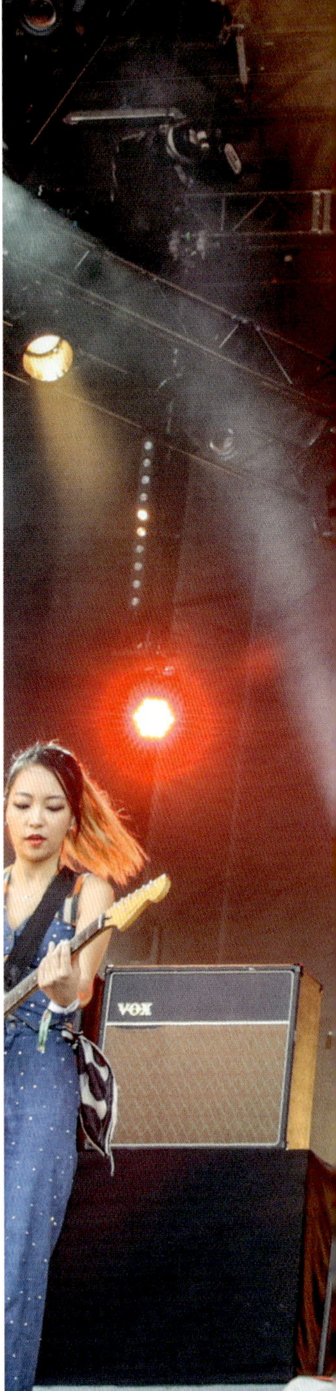

Performing at Osheaga Music and Arts Festival, Montreal, August 2015

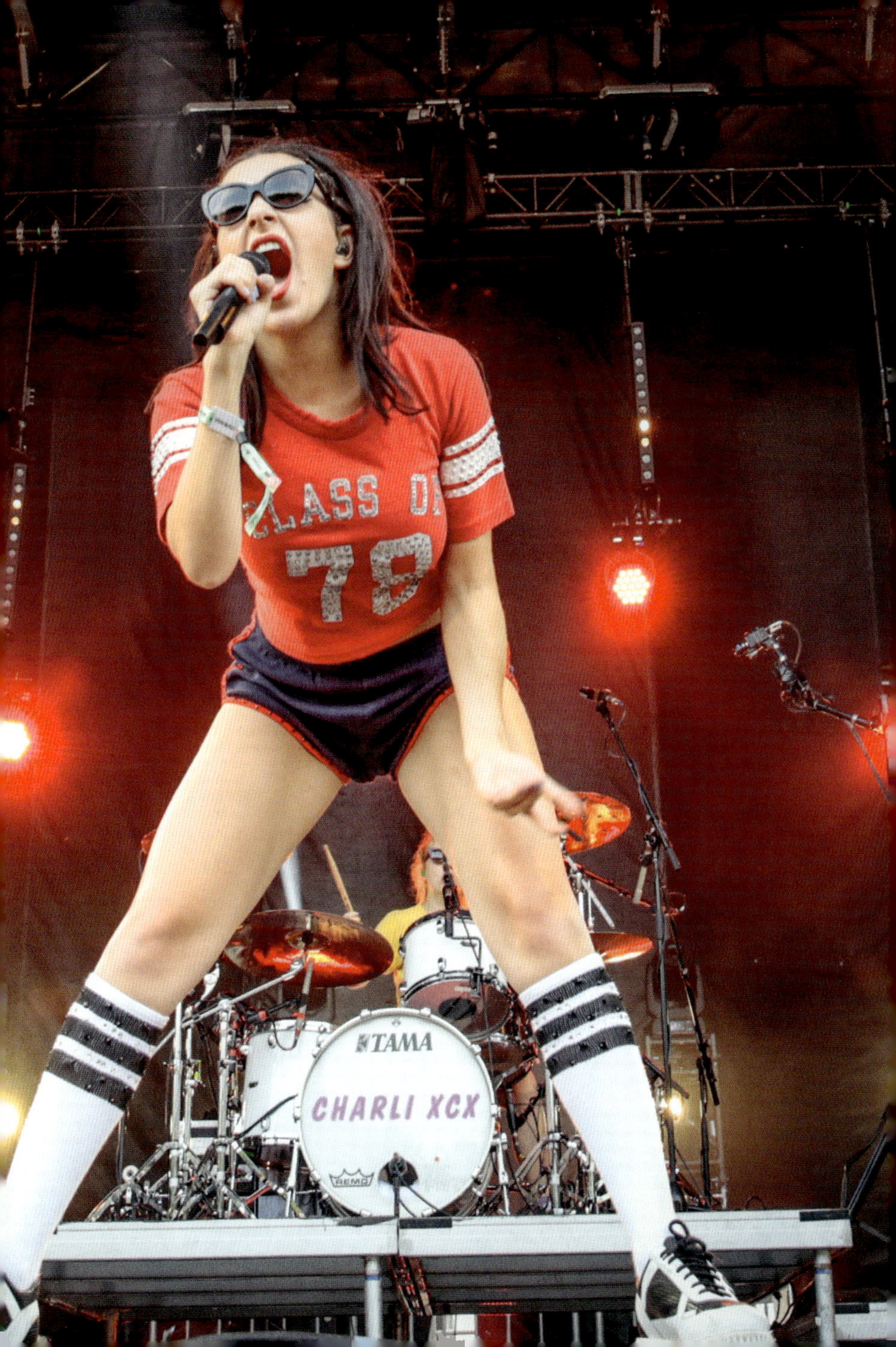
TAMA
CHARLI XCX

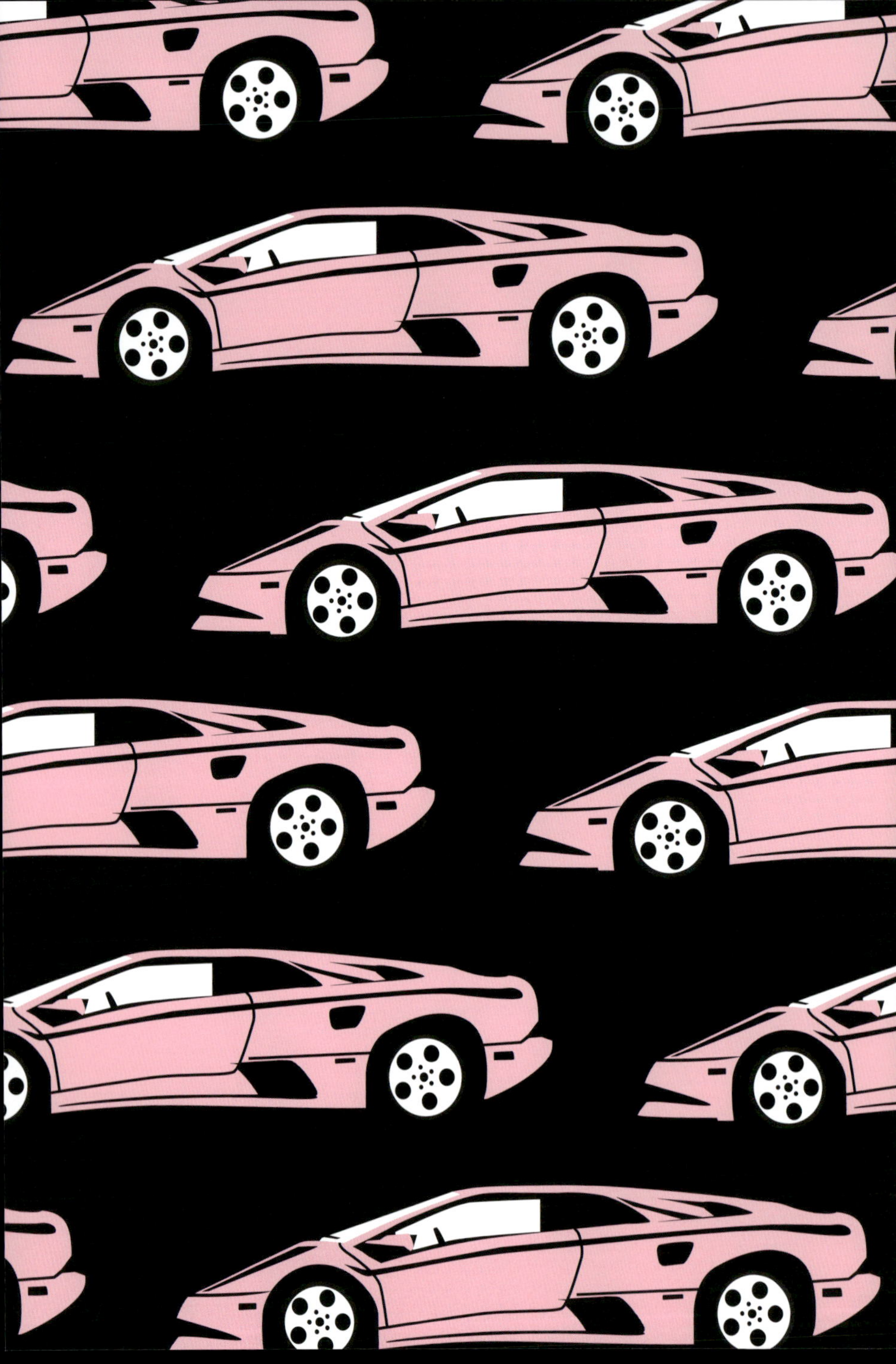

SHIFTING GEARS

Mixtapes and Mission

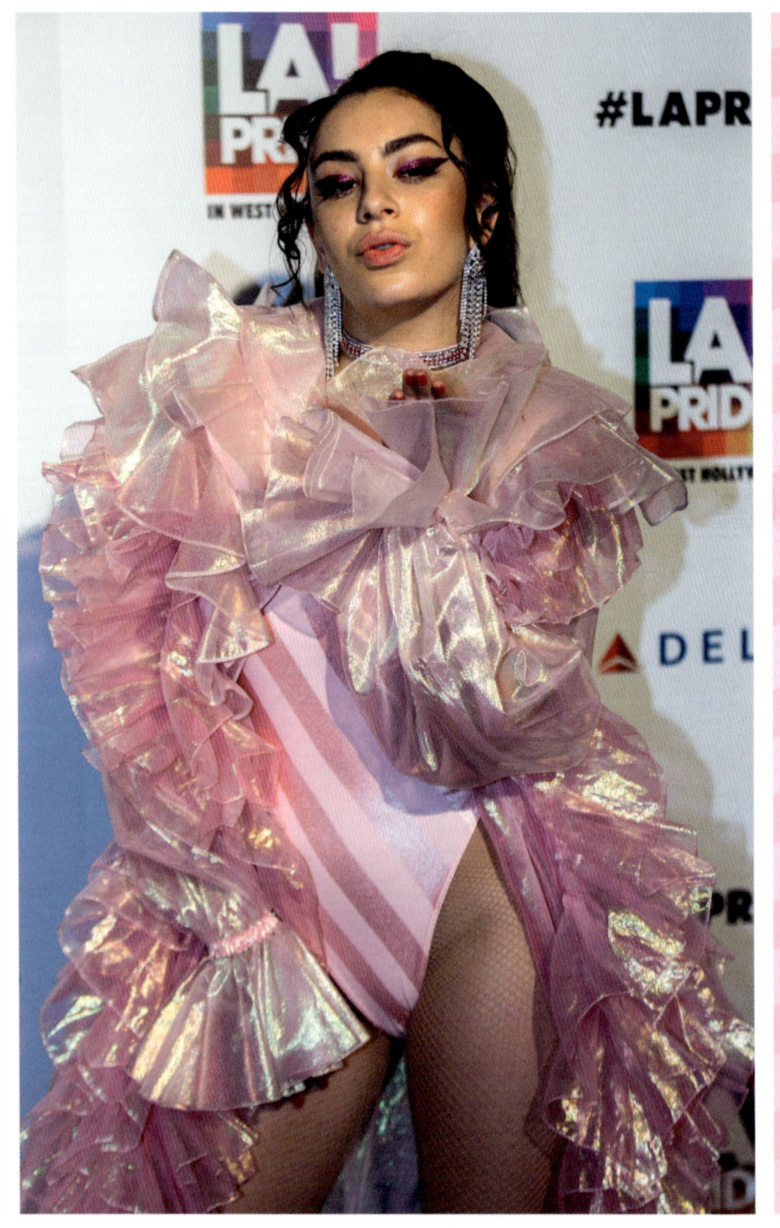

'It took some people who thought quite drastically outside the box to make my ideas reality. I found that at PC Music.'

Part of the reason Charli found touring *Sucker* so hard was that she had unfinished songs she was itching to release – tracks she was buzzing about, music that would go on to define her sound and build her a new cult following. After Huck Kwong had played her SOPHIE's 'Lemonade', she became obsessed with its childlike vocal and experimental production. Tracking SOPHIE down via her Soundcloud page, Charli wrote her an email. To her surprise, SOPHIE wrote back.

In early 2015 Charli had some time off before she hit the road and was keen to get back in the studio. She organized a songwriting camp in the Swedish countryside called Camp Skimret and asked SOPHIE along. To her delight, the producer and songwriter packed her bags and hopped on a plane. The plan was to write a bunch of tracks – some to pitch to other artists and some for Charli to keep herself. Joining Charli and SOPHIE were Swedish songwriter Noonie Bao and Miike Snow producer Pontus Winnberg, who had both written with Charli on *Sucker*. The gang spent a week writing together and the result was Charli's *Vroom Vroom* EP – a collection of songs that yet again took her sound in a completely new direction. But who was SOPHIE? And why did she have such an influence on Charli?

SOPHIE AND HYPERPOP

British artist Sophie Xeon had been uploading music to the internet for a brief time when fellow electronic musician A.G. Cook stumbled across her Soundcloud page and an early demo of single 'BIPP'. A.G. was intrigued. He was studying Music Computing at Goldsmiths, University of London, and making tunes with his pal Danny L Harle under the moniker Dux Content. Their schtick was mashing up electronic beats, video-game synths and pitched-up, saccharine vocals to make tracks that sounded like a bonus round of Sonic the Hedgehog on acid. In SOPHIE, he saw a synergy. 'I couldn't believe that there was someone out there, let alone someone in London, with such a strong vision and almost no regard for the walls between pop and experimental art,' he would later write on his blog.

Arriving at the LA Pride Festival and Parade, Los Angeles, June 2016

The pair exchanged emails and eventually met up in London, sharing a passion for experimental music production and the limitless boundaries of electronic sound design. Why use a piano or guitar when a computer allows you to create entirely original sounds?

The following year, 2013, A.G. founded his own record label, the highly influential PC Music, and while SOPHIE never signed, she remained a close collaborator, while A.G. began collecting a roster of artists who shared their hyperpop sensibilities: Hannah Diamond, GFOTY and old buddy Danny L Harle. SOPHIE and A.G. played a number of shows together and the crowds slowly grew, fans getting high on the sugary, outré pop world they were creating.

While A.G. focused on growing his label, SOPHIE continued to write and collaborate. There was a team-up with kawaii J-Pop artist Kyary Pamyu Pamyu, a joint project with A.G. called QT (which produced the undeniably brilliant fictional fizzy drinks campaign single 'Hey QT') and then came 'Lemonade', which is where Charli caught on. 'Lemonade' was SOPHIE's first glimpse of critical and commercial success, making several critics' lists at the end of 2014 and even featuring on a McDonald's advert.

By the time she arrived at Camp Skimret, SOPHIE was no longer a complete outlier. She'd proven her production chops and grown in confidence. She was ready to make a pop record.

Charli and SOPHIE clicked. SOPHIE was able to challenge Charli in a way that label-assigned producers and songwriters weren't. She was supportive and had a knack for knowing exactly where to take a song. That year, they both moved to LA – Sophie to live in a pool house-cum-studio with partner Hayden Dunham, and Charli to a house she bought in the celebrity-packed Beachwood Canyon neighbourhood of Hollywood Hills.

Like any self-respecting party girl, Charli threw a huge housewarming and SOPHIE was top of the invite list. She brought along Dunham and A.G. A.G. was yet to meet Charli in the flesh but was aware of her work, and this party would be the catalyst for years of friendship and collaboration. As A.G. wrote online, 'it was satisfying to finally be in the same place and to feel that we were all on the verge of individual journeys that had somehow collided.'

SOPHIE performs at Village Underground, London, January 2016

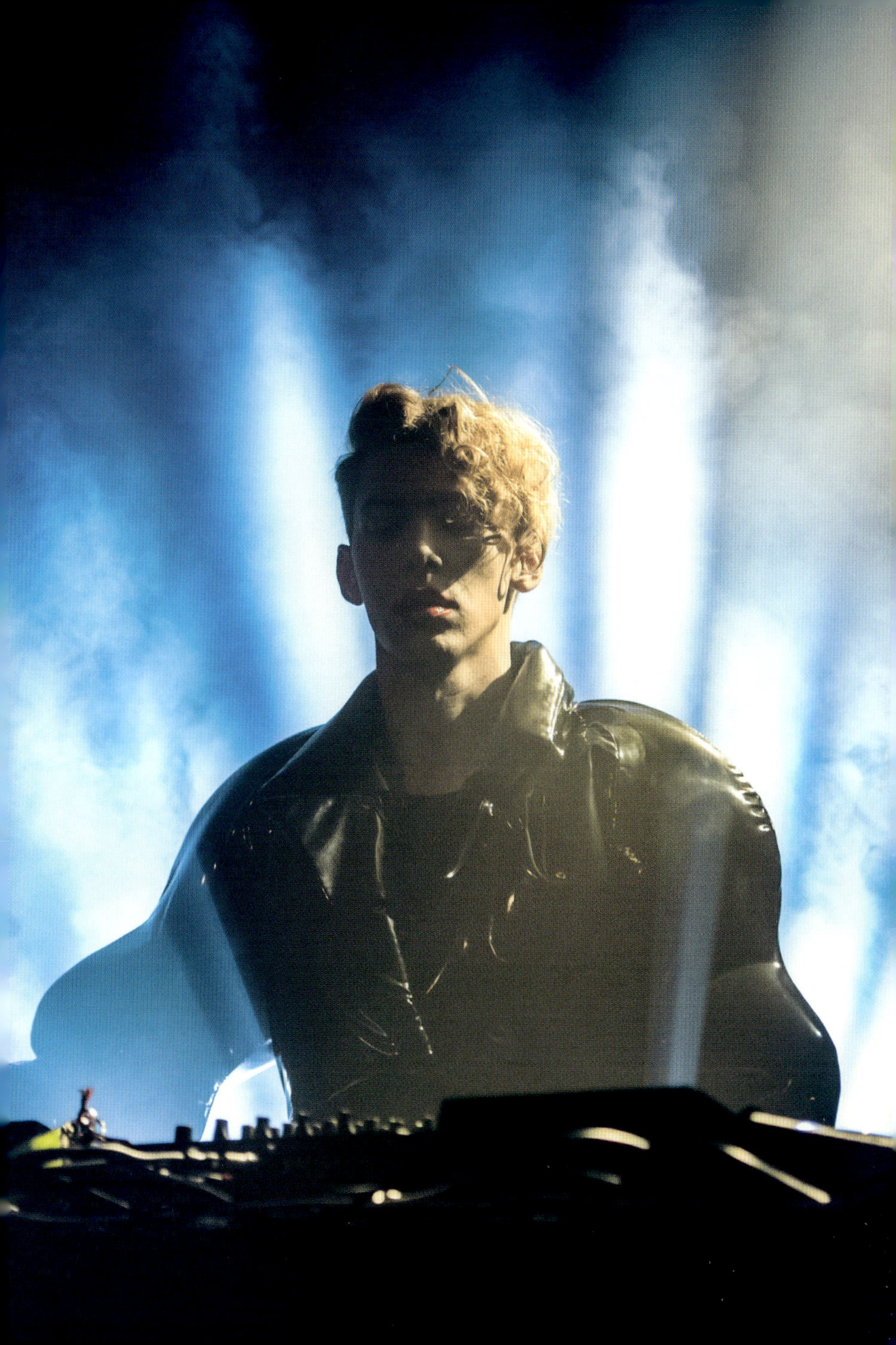

VROOM VROOM!

At school, Charli had been something of a loner, but finally she had a crew of creative people who understood her vision. There was no going back. The single 'Vroom Vroom' dropped in February 2016, with the mixtape following in the spring. The single was an undeniable bop with a flirty earworm of a chorus. It was unlike anything Charli had released before – futuristic pop at its finest. 'Vroom Vroom Recordings is my new, experimental pop label and it will combine my love for bubblegum pop with mystery and darkness,' she wrote in a press release. 'The artists coming up through it will be sharp, potent, deadly, and ultimately, will leave their mark on pop music.'

'I've worked with SOPHIE on the new EP and what we create together speaks for itself. Sometimes we get aggressive, sometimes we get beautiful; [s]he pushes me and I push him [her]. I'm making beautiful party songs right now and this is just the start. The album goes to other places and I can't wait for people to hear it. I feel the most creative I have in a long time and I couldn't be more excited for the next chapter.'

The next single to drop was 'Trophy'. 'Yeah, bitch, I'm here to take that crown,' sneered Charli's autotuned vocal. She meant business. With SOPHIE as the sole producer across the EP's four tracks, there was a unifying sound that had been missing from Charli's first two records. Not only that, it was refreshingly new. *Pitchfork* claimed 'few things are as wearying as pop culture that constantly congratulates you on how clever you are for "getting it," and Vroom Vroom is nothing if not exhausting', but they'd missed the point. Charli had created a world that fans were begging to be a part of. It felt cool, and exciting – the antithesis to the chart-dominating EDM from the likes of Calvin Harris and Mike Posner that was inescapable at the time. No longer was she just the party girl with shouty choruses – she had edge.

LET'S RIDE

With her experimental new sound came a new look. Charli recruited Lisa Katnic, the stylist who had been responsible for Miley Cyrus's post-Hannah Montana transformation, to give her a sartorial overhaul. When the music video for 'Vroom Vroom' was revealed, on 3 May, so was her new look. It featured Charli in a leather crop top and miniskirt, swinging her ponytail back and forth. The PC Music gang, Hannah Diamond, A.G. and Sophie, all had guest spots in the background. It served as a mission statement: Charli 2.0 had arrived, 'so let's ride'.

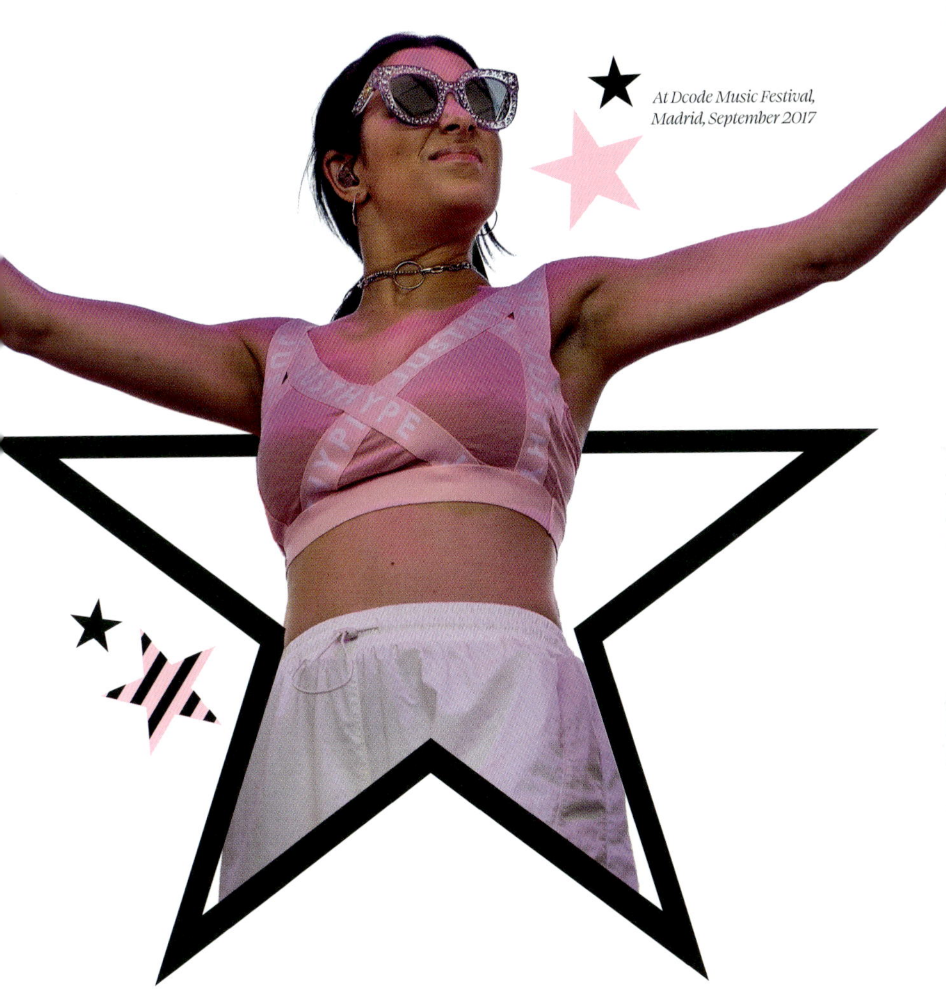

At Dcode Music Festival, Madrid, September 2017

Before long, A.G. had signed on to become Charli's creative director and the pair started to work on a manifesto for her third album. The vision was to create an XCX universe that saw Charli in a rotation of familiar settings including 'XCX Towers, a Vroom Vroom car workshop and an "underground lair nightclub"'. The pair weren't interested in just making a record – they were world-building. But Charli was still under contract with Atlantic, and not everyone shared her vision for where she should go next.

NUMBER 1 ANGEL

Since 2015, Charli had been working on sessions for her third album with SOPHIE, A.G. and – at the label's request – Stargate (the Norwegian duo who had produced hits for the likes of Katy Perry and Beyoncé). But when Atlantic Records heard the *Vroom Vroom* EP they began to worry about the direction of the new tracks. They were still waiting for their chart smash – a Charli XCX record of wall-to-wall hits that could match the success of 'Fancy' or 'I Love It'. Were they going to get it with this futuristic, experimental electronic music? They had doubts.

The intention had been for some of the *Vroom Vroom* tracks to appear on the next record, but Atlantic had other ideas. In October 2016, Charli dropped 'After The Afterparty', a radio-friendly hit featuring Soundcloud rapper Lil Yachty, whose track 'One Night' had put him on the map the previous year. It was billed as the first single from Charli's upcoming third album. But Charli had her own vision for the rest of the record; she didn't want her creativity to be stifled. She was determined to create, and headed back into the studio.

In February, Charli tweeted 'you have no idea how fucking hard it is to just release a free fucking mixtape in 2017.' The label were getting wise to her tactics of continuing to put out free music rather than finishing the album she was contracted to deliver. A month later, she dropped *Number 1 Angel*, a 10-track collaborative project produced by A.G., SOPHIE and Danny L Harle. However, it wasn't free as she'd promised. Instead, it was listed for £4.99 on iTunes – a way for the label to exercise some control over her prolific and uncompromising songwriting.

Number 1 Angel had the hallmarks of a PC Music record – helium vocals, twinkling synths, frenetic beats – but lyrically, the mixtape also showed a new, vulnerable side to Charli. Tracks such as 'Blame It on U' and 'Emotional' found her wrestling with toxic love and romantic what-ifs. Of the project, she told *NME*, 'It's just songs that me and AG Cook made in two weeks in LA when I was, like, feeling really depressed.'

At radio station Hits 97.3 Live, Florida, January 2017

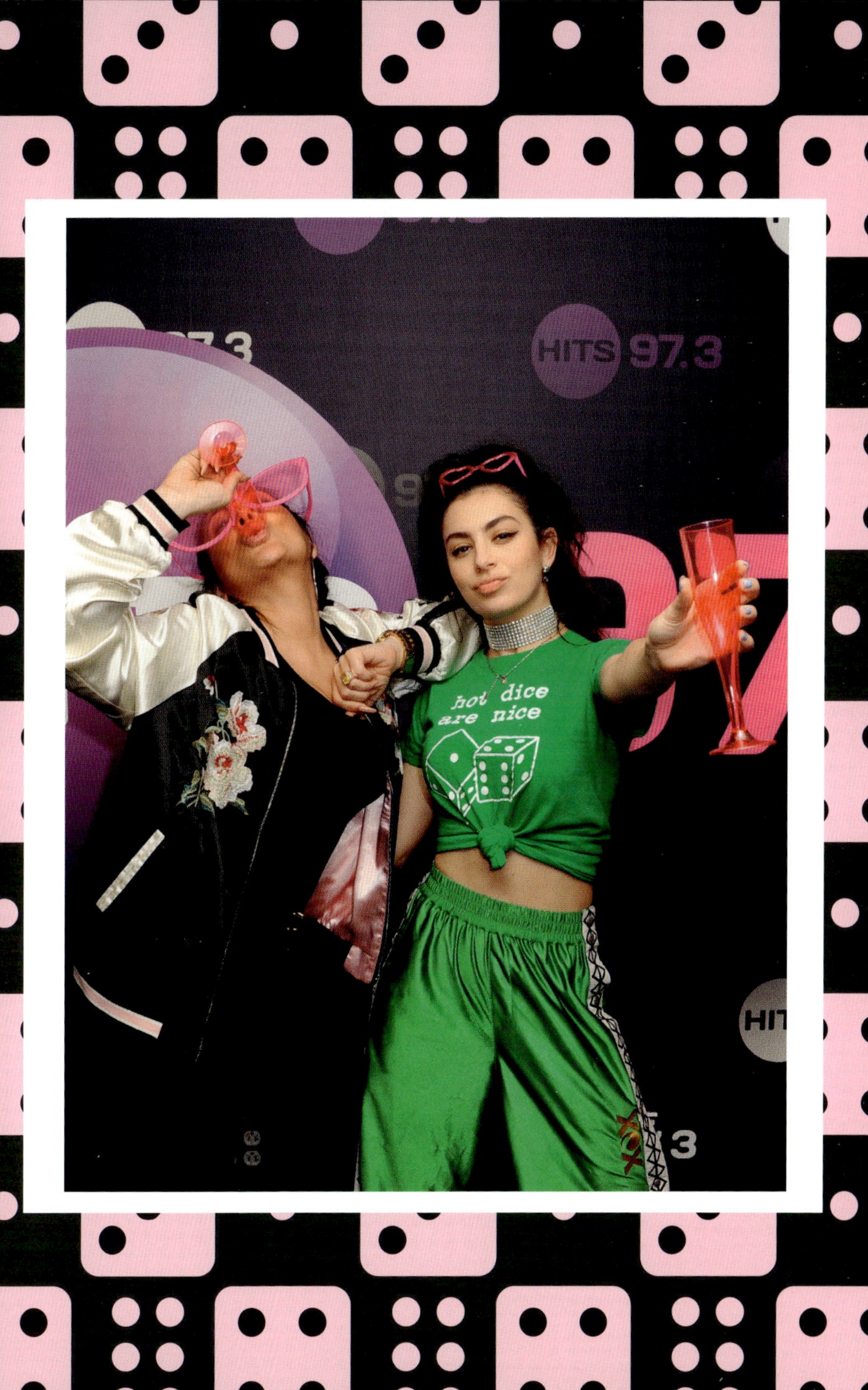
HITS 97.3
hot dice
are nice

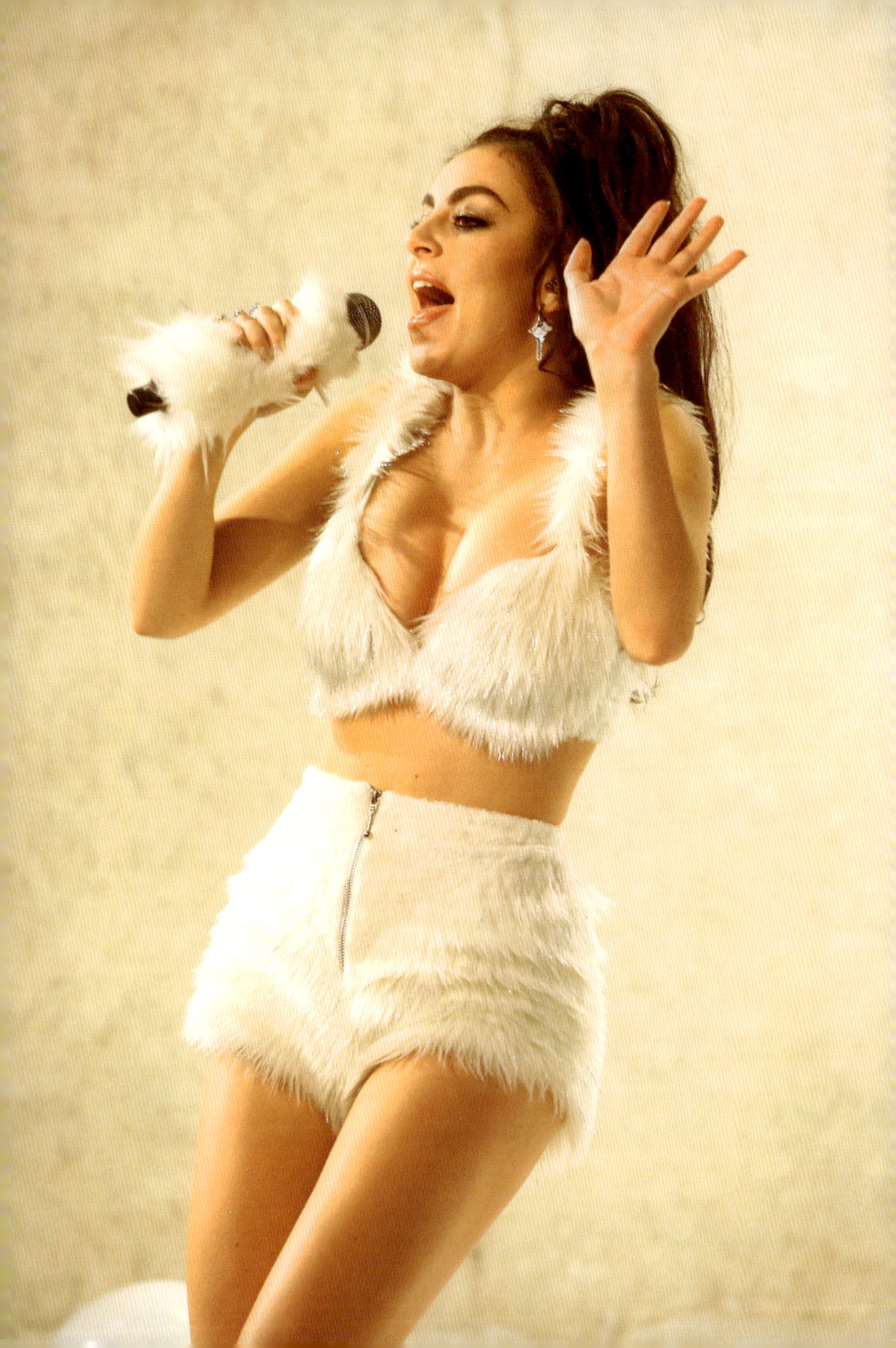

NON-STOP PARTY GIRL

All the back and forth with Atlantic was getting Charli down. She was feeling the effects of her lifestyle, too. The partying had been non-stop for over a decade and now, at 26, it was starting to wear thin. 'Partying is sometimes a really important and cathartic moment for people, but sometimes it can be really lonely,' she told *The Fader* at the time.

That push-pull is felt across *Number 1 Angel*: the giddy highs of nights out versus the crushing lows of the morning after. It's something Charli would continue to write about throughout her career. Record highlights included the cunnilingus-celebrating 'Lipgloss', featuring fabulously filthy Chicagoan rapper CupcakKe, and 'Babygirl', with Charli's earliest idol, Uffie; alongside these were tracks with MØ, Raye and Abra.

It was the first time the critics were unanimous – this was inventive, exciting pop from an artist not afraid to take risks. But fans were getting confused: do these 10 new tracks, that we need to pay for, not constitute an album? Still the fans paid up and waited. At the end of 2016 Charli had played a show at Exchange in Los Angeles, where she debuted some unreleased songs – including 'Bounce', 'Taxi' and 'Hey Boy, Hey Girl'. Fans had no idea it would be the only time they'd hear them live. All clues pointed to 'Bounce' being the next single, particularly when she performed it on Jimmy Kimmel in a white furry bikini, while A.G. lay passed out on the floor behind her: performance art at its finest.

When the tracks failed to appear on *Number 1 Angel*, fans were sure they wouldn't have too long to wait before their official release. But publicly the messages were mixed. In interviews, Charli admitted to the album being finished, but the release dates she hinted at came and went. What was going on?

Atlantic wanted more radio-friendly hits and Charli played ball, to an extent. Rather than the next single being her preferred 'Bounce', next came 'Boys' with its zeitgeist-capturing (and incredibly thirsty) video that served as a who's who of teenage crushes, including Joe Jonas, Diplo, Oli Sykes and Tom Daley. 'I been busy thinking 'bout boys,' came the bubblegum chorus, followed by a *Super Mario Bros* sample. It was a perfect blend of mainstream pop and PC Music.

Performing as the musical guest on Jimmy Kimmel Live, *7 February 2017*

THE LOST ALBUM

Just one month later, everything changed. A hacker managed to guess the password to Charli's Google Drive and leaked the album online. Charli felt violated. Her work with A.G. had taught her that releasing an album was about so much more than just the music, it was about creating a universe in which her art could exist. When that control was taken away from her, it ruined everything. 'It felt like an invasion of my life, my personal space, my personal property,' she told *ES magazine* in an interview in 2019. 'It was just really sad, and I was really hurt.'

Fans had lovingly started referring to the album as 'XCX world' and even made album artwork to accompany the 12 leaked tracks. But the record in its finished, mixed and mastered form would never officially see the light of day, with Atlantic and Charli making the painful decision to scrap it and start over again.

So, what now? The album Charli had been waiting years to release was in the bin. Whereas some artists would have been broken, Charli headed right back into the studio.

Since *Vroom Vroom*, her fanbase, the Angels, had grown rapidly. Her edgy new pop was resonating with new audiences, most notably queer club kids who felt represented by her sugary, underground pop. They were hungry for more music in the same vein. And Charli was ready to deliver.

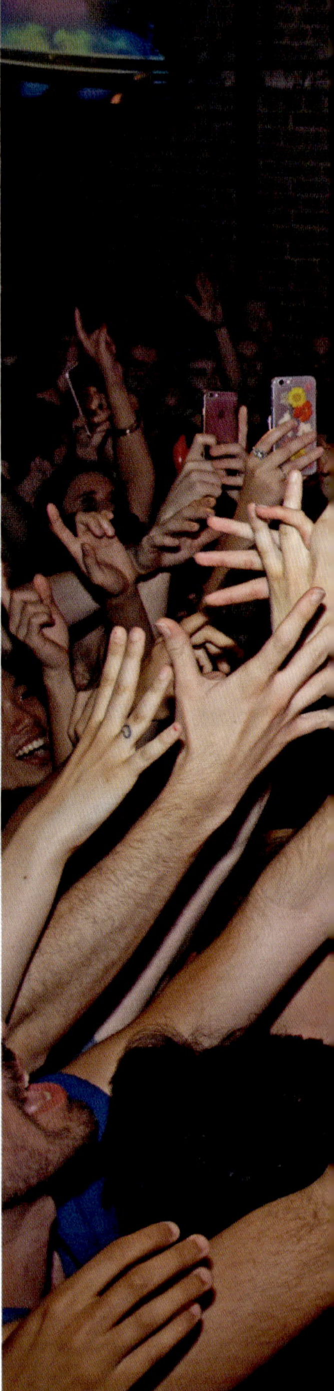

Performing at G-A-Y nightclub, London, August 2017

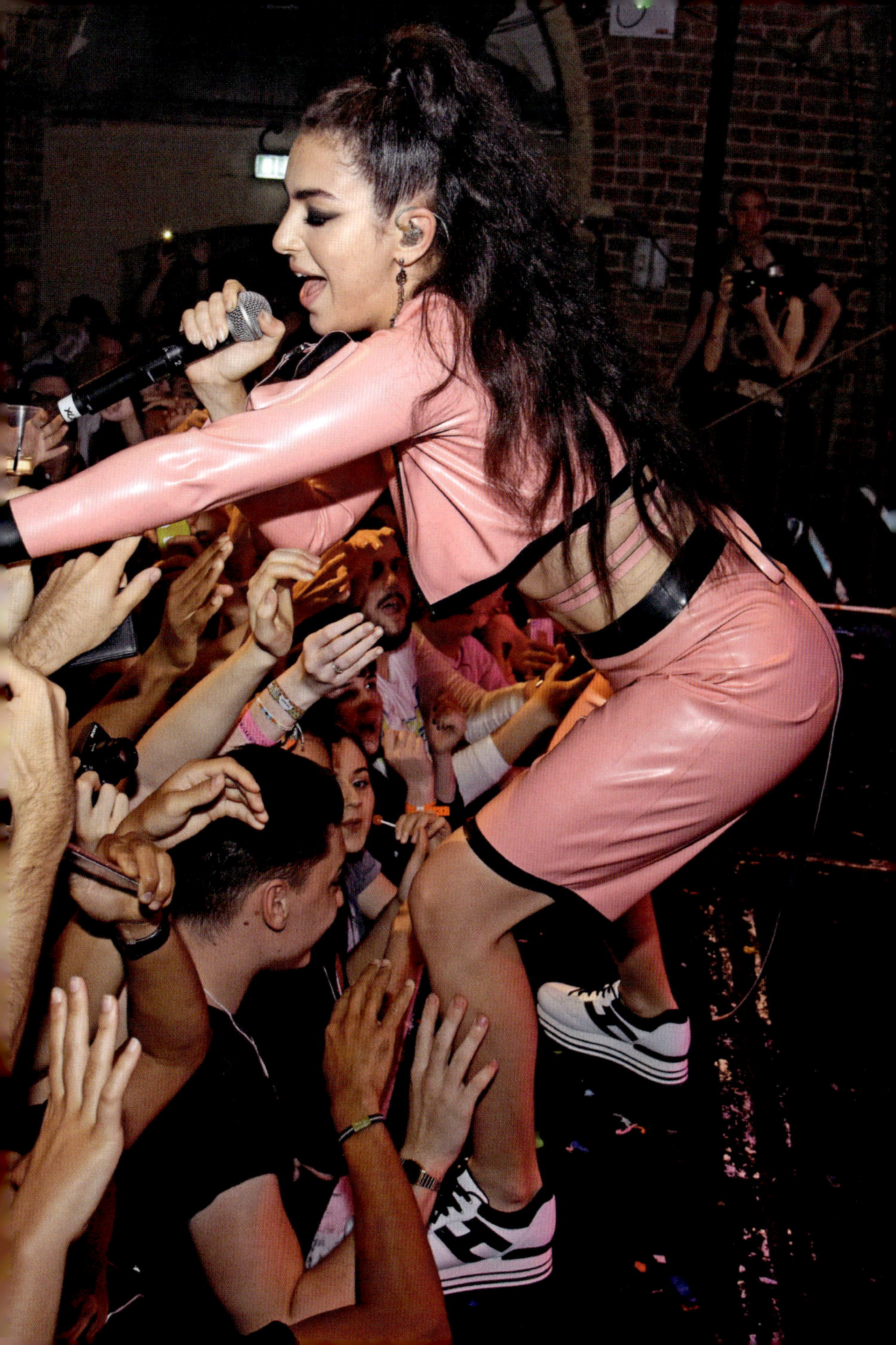

NEW ALBUM, NEW LOOK

In December 2017, Charli dropped a new mixtape, *Pop 2:* 10 collab-boasting tracks featuring peak pop powerhouses Carly Rae Jepsen and Tove Lo alongside subversive artists such as Estonian rapper Tommy Cash and gender-fluid avant-pop provocateur Dorian Electra. The vocals were autotuned, breathy and emotional, the production glitchy, experimental and completely at odds with anything in the charts. Despite the revolving door of cool-kid features, there was a cohesiveness to the project that had been missing in some of her earlier work. As the *Guardian*'s Alexis Petridis aptly put it at the time: 'Pop 2 does an impressive job of convincing you that Charli XCX is infinitely better when freed from record company interference.'

Charli had found her sound – it may not have been one her label liked, but everyone else saw she was an artist reaching new creative heights.

Stylist Rebecca Grice was brought on board to bring *Pop 2* to life. The sartorial manifestation involved pastel-coloured, synthetic fabrics that felt both girly and hyper-modern, mirroring the glossy, warped production of the mixtape. Charli leaned into a futuristic form of athleisure – outfits that suited her high-octane live performances while still creating a distinct vibe.

*'**Charli XCX** is **infinitely better** when **freed** from record company **interference.**'*

To this day, *Pop 2* is revered as one of Charli's finest bodies of work. Beloved by fans and critics, it is a masterpiece in expressive pop. It also doubled down on Charli's love of cars – references she'd been seeding in her music since *True Romance* but which had gradually become more overt on tracks such as 'Backseat' and 'Porsche'. This pedal-to-the-metal symbolism was representative of Charli's creative 'drive', a desire to go, to make, to see where the road takes her, with the label as the speed bumps and roadblocks on her journey.

Performing at Glastonbury Festival, Worthy Farm, June 2017

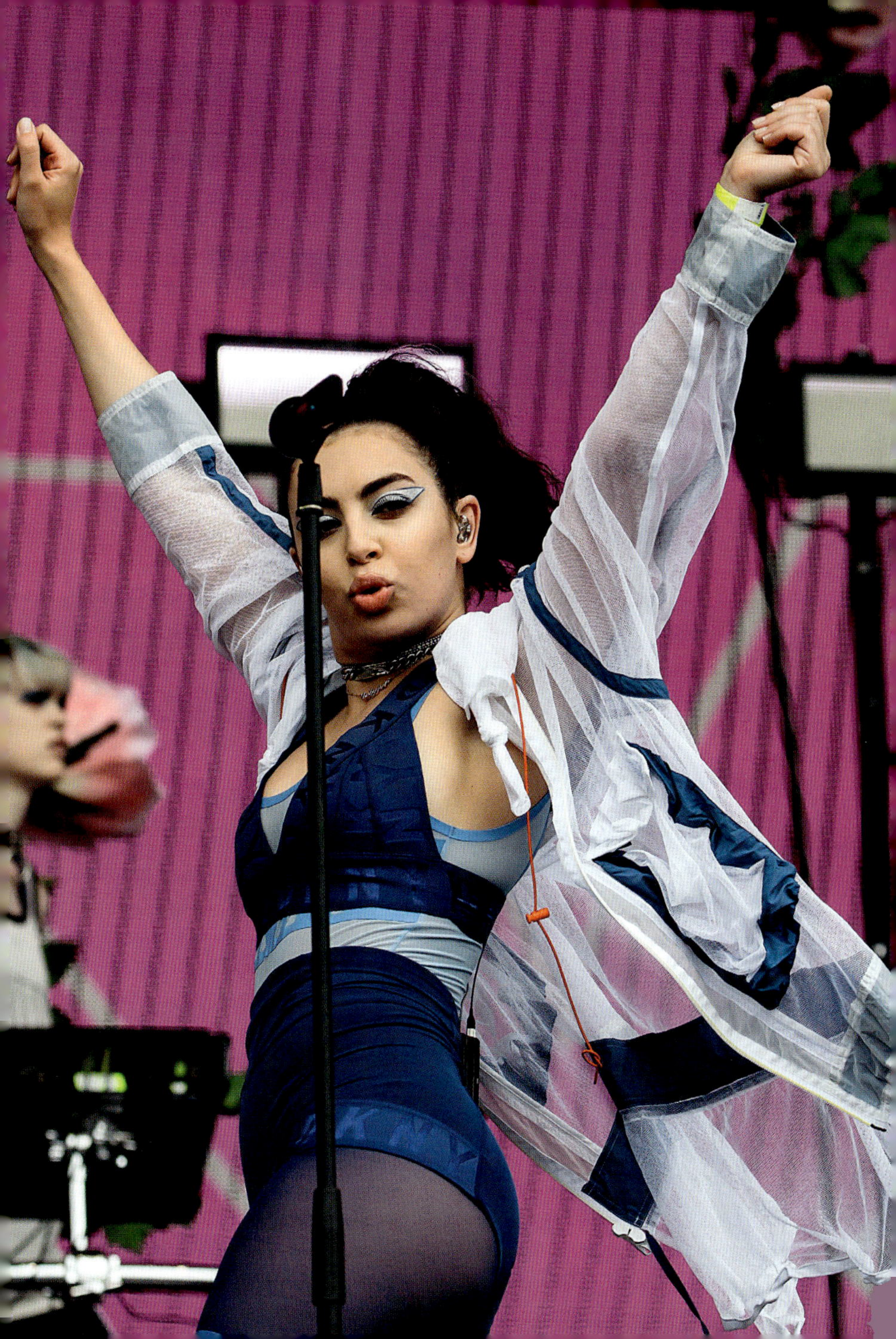

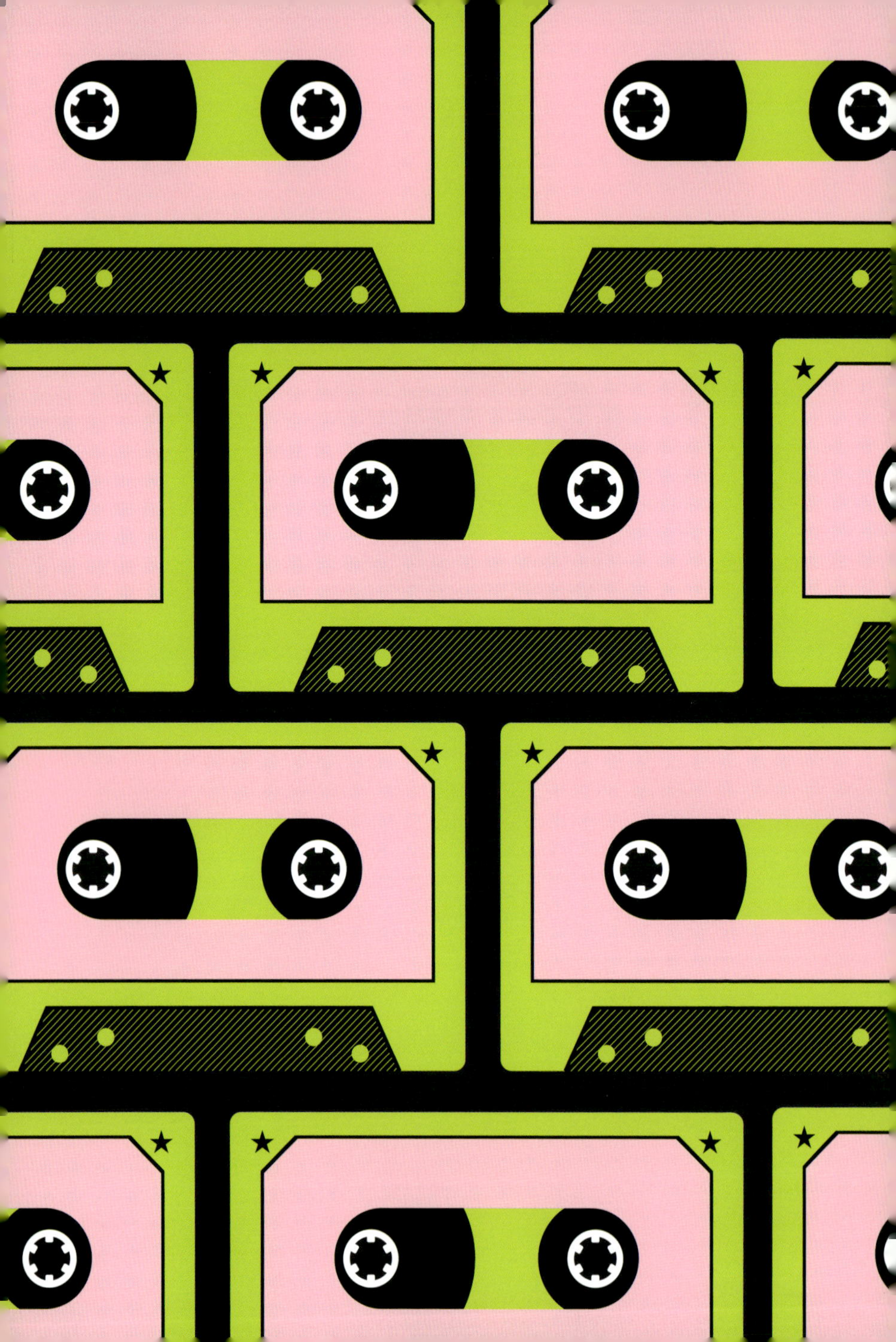

NEXT-LEVEL CHARLI

Opening Up and Hitting the Road

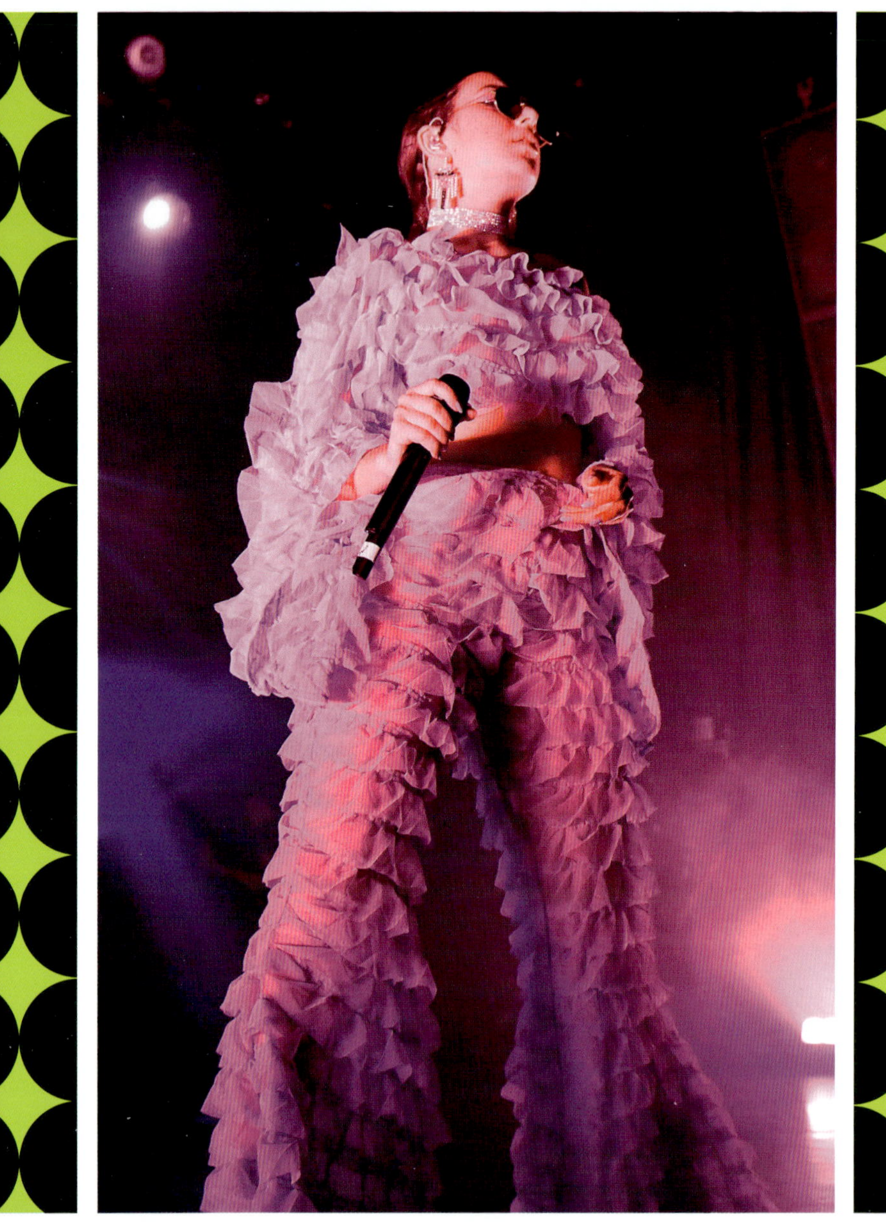

The response to *Pop 2* reinforced Charli's belief in her own artistic vision, with a little help from A.G. and SOPHIE. 'They've made me more confident in who I am as an artist,' she told *Vulture* in 2018, 'in my ability to commit, make decisions, and be fearless.'

But she was also fed up with the industry and the traditional way she was required to release music. In interviews at the time, she shared doubts as to whether she'd ever return to the album medium, the fluidity of dropping mixtapes being much more suited to her and the spontaneous way she writes songs.

The start of the year brought a bout of awards season parties and one legendary LA gig at LA's El Rey theatre. Joined by Tove Lo, Abra, Mykki Blanco, Bibi Bourelly, Brooke Candy and Carly Rae Jepsen, Charli threw one hell of a *Pop 2* party, even crowdsurfing in a ruffled lavender two-piece.

REPUTATION

By spring the album leak was a distant memory and Charli was preparing to hit the road with Taylor Swift on the *Reputation* tour. Booked with Camila Cabello as the tour's only openers, for 56 nights Charli played seven of her 'hits' to half-empty stadiums of tweens around the world. Of her recent releases, only 'Boys' and 'Unlock It' made the setlist, showing Swifties the more palatable side of her oeuvre. The booking would mean huge exposure, with Charli and Cabello frequently joining Swift on stage to sing her biggest hit, 'Shake It Off', but would the Swifties really get her?

To Atlantic, eyeballs were eyeballs and it was vital they took advantage of being in front of so many new faces. Charli started releasing monthly singles. First, came '5 in the Morning', a moody trap song about partying all night that made its way onto the *Reputation* tour setlist. Club-ready pop tracks 'No Angel' and (an XCX World-reboot) 'Focus' were next to drop, followed by 'Girls Night Out', another track salvaged from the wreckage of album three. None of the tracks saw huge chart success but the fans gobbled up more music from their fave.

Performing Pop 2 *at the El Rey Theatre, Los Angeles, March 2018*

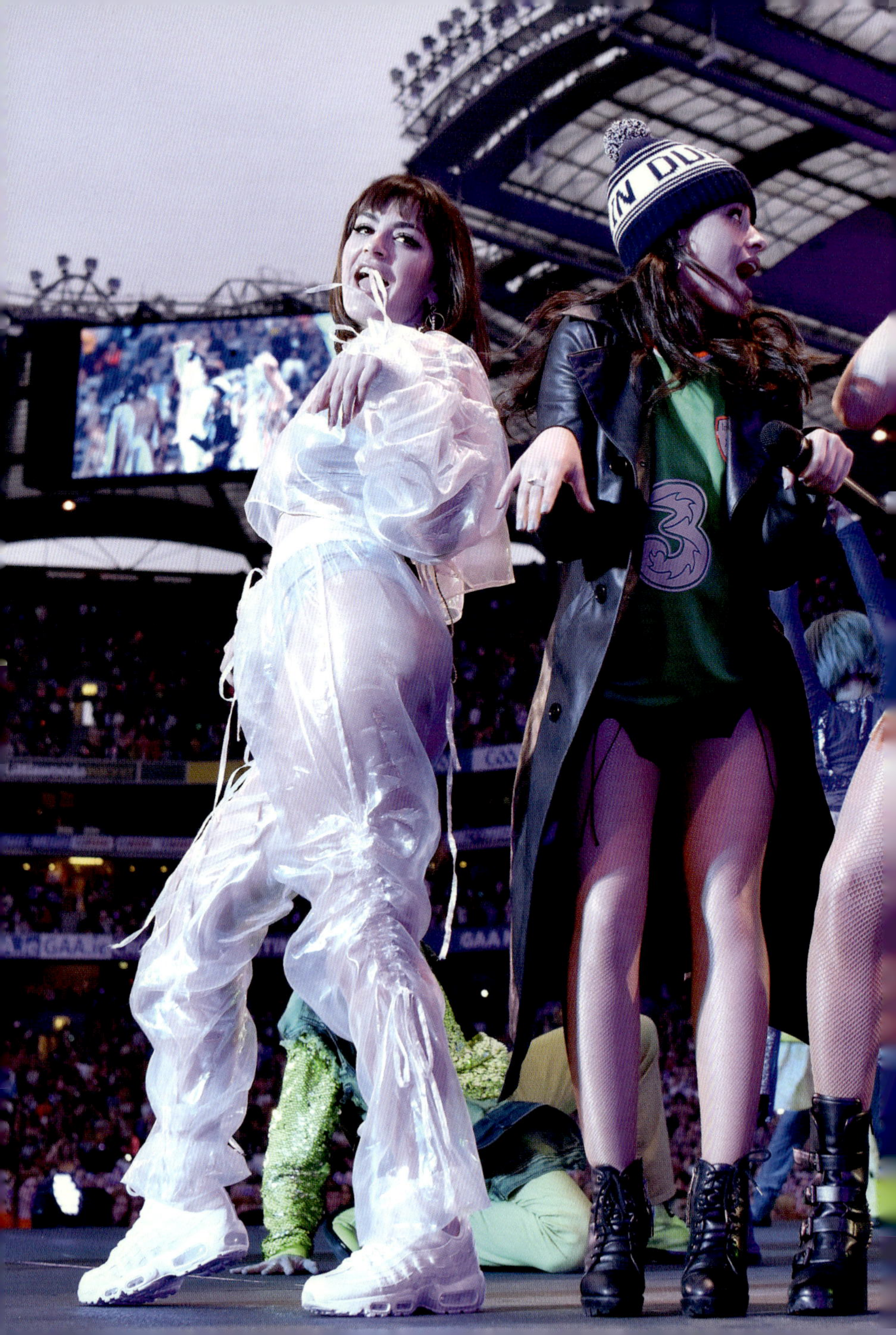

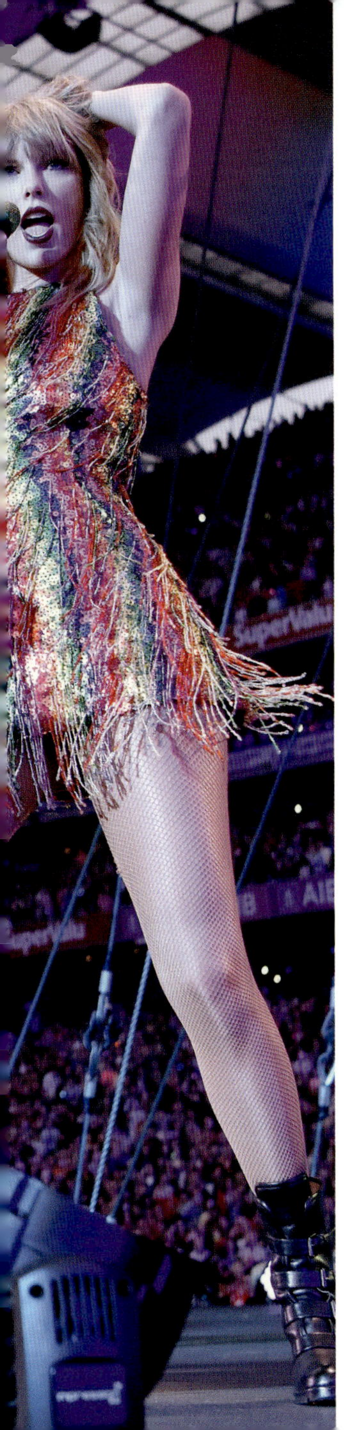

In October came a real treat. Charli dropped '1999', featuring up-and-coming Aussie pop star Troye Sivan, along with a nostalgia-packed music video that referenced *Titanic* (1997), The Sims, Backstreet Boys, *The Matrix* (1999) and other late '90s cultural moments. The track reached number 13 in the UK charts and was a bona fide bop.

By the time the *Reputation* tour wound up in November, Charli was ready for something new. In early 2019 she headed to the studio with A.G. with the intention of making the third in a trilogy of mixtapes, but the sessions were flowing well and so she decided to step things up and aim for an album.
It took just two weeks to mastermind Charli's self-titled third studio album proper. She went into the studio with no expectations and came out with 15 new tracks. In June, Charli announced the record to the world: 'Angels, my new album "Charli" is out September 13th. I am so proud of this music and I cannot wait for the world to hear it,' she tweeted to fans, alongside its cover art, which saw her naked but for a CGI, metallic pink snake curled over her breasts.

The same month another song would drop that would help her bank balance, but perhaps not her ego. In a writing session the previous year, Charli had penned steamy Latin-pop hit 'Señorita'. Initially recording a demo for herself, she decided to give it away to Camila Cabello and Shawn Mendes. When the pair released the track – impelled a little

Performing with Camila Cabello (centre) and Taylor Swift (right) on the Reputation *tour, Dublin, June 2018*

by a blossoming real-life romance – it landed at number 2 on the US charts, eventually climbing to the top spot. Charli again felt conflicted about the reception. She should be pleased she'd written yet another hit. So why did it sit uneasily?

SELF-TITLED SUCCESS

Charli was happiest when working with like-minded creatives, and for *Charli* she once again tapped into her community, featuring 12 guests across the record, including Lizzo, Haim, Clairo and Sky Ferreira's first return to music in years – a testament to her musical creds. Another early single, 'Gone', featured Christine and the Queens. 'I feel so unstable, fucking hate these people, how they're making me feel,' came the refrain. It was a raw and vulnerable song about party paranoia, at odds with her usual saccharine and hedonistic lyricism. Elsewhere on the record, 'White Mercedes' found Charli feeling undeserving of a lover. Was our self-confident queen feeling self-doubt?

'It's my most ***personal*** *body of work.'*

'It's an unoriginal statement, but it's my most personal body of work,' she said at the time. There were always two sides to Charli, but this was the first time fans were hearing them pushed up against each other. Who knew the life and soul of the party was in truth riddled with angst?

It's a familiar story and one Charli felt ready to open up about. In the run-up to the record's release she tweeted 'Can't stop crying', with no context. Fans rushed to post messages of support. Later she admitted to feeling silly about the tweet, but she was deep in her feels. Perhaps it was the pressure of the record, maybe it was the strain of the long-distance relationship she had with Kwong, or the fact that she'd barely stopped working and partying since she was 14.

Performing on the Reputation *tour, Toronto, August 2018*

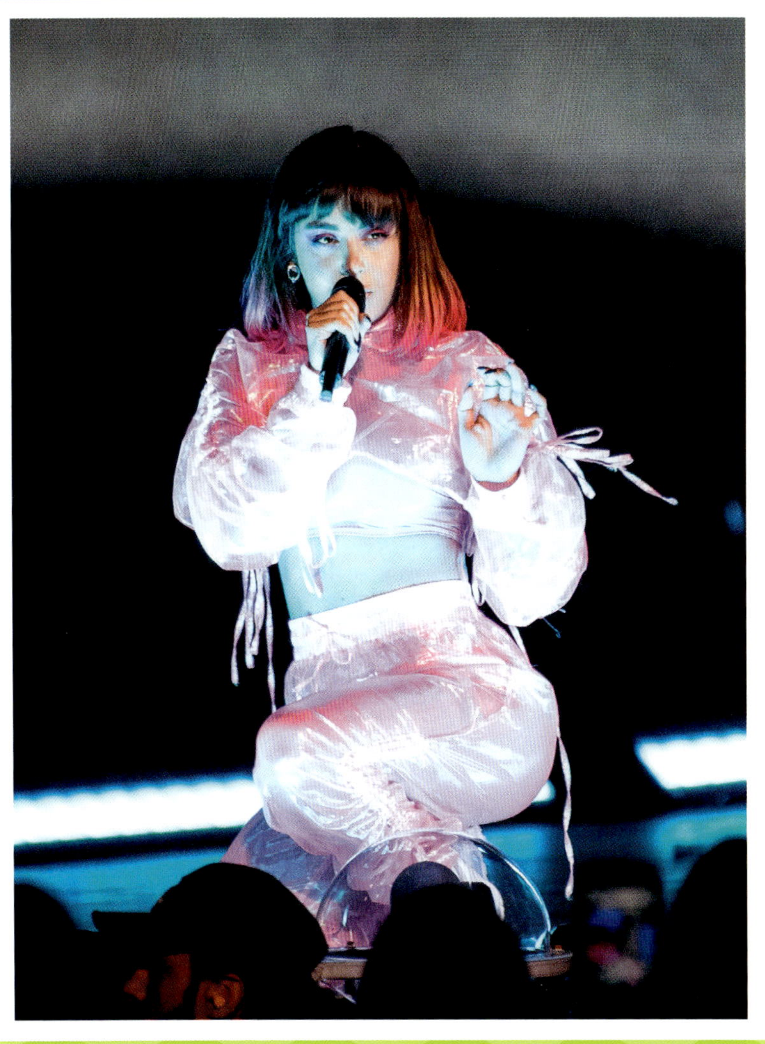

'I didn't set out to make a record about my vulnerability or emotional state, it just happened,' she told *The Fader.* Charli's authenticity meant she had no choice but to let her fans in, leaning on her peers and the LGBTQIA+ community who had embraced her for support as she wrestled with the sadness and loneliness on the flipside of every big night out. The connection she was building with her fans was deepening. From meme-fuelling moments (such as fans asking her to hold a bottle of poppers and yell 'Gay Rights') to truly being there for her at her lowest ebb, the Angels had a connection with the star that she didn't take for granted.

Critically, *Charli* was well received, the blogs and broadsheets praising her new-found vulnerability. The record debuted at number 14 on the UK singles chart – her highest British chart position – and 42 on the Billboard 200, underperforming *Sucker* by 14 spots. Charli was making peace with the idea that her people operated outside of the mainstream and that connecting with them was more important to her than chart success. But as ever, her label had other ideas.

CHARLI, POP SVENGALI

With the album done long before its release, Charli's workaholic mind was in 'what next?' mode. But did anyone have reality TV series and evolution into a Simon Cowell-esque music svengali on their bingo card?

Along with thoughts of album four, Charli's brain had been ruminating on an idea for some time: what if she could create a girl band from scratch and make them into stars? Enter Nasty Cherry, a four-piece group put together like a pop pick 'n' mix. And this wasn't a low-key experiment in music management; Charli plucked the individual members from relative obscurity, put them up in a house in LA and documented the whole process via Netflix series *I'm With The Band: Nasty Cherry*.

Two Brits – Georgia (Charli's childhood friend) and Debbie, a drummer on Charli's tour – were teamed with Chloe, guitarist and hyperactive frontwoman of the band Kitten, and Gabbriette, a then model who had starred in a couple of her videos. None of the gang knew each other. Gabbriette had never been a singer, and Georgia learned bass for the band. It was a risky strategy.

Charli's mission for the band was to inspire young women to feel like they can do anything. It made for some good TV and the series launched with a six-track EP, released on Vroom Vroom Recordings – indie pop that was fun, but lacked a little depth. A couple more EPs followed but the band weren't to last, splitting up somewhat acrimoniously in 2021.

Still, Charli remained tight with at least one of the band – Gabbriette, the BRAT-referencing It girl and Matty Healy of The 1975's betrothed. Funny how things turn out.

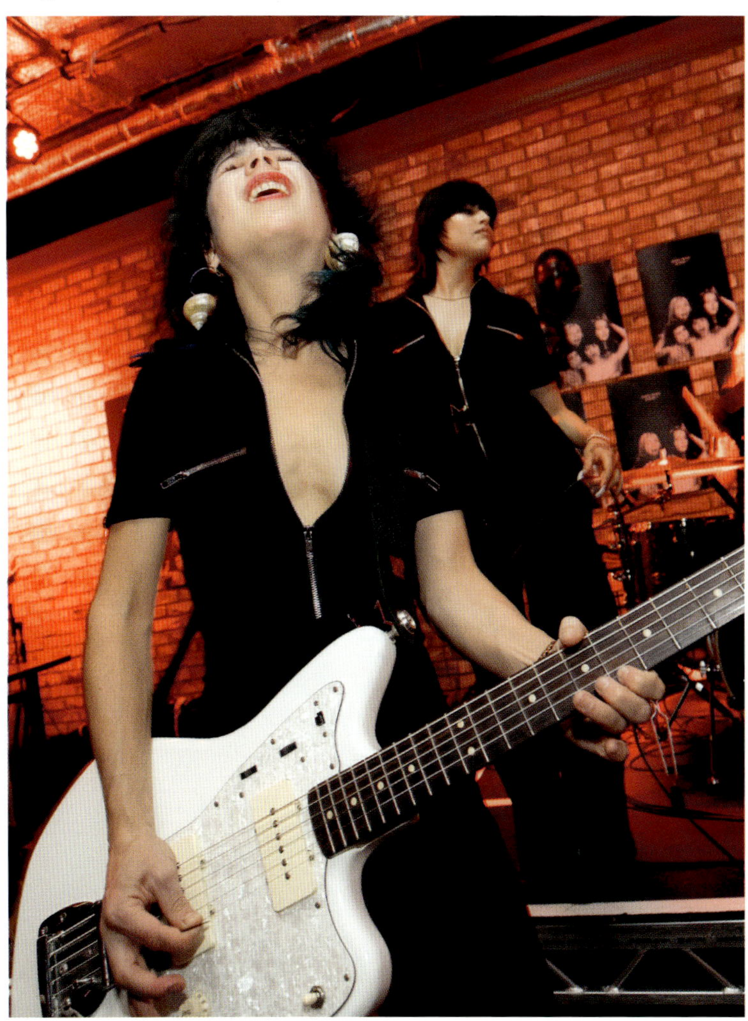

Nasty Cherry perform at members club The Curtain, London, November 2019
Overleaf: Performing at Village Underground, London, June 2018

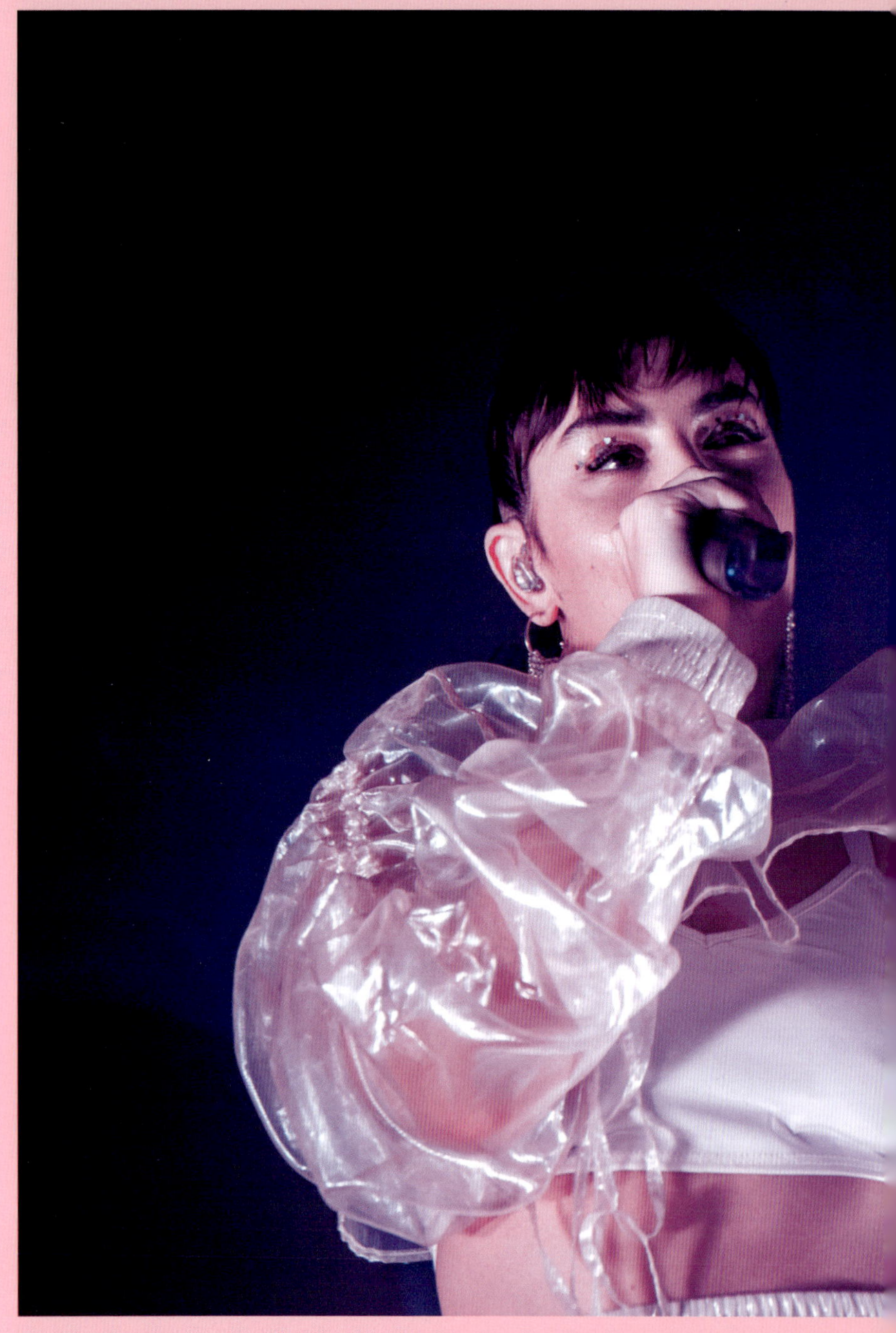

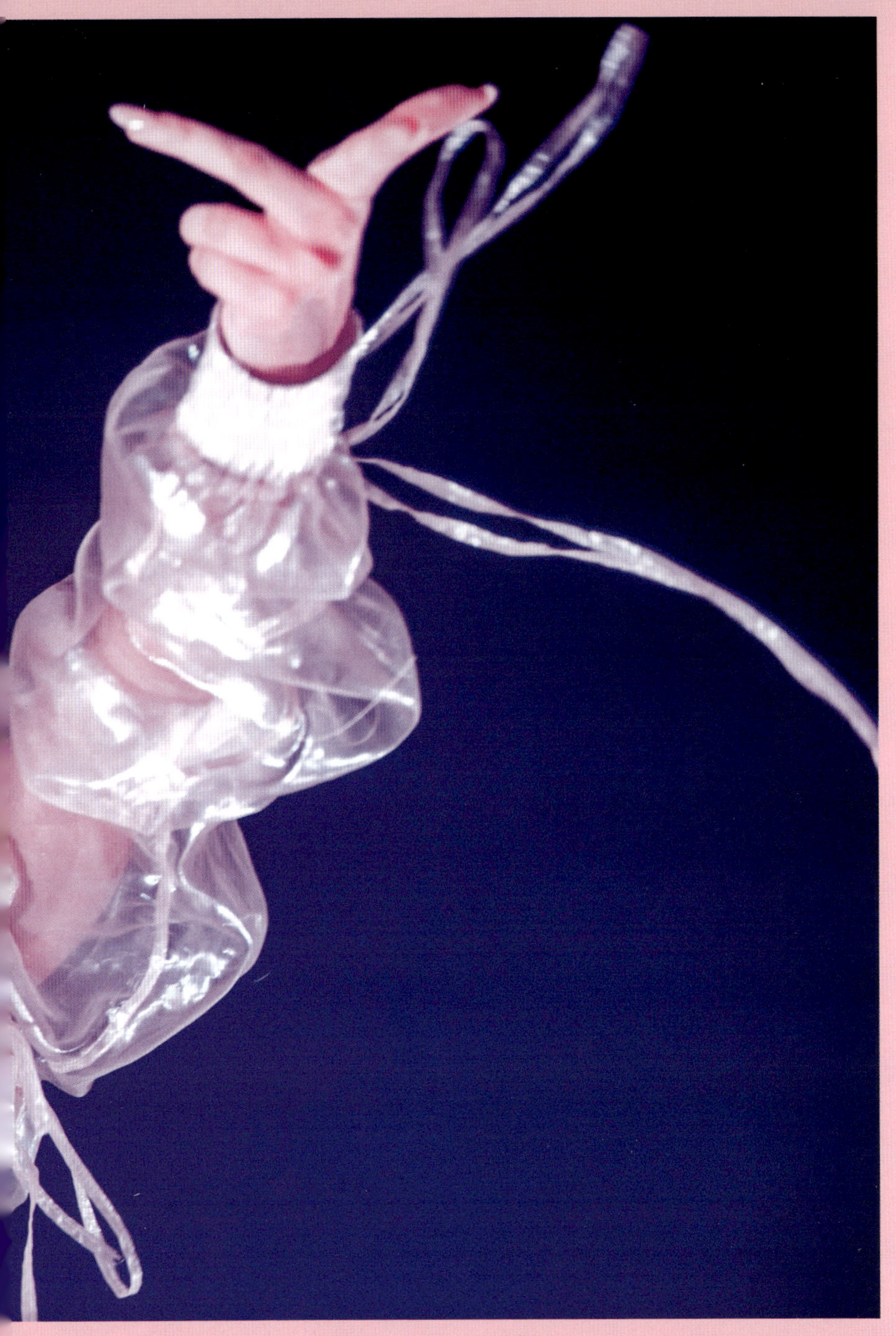

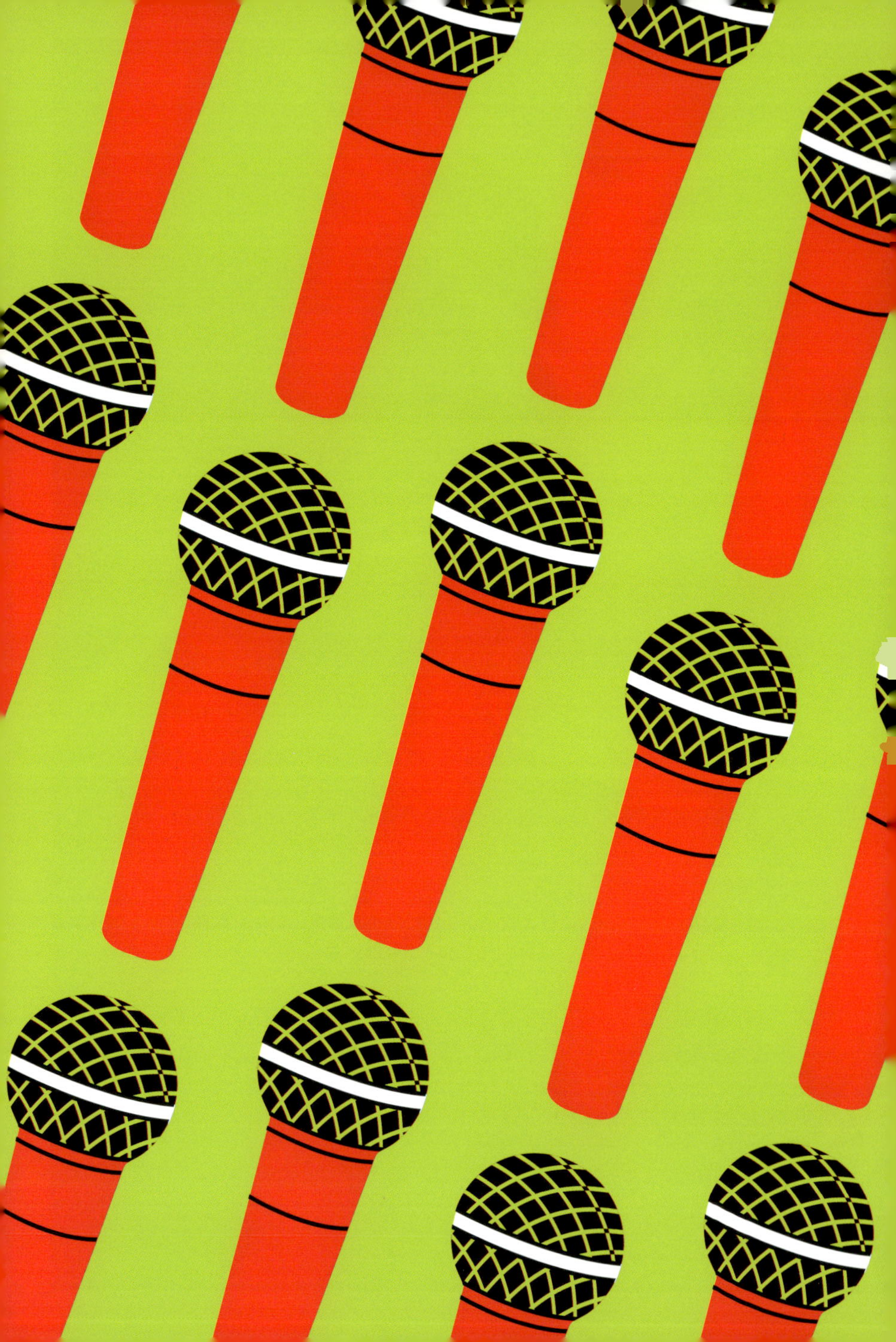

YOU'RE MY FAVOURITE
Reference

Charli's Musical Influences

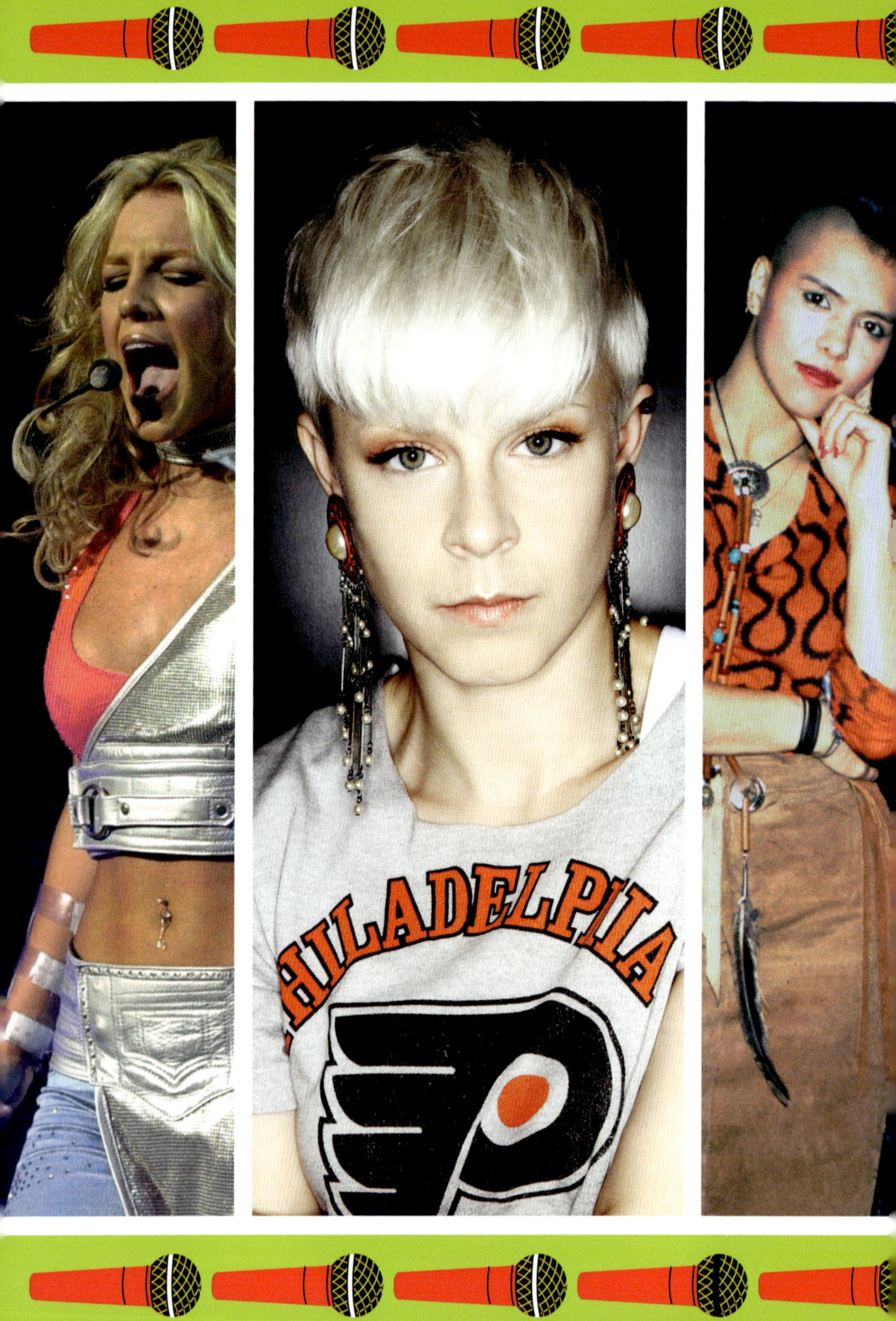
HILADELPIA

From Baby Spice to Bow Wow Wow, Britney to Lou Reed – Charli XCX's record collection is as chaotic and iconic as she is. A student of pop in all its forms, her influences span sugary chart hits, bratty punk and underground electronica. Welcome to the crash course in what made Charli Charli – a one-of-one artist.

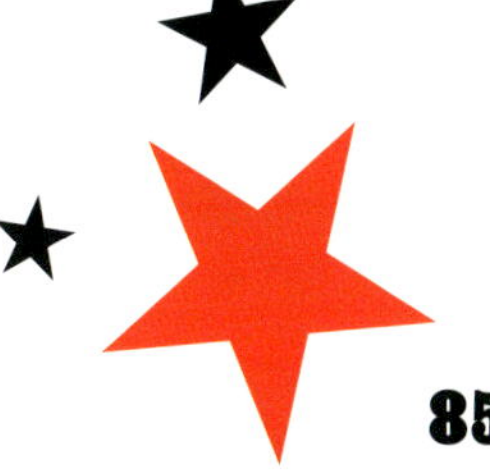

★ A.G. COOK ★

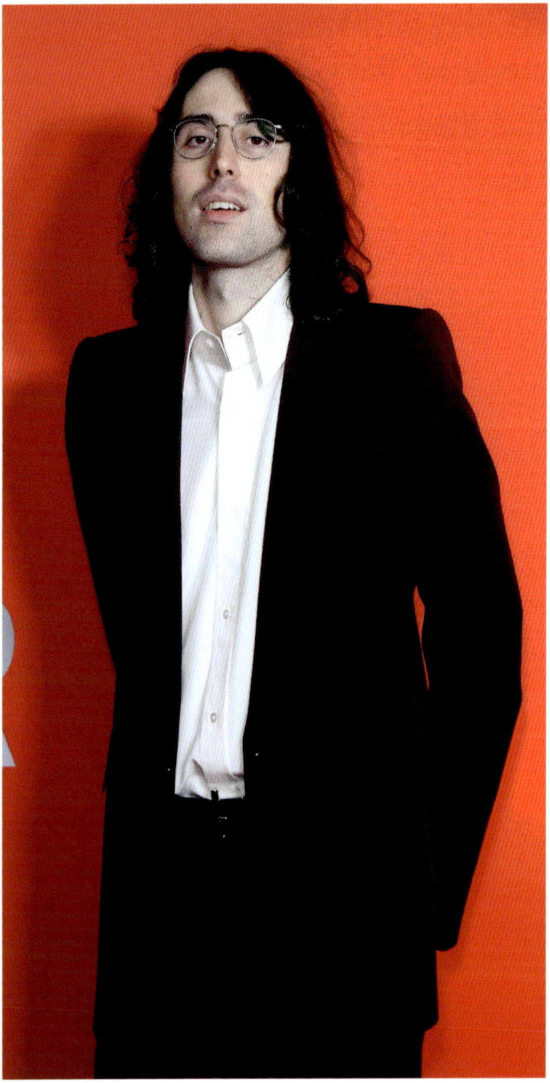

Charli's longest-standing collaborator, Alexander Guy Cook, was the founder of PC Music – a label that blended pitched-up video-game sounds with sugary pop production and autotuned vocals. A.G. has been an influence not only on Charli's sound but on the way she thinks about artistry. A firm believer in manifesto-writing and world-building, A.G.'s approach has shaped the way Charli thinks about pop.

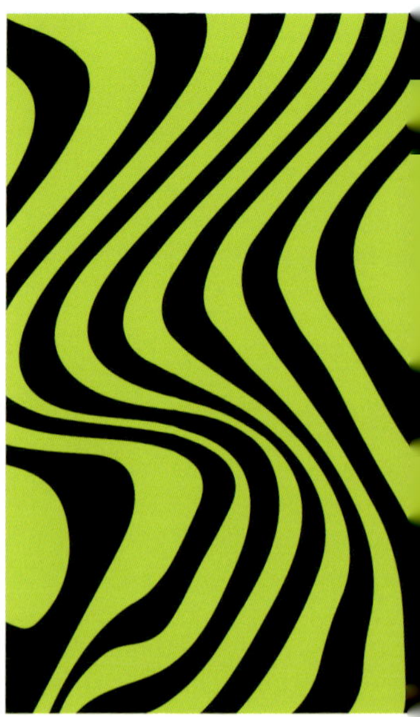

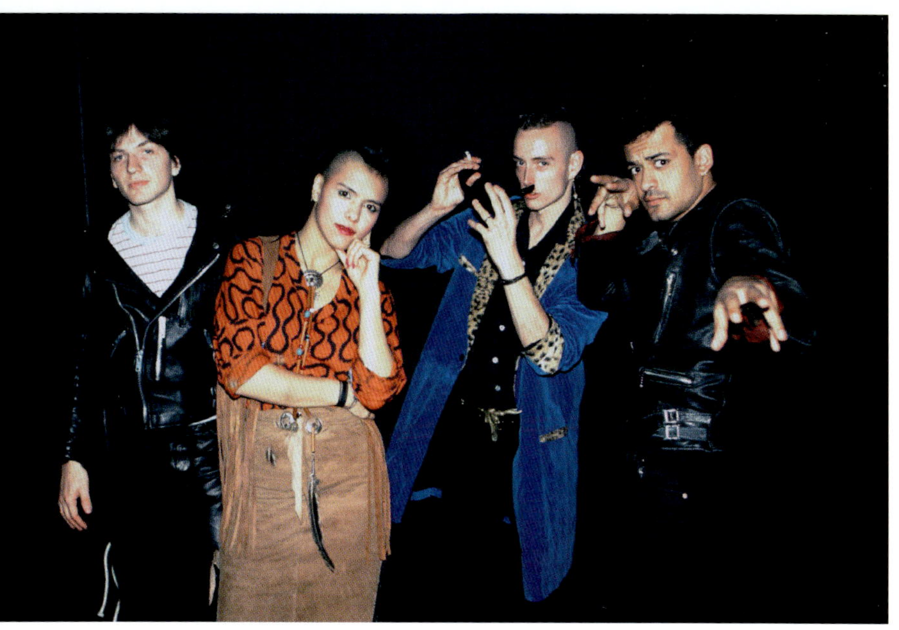

During the *Sucker* era, Charli was listening to a lot of Bow Wow Wow. The New Wave band were formed by former Sex Pistols manager Malcolm McLaren in 1980, taking members of Adam and the Ants and pairing them with feisty 13-year-old vocalist Annabella Lwin. Charli saw something of herself in the young frontwoman and admired her punk energy and style.

★ BOW ★ WOW WOW

★ BRITNEY SPEARS ★

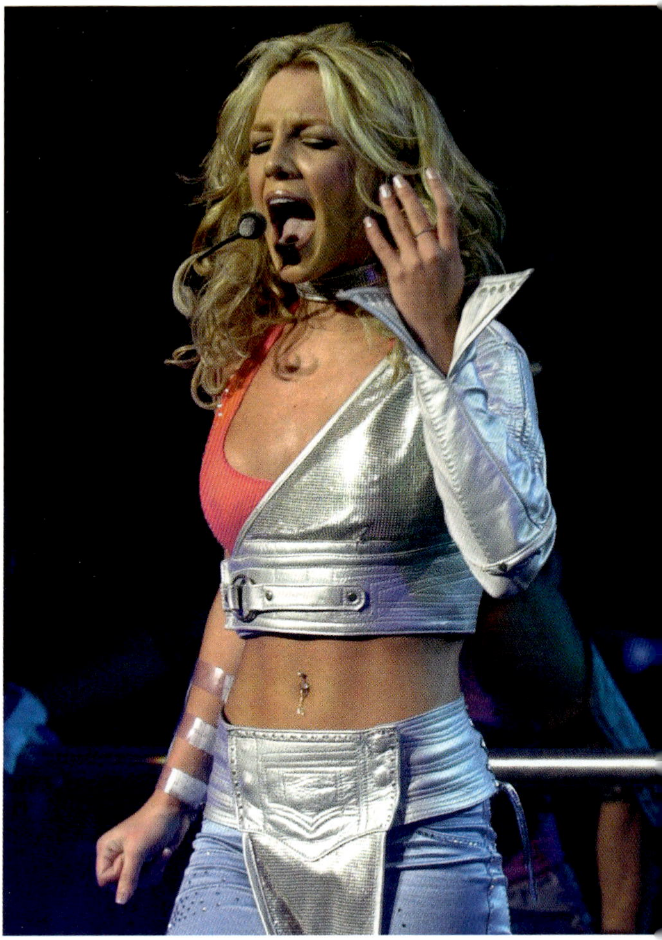

Britney was one of Charli's earliest influences and one of the reasons she wanted to become a pop star. Back in 2022, while on *The Tonight Show Starring Jimmy Fallon*, she declared 'Baby One More Time' to be the greatest song of all time, and has also frequently called Spears's *Blackout* one of her favourite albums.

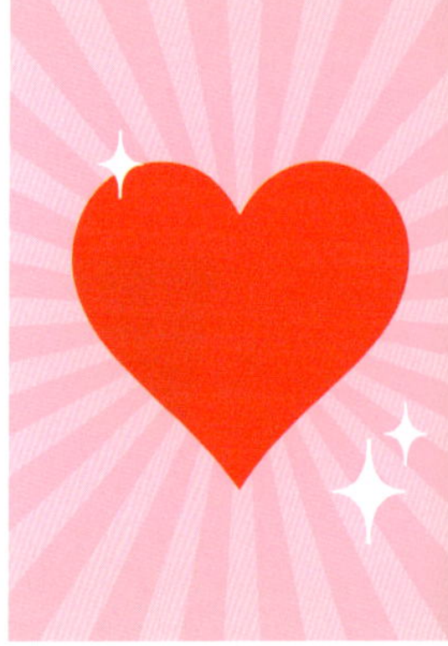

★ ROBYN ★

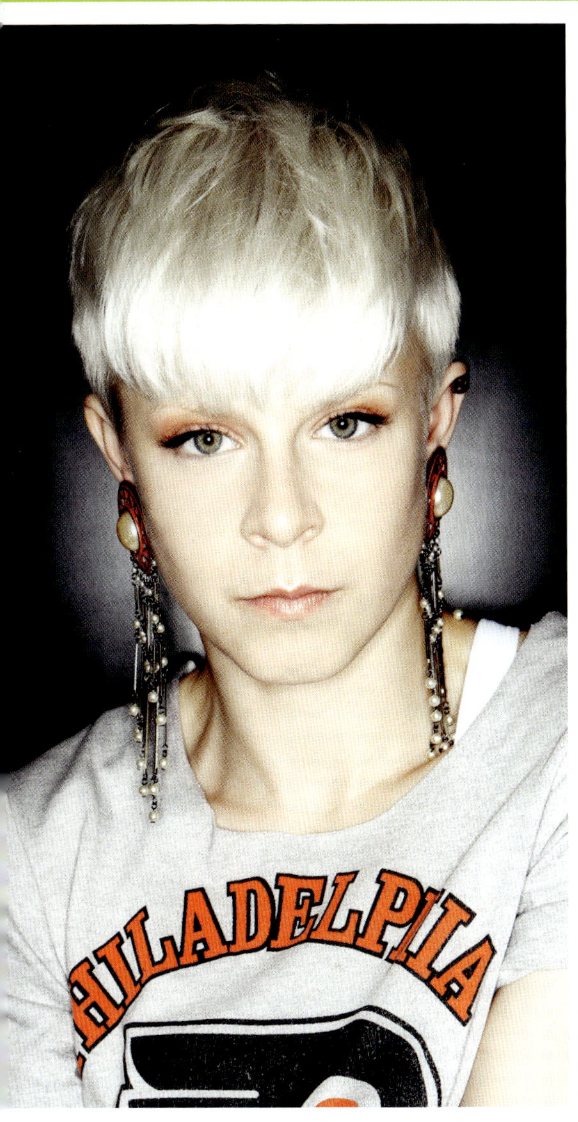

Charli XCX and Robyn have a friendship that goes back years. Speaking to *NME* in 2020, Charli recalled early encouragement from Robyn, who told her 'Don't worry about what anyone else thinks of you' – a lesson that stuck with Charli as she continued to forge her own path in pop music.

Robyn features on the 2024 remix of Charli's track '360' alongside Yung Lean, which was released as part of the remix album *Brat and it's completely different but also still brat*. During Charli's *Brat* tour, Robyn joined her on stage at London's O2 Arena, performing both '360' and her own huge hit 'Dancing On My Own'. Robyn's vulnerable lyricism and club-ready anthems continue to shape Charli's vision of experimental pop.

★ LOU REED ★

Charli's in her Lou Reed era right now, sporting a tee to Coachella and namechecking him in interviews. Despite his cantankerous reputation, the Velvet Underground frontman is considered one of the greatest songwriters of all time – Charli definitely thinks so, telling Howard Stern as much at the end of 2024. From garage rock anthems such as 'I'm Waiting For My Man' to the tender brilliance of 'Pale Blue Eyes', Reed's conversational songwriting, which brings the listener into the people and places that make up his world, was a direct influence on *Brat*.

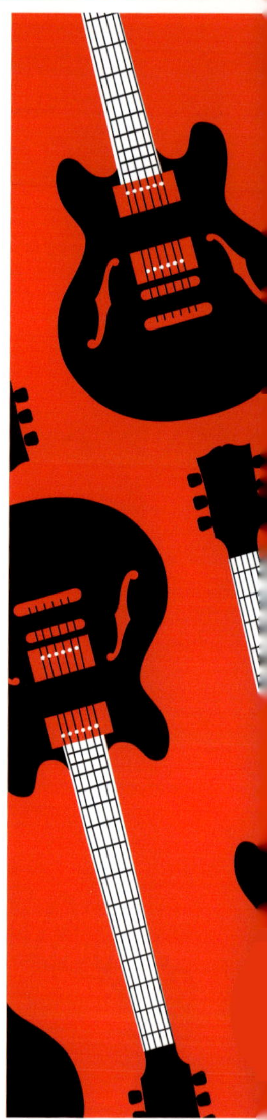

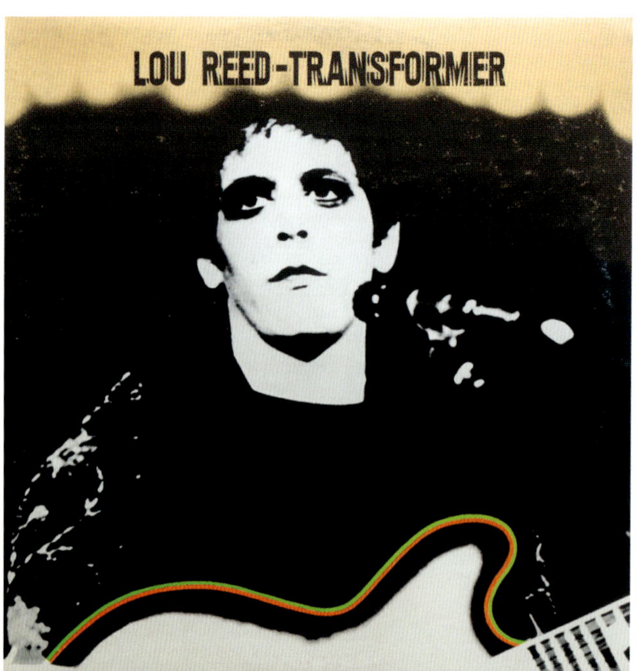

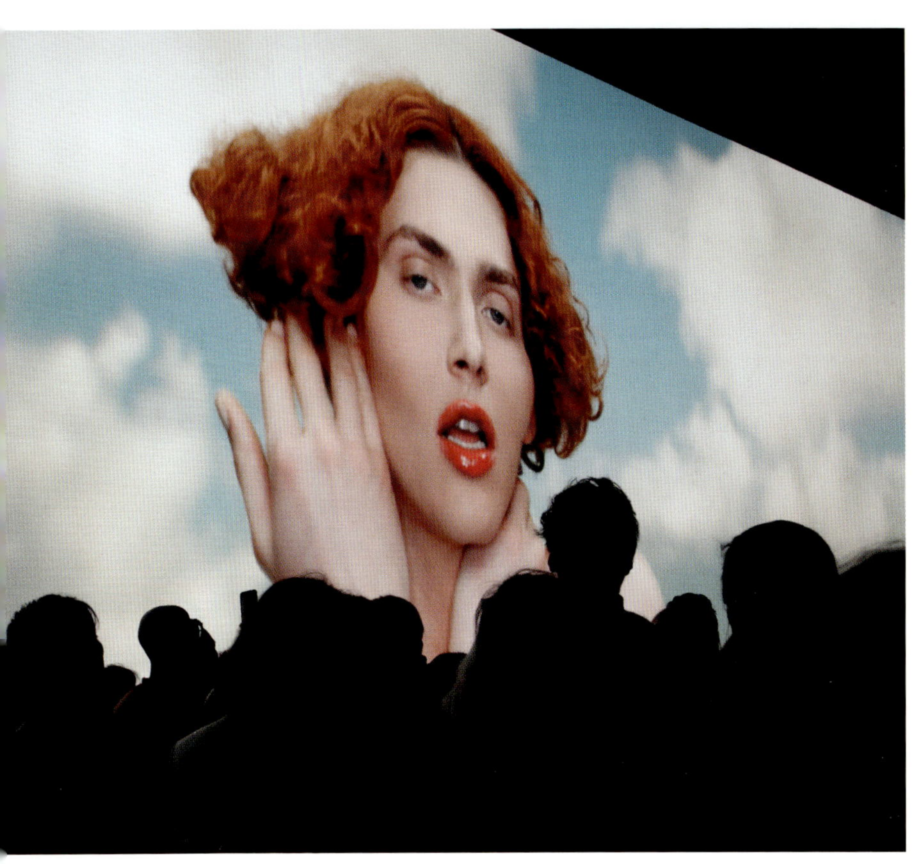

There's pre-SOPHIE Charli and post-SOPHIE Charli. Working with the late producer marked a turning point in Charli's sound, starting with the *Vroom Vroom* EP. SOPHIE's sharp, futuristic production pushed Charli towards something more experimental, more synthetic and more extreme. Charli has spoken about SOPHIE as both a creative influence and a personal inspiration – someone who shifted how she thought about pop, creativity and possibility.

★ SOPHIE ★

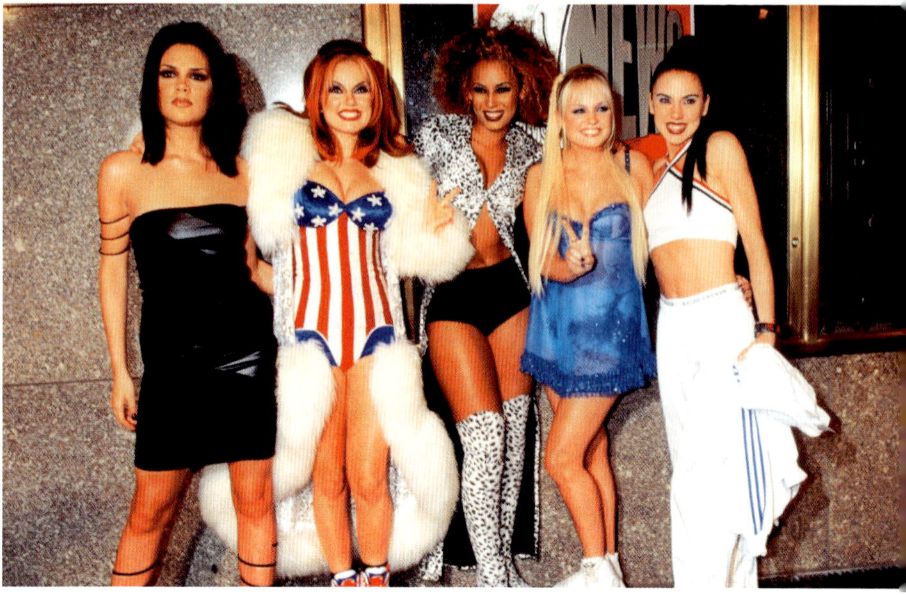

Little Charli loved the Spice Girls – Baby was her favourite – and often sang and danced around to their songs at home. She credits the group as being her first introduction to feminism, their 'Girl Power' slogan and strong female friendship being a blueprint for what Charli wanted in her life. In 2019, she joined forces with Diplo and Herve Pagez for a reworked version of 'Wannabe' called 'Spicy'.

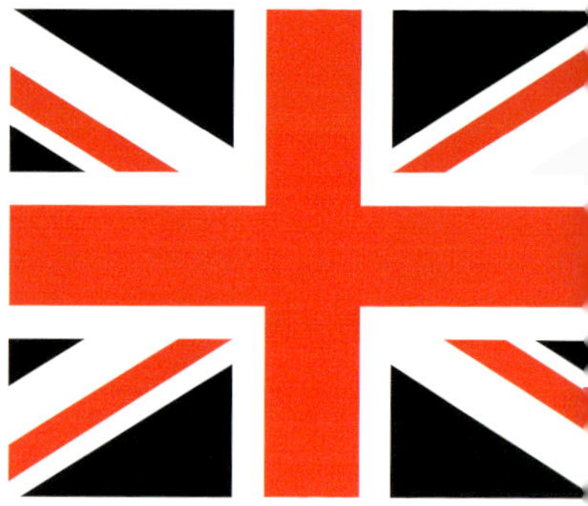

★ SPICE ★ GIRLS

★ UFFIE ★

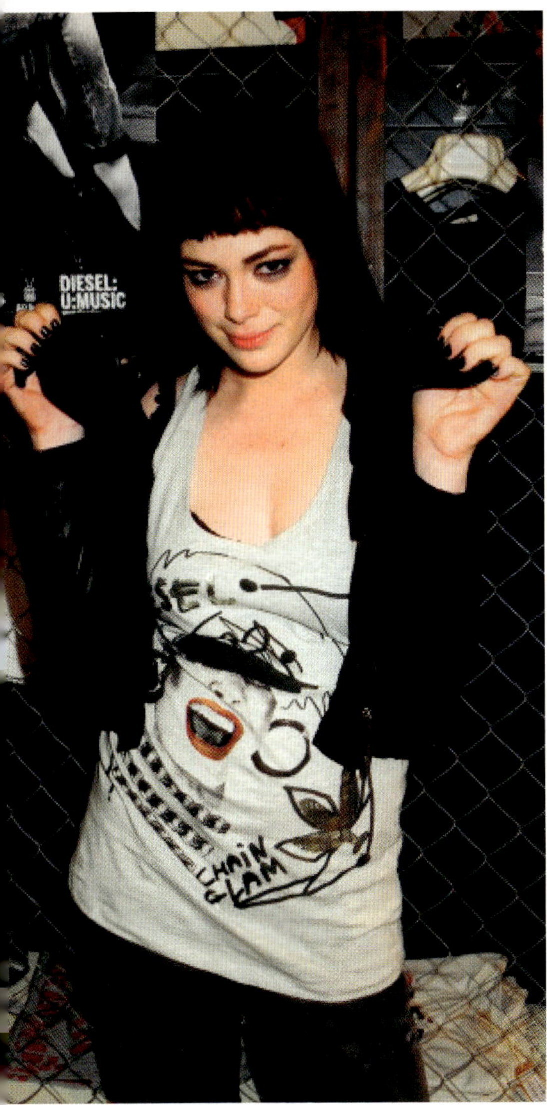

An early influence on Charli's sound, Uffie (Anna-Catherine Hartley) signed to French electro label Ed Banger Records in her teens, and had a hit with autotuned bop 'Pop the Glock'. Charli credits the song as the reason she got into music, and the pair later teamed up for *Number 1 Angel* track 'Babygirl'.

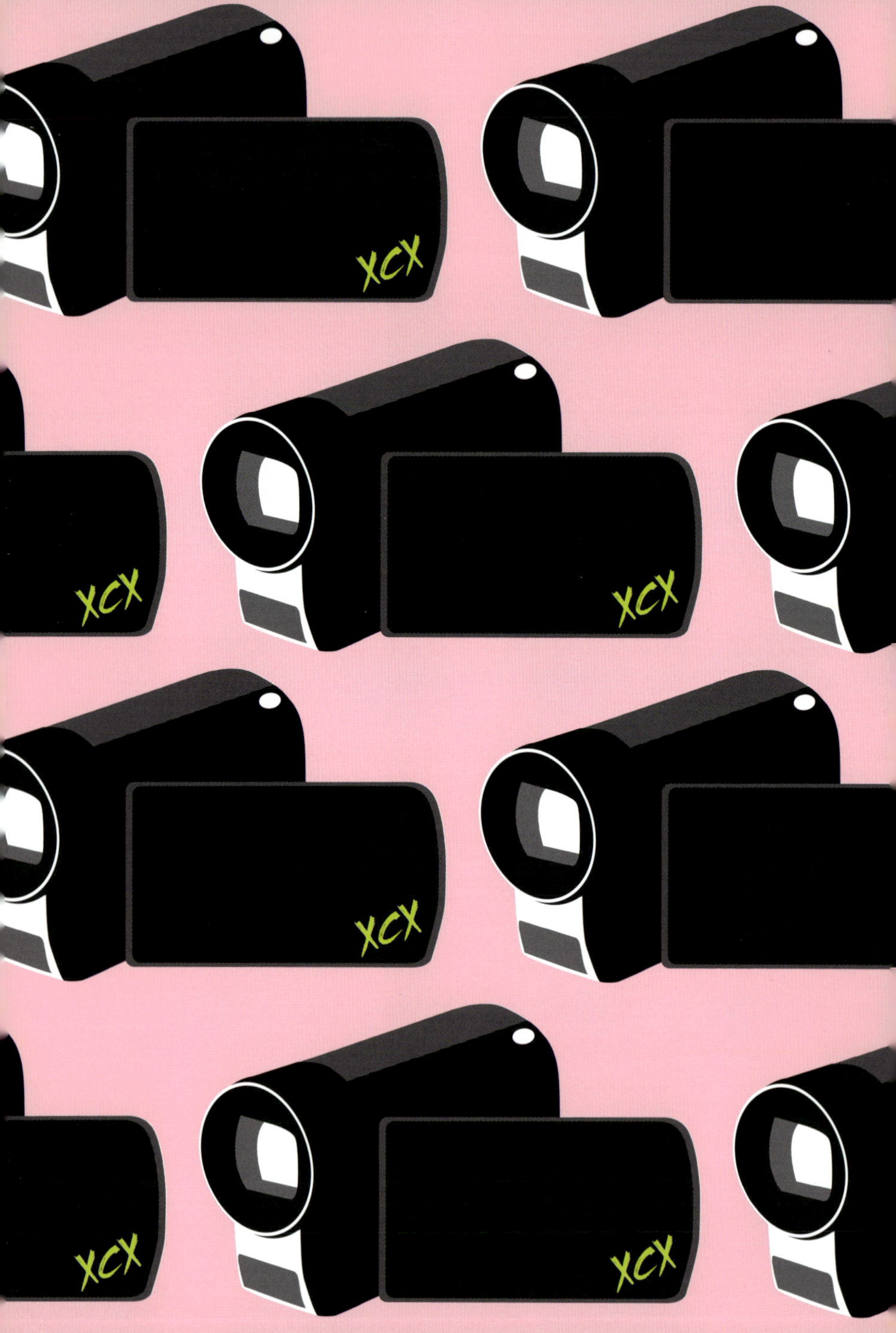
XCX
XCX
XCX
XCX
XCX
XCX
XCX
XCX

FROM LOCKDOWN *to* LIFT-OFF

Charli's Pandemic Project

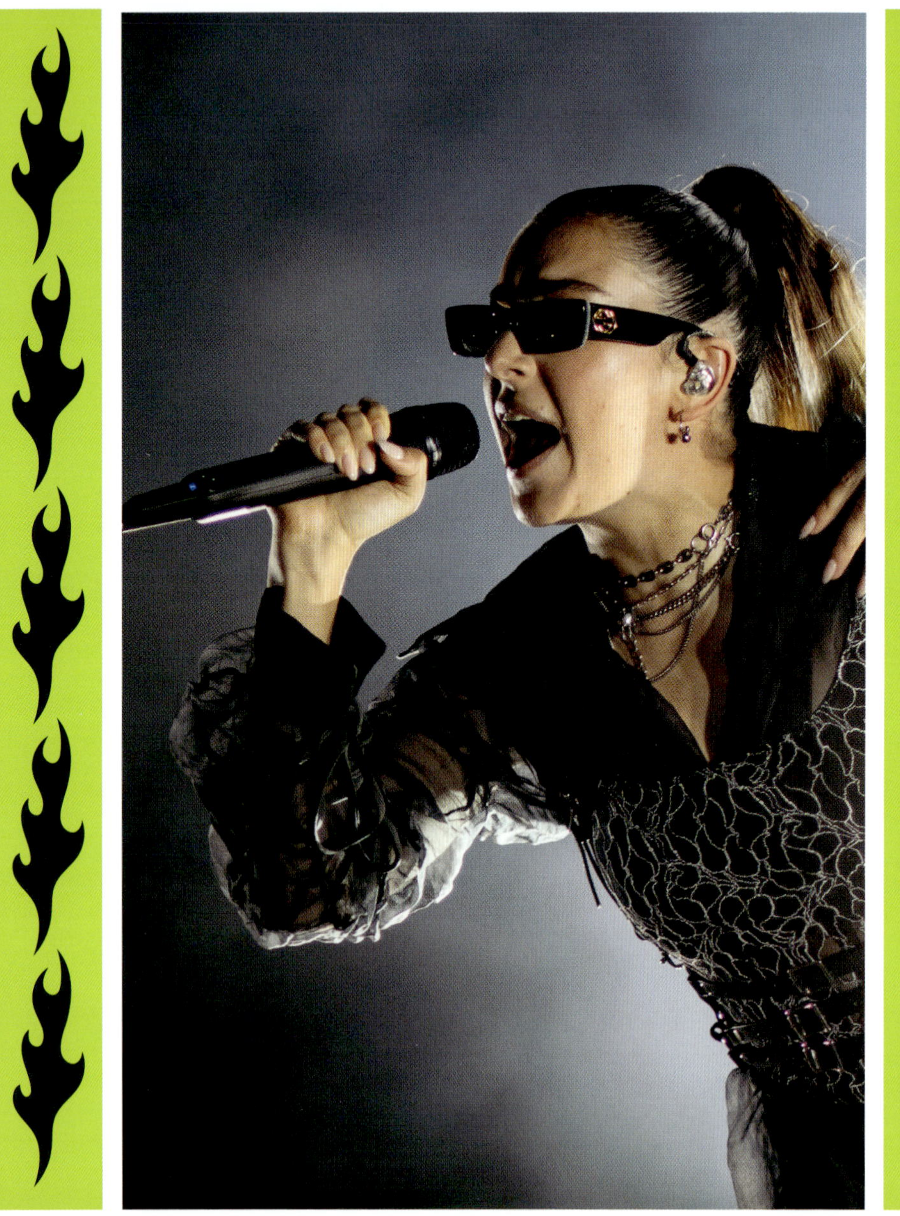

Charli kicked off 2020 by performing at Laneway Festival in Melbourne, Australia. She was second on the bill, just below The 1975.

Backstage, she got to know the band's keyboardist, George Daniel (now her fiancé). Matty Healy teased her that she had a crush, but Charli was still in a relationship with Huck Kwong at the time so put it out of her head. After flying straight from the festival to party at the NME and BRIT awards, she returned home to LA as news of a deadly and highly contagious virus started to reach all corners of the globe.

As LA went into lockdown, Charli hunkered down at home with her boyfriend and her managers, Twiggy and Sam. Forced to take a breather for the first time since her teens, she was spiralling. Who was she without her work? 'I feel true anxiety when I'm not working and I think it comes from feeling fearful or feeling like I'm purposeless, or not good enough,' she told journalist Ben Homewood at *Music Week*. Not one to let a little thing like a global pandemic stifle her creativity, Charli hatched a plan. While the rest of us were baking sourdough and jumping up and down to Joe Wicks, she decided to see if she could make an album, from home, in just five weeks.

Since the mixtape eras, Charli had used social media to be in constant conversation with her fans. Her no-filter tweets built a close bond with her community, many feeling as though they knew her intimately. She shared how she was feeling in group chats, invited fans to meet-ups and had an open dialogue that blurred the lines between artist and fan. As the *Charli* tour wrapped at the end of 2019, she felt closer to her Angels – who camped outside her sold-out shows – than ever. In an emotional moment on stage at London's Brixton Academy, she wept on stage, thanking them for allowing her to be herself and make the music she wanted to make.

During these months of isolation, when so many of us were yearning for human connection, Charli leaned into her community. She hosted Instagram Lives with Chris, Clairo and Ashnikko, painting and working out. She was vulnerable, sharing feelings of anxiety and sadness on video streams, often in tears. Eighteen days into lockdown, she decided she needed a focus.

Performing at St Jerome's Laneway Festival, Brisbane, February 2020

ALONE TOGETHER

Sharing a Zoom code on Instagram, she announced the news to 1,000 fans: she was making a new album. It would be out in five weeks. There would be artwork, videos and a record's worth of new songs, all created from her Los Angeles home – and she needed their help. 'I'm going to be sharing demos with you, a cappellas with you asking you to help me make videos,' she told her giddy fans. 'It's going to be called "How I'm Feeling Now".'

The usual process of planning a major-label album release can take up to a year. Charli's team were used to her not playing by the book – but could she really pull this off? There were not only technical hurdles to overcome but her creative process had been one that thrived on collaboration. Could she do it alone? A.G. was locked down in Montana but was on board to produce the record, albeit over Zoom.

*'I'm going to be **sharing demos** with you ... asking you to **help make videos.**'*

Charli ordered a bunch of microphones and cables to fit out her home studio, which would become a creative milieu for the next few months. She planned to document the whole process, the result of which is the BBC documentary *Charli XCX: Alone Together*.

At a time of global chaos, it was revolutionary thinking. Many artists would use the time to be creative, spawning pandemic projects aplenty over the next few years, but Charli was the first, and prioritized finding new ways to connect with her fans when they needed it most.

It was a savvy business move. Charli had always understood that online fandom translated into ticket and album sales, but it was also a lifeline – for Charli and thousands of kids. Many of her LGBTQIA+ fans had been forced to return to family homes, away from the friends and chosen family that made them feel safe and seen. Others were locked down alone, mental health declining. Charli's daily livestreams gave them a reason to get up in the morning.

Right: Promotional image for the documentary Charli XCX: Alone Together
Overleaf: Stills from BBC documentary Charli XCX: Alone Together, *2021*

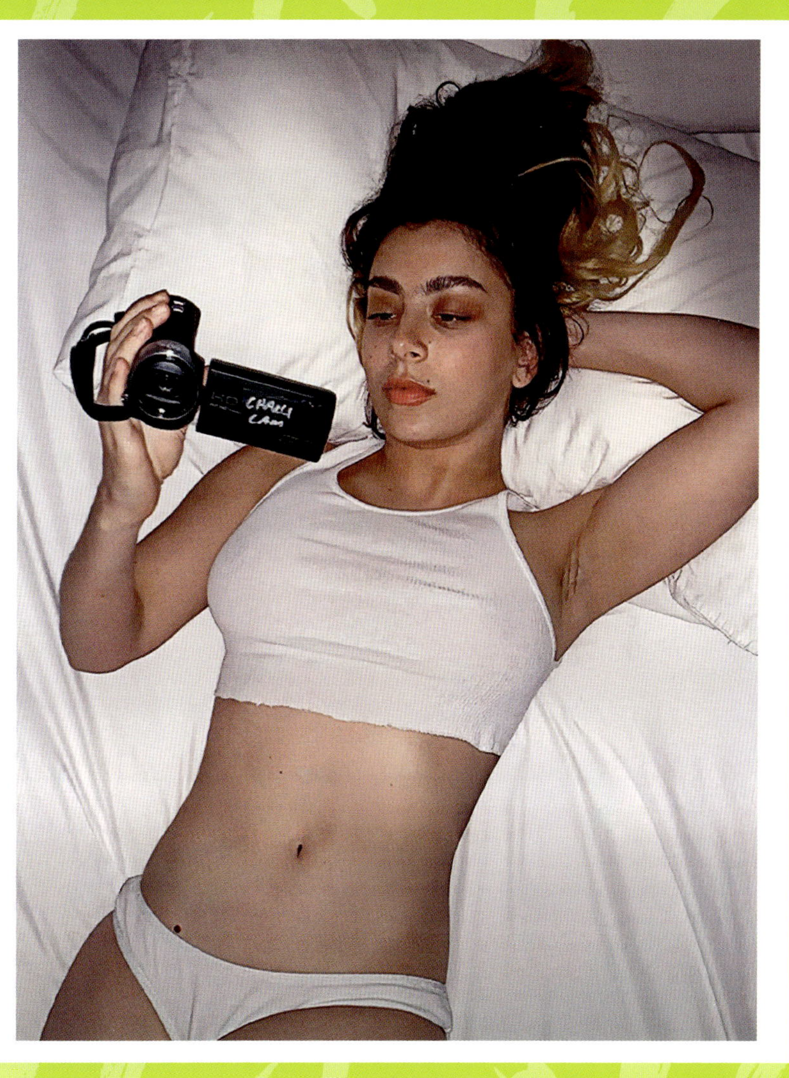
HD
CHARLI
CAM

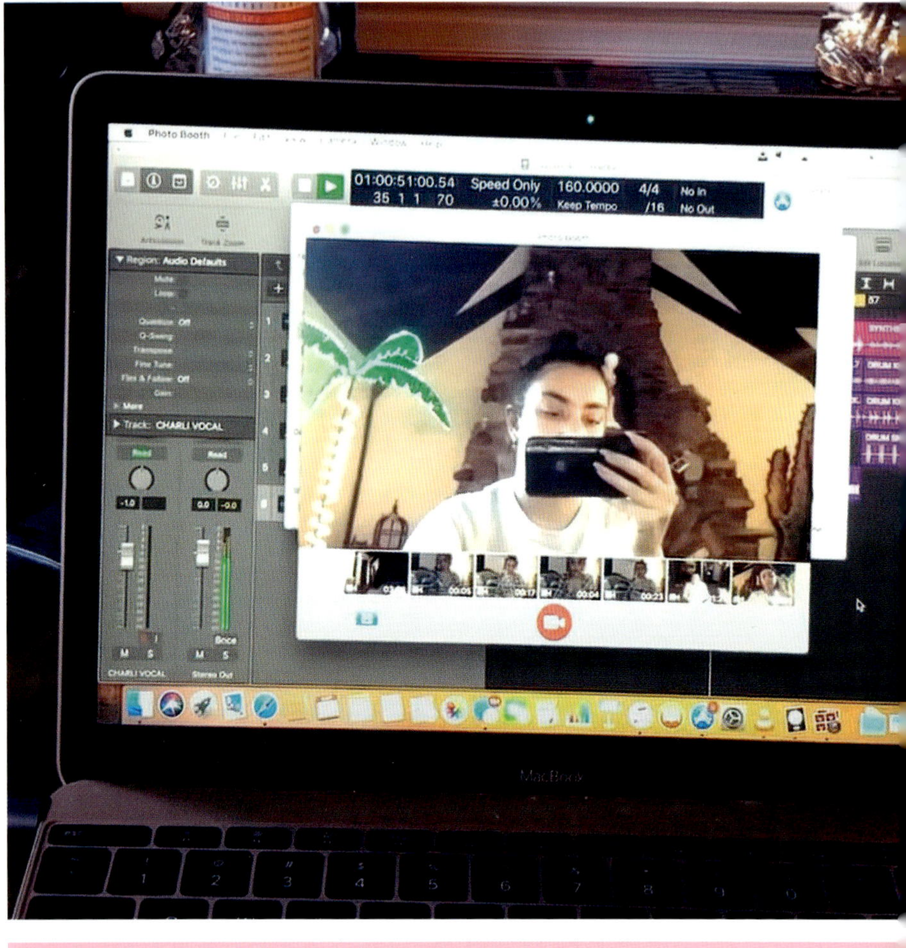

Many artists would use the time to be creative, spawning ***lockdown projects*** *aplenty ... but Charli was* ***the first***.

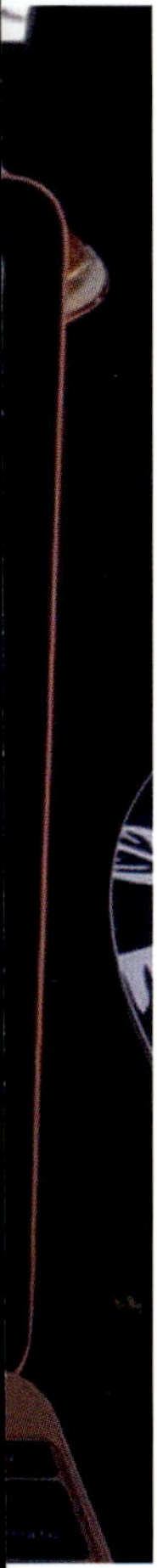

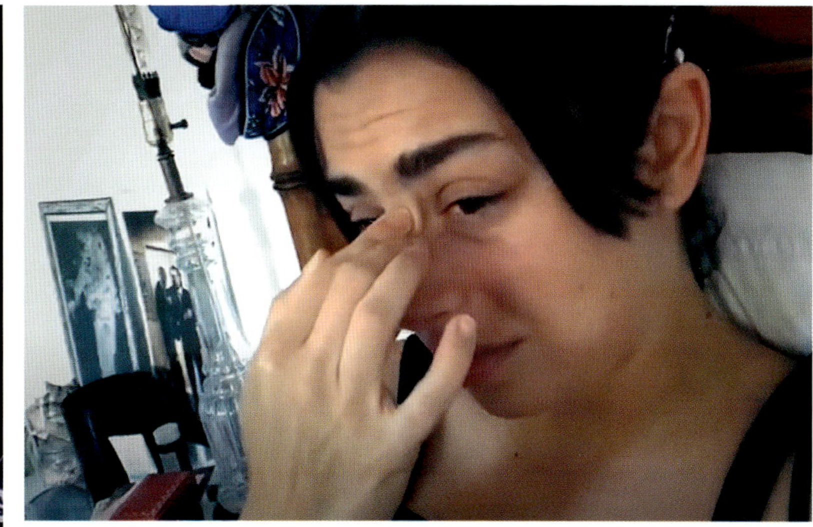

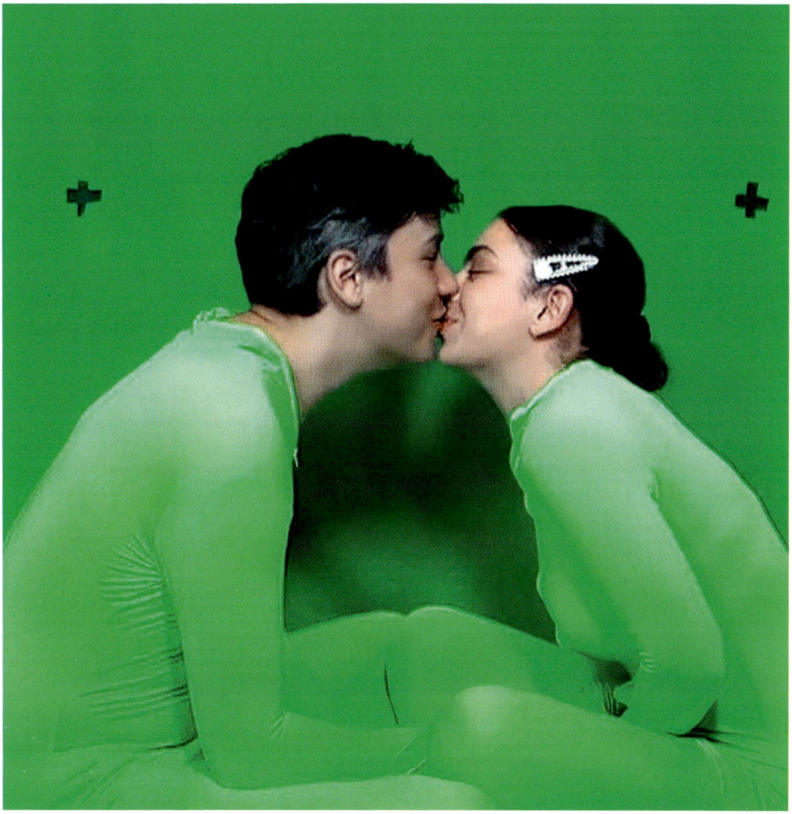

Thematically, the album was about her relationship with Kwong. As the world shut down, he had moved from New York City to LA to isolate with Charli. It was an intense decision, as despite being together for seven years, the couple had never spent more than eleven consecutive days together. Charli was open with her fans that 'they had stuff they needed to work on.' And with no escaping each other, it would be make or break.

Friends such as 100 gecs's Dylan Brady and Danny L Harle sent Charli beats to record vocals to. It was to be a party record, but one that was about love and longing. Jumping on livestreams, she crowdsourced lyrics and opinions on her work, her online community replicating the creative volley of the studio. Videos were recorded on a green screen in the living room. Stems were uploaded for fans to remix. Emotionally, Charli was up and down, sometimes feeling hyped over the process, other times questioning herself in emotional voicenotes shared to social media. She had started going to therapy just before lockdown and it was emotionally draining; the work centred around her negative self-perception and deep-rooted feelings of self-loathing which, at her lowest ebb, were all-consuming.

As the album deadline approached, she began to feel the pressure. She had dropped a few singles – 'Forever', 'Claws' and 'I Finally Understand', hyperpop anthems with DIY visuals. The party-starved fans lapped them up, but now was crunch time. She had an album to finish.

A week ahead of its release, she shared this with fans on Instagram:

> *I can't believe How I'm Feeling Now is out this Friday! this whole process has been so incredible & I'm so happy you've all been such a crucial part of the creative process! co-writing verse 2 of 'anthems' on insta live; making the 'forever' video together from all your amazing clips, your green screen versions of 'claws', the remixes & edits you made using the stems I dropped* [...] *helping me with production decisions & so much more... i couldn't have made this album without you!*
>
> *howimfeelingnowinbox@gmail.com has been bombarded with wild beats, artwork & ideas & it's been so inspiring going through it all.* [...] *This process has introduced me to new work & I'm so grateful for that.* [...] *I can't believe this album is nearly out! We did it!*

I can't believe ***How I'm Feeling Now*** *is out this Friday!! this whole process has been* ***so incredible*** *& I'm so happy you've all been such a crucial part of the* ***creative process****!*
... i couldn't have made this album ***without you****!*

On 15 May 2020, Charli dropped *How I'm Feeling Now*: 11 tracks that stayed true to the 8-bit artistic journey she'd begun on the *Vroom Vroom* EP. The record inspired 5,000 music video clips, 2,000 cover artworks and 3,000 remixes from fans, and the critics were unanimous – this was important, boundary-breaking work. As Dua Lipa's *Future Nostalgia* topped the charts, Charli's record failed to get a look-in, but much more than a career play, this album was a gift to her community and herself.

As 2021 unfolded, Charli teased a shift in her aesthetic, dropping cryptic messages about her 'selling out' and referencing the concept of mainstream pop in a way that felt both tongue-in-cheek and entirely serious. If *How I'm Feeling Now* had been a testament to her cult following, her next project would be a declaration: Charli XCX could play in the big leagues and still maintain her identity. That project was *Crash*.

After lockdown, Kwong had moved in with Charli in LA, but it didn't last and, after seven years together, the couple called it quits. Not long after, she began dating George Daniel. It was a period of immense personal upheaval. But the worst was still to come.

On 31 January 2021, SOPHIE died after falling from a rooftop in Athens, while trying 'to watch the full moon'. The loss was seismic, felt by fans and artists across the world, who had been forever changed by her groundbreaking approach to pop music. SOPHIE had created a genre, pioneered new sounds and made Charli into the artist she is today. She was devastated. On 2 February, she paid tribute via social media, posting:

> *It's really hard for me to sum up the special connection I felt with such an amazing person who completely changed my life. There are so many memories, so many small details, so many different views and incredible feelings and stories ... Even the most insignificant thing felt enormous ...*
>
> *For now, all I can* [say] *is that I will miss her terribly; her smile, her laugh, her dancing in the studio, her gentle inquisitive voice, her cutting personality, her ability to command a room without even trying, her incredible vision and mind. She taught me so much about myself without even realizing ...*
>
> *I love you and I will never forget you Sophie.*

In interviews, Charli spoke of a distance that had grown between them, of not feeling cool enough for her company outside of the studio – something she now regrets.

SOPHIE performs onstage at Coachella Valley Music and Arts Festival, Indio, California, April 2016

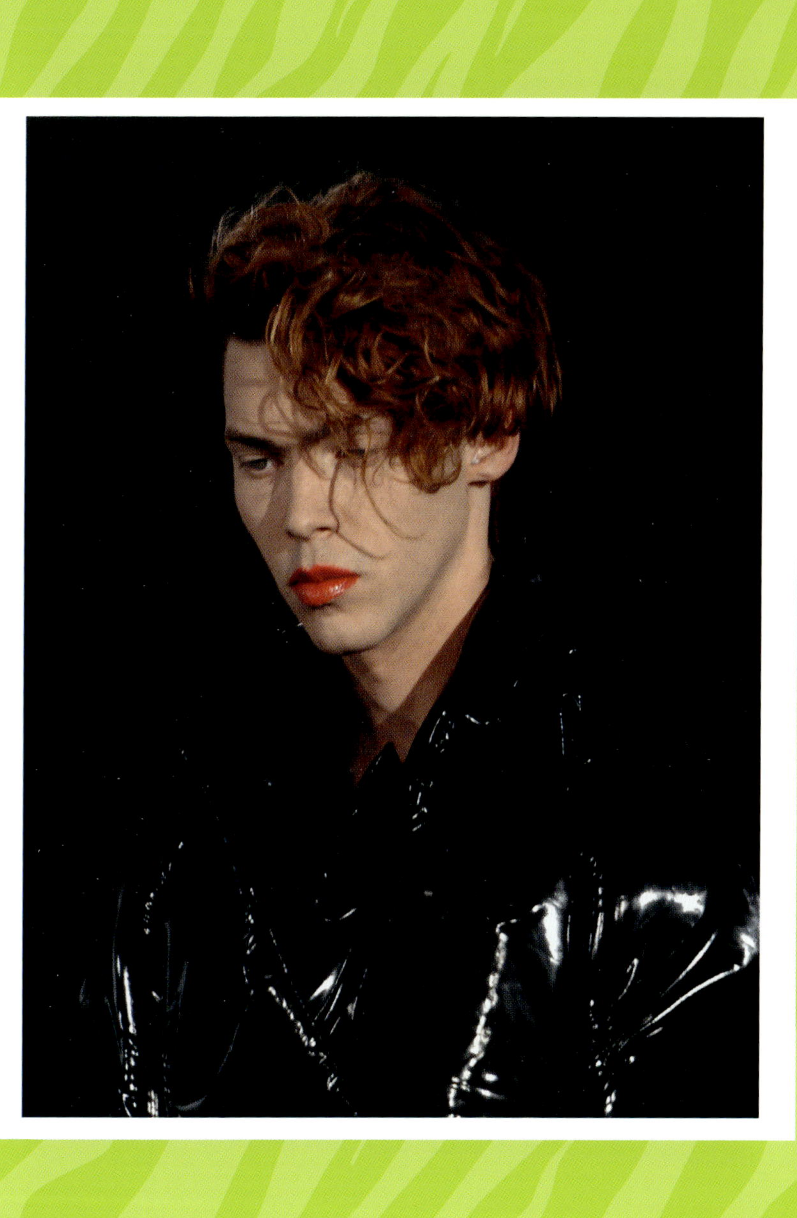

CRASH

Announced in November 2021 and billed as her 'final album' with Atlantic Records, *Crash* was both a send-off and a statement. It leaned into the hallmarks of mainstream pop – pristine production, glossy visuals, structured rollouts – but never lost the off-kilter charisma that made Charli, well, Charli. In prep for new music she reactivated her Tumblr – a cool marketing move that harked back to her humble beginnings. She began to share behind-the-scenes photographs at shoots and music videos, dropping hints at the album's aesthetic.

The lead single, 'Good Ones', was a tightly wound, synth-heavy banger. Gone were the bleeps, bloops and autotune: this was a mainstream pop track through and through. Draped in the kind of dark glamour she had been hinting at for months, the video featured a new, super-sexy aesthetic from Charli, hair big and blown out like a Hollywood siren, writhing around on a grave in a leather bikini.

Follow-up track 'New Shapes' (featuring Christine and the Queens and Caroline Polachek) played with an '80s aesthetic and in-step choreography. And 'Beg for You' (a UK garage-indebted duet with Rina Sawayama) cemented the idea that Charli was playing with pop conventions, taking recognizable formulas and warping them just enough to keep things interesting.

With each new single, it became clearer: *Crash* was an album about control. About taking the major-label machinery that had often felt like a hindrance and making it work for her. About embracing the full, unashamed force of pop music – not as a guilty pleasure, but as an art form worthy of deconstruction and reimagination. And it worked.

Released on 18 March 2022, *Crash* debuted at number 1 on the UK Albums Chart, her first-ever chart-topping album. In the US, it landed at number 7 on the Billboard 200, her highest position yet. For an artist who had spent over a decade straddling the line between cult icon and reluctant pop star, it was a definitive victory. Charli XCX had done what many thought impossible: she had embraced the mainstream without losing herself in it.

The title – much like the music – drew on over a decade of experience in pop. It again referenced cars (now a much-loved in-joke with her fandom). It was onomatopoeic, like *Vroom Vroom* and 'Boom Clap', and it was knowing, giving a wink to all those who thought she'd reached her heights and sold out.

Performing at the Crash *album launch party with Amazon Music, London, March 2022*

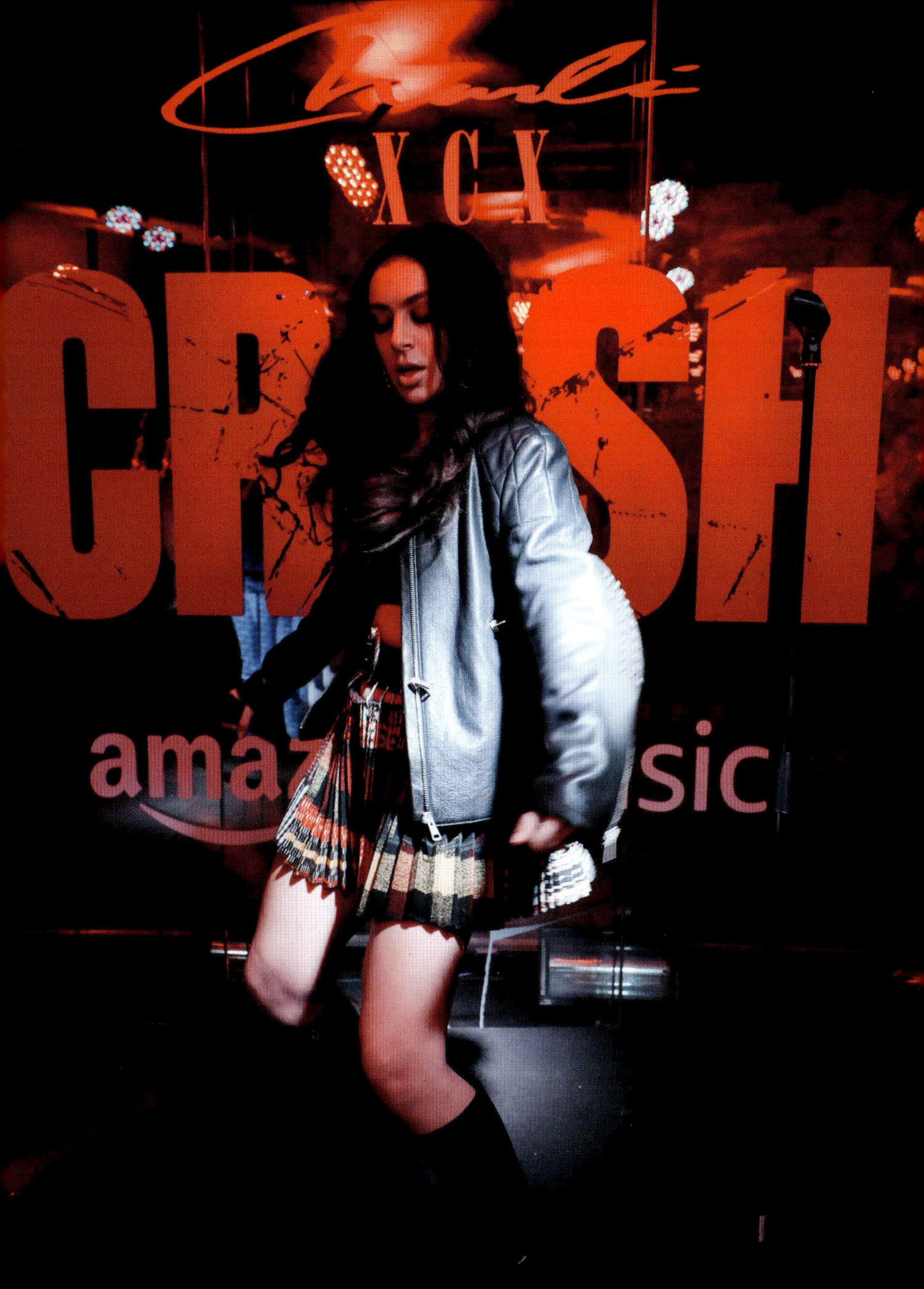
Charli
XCX

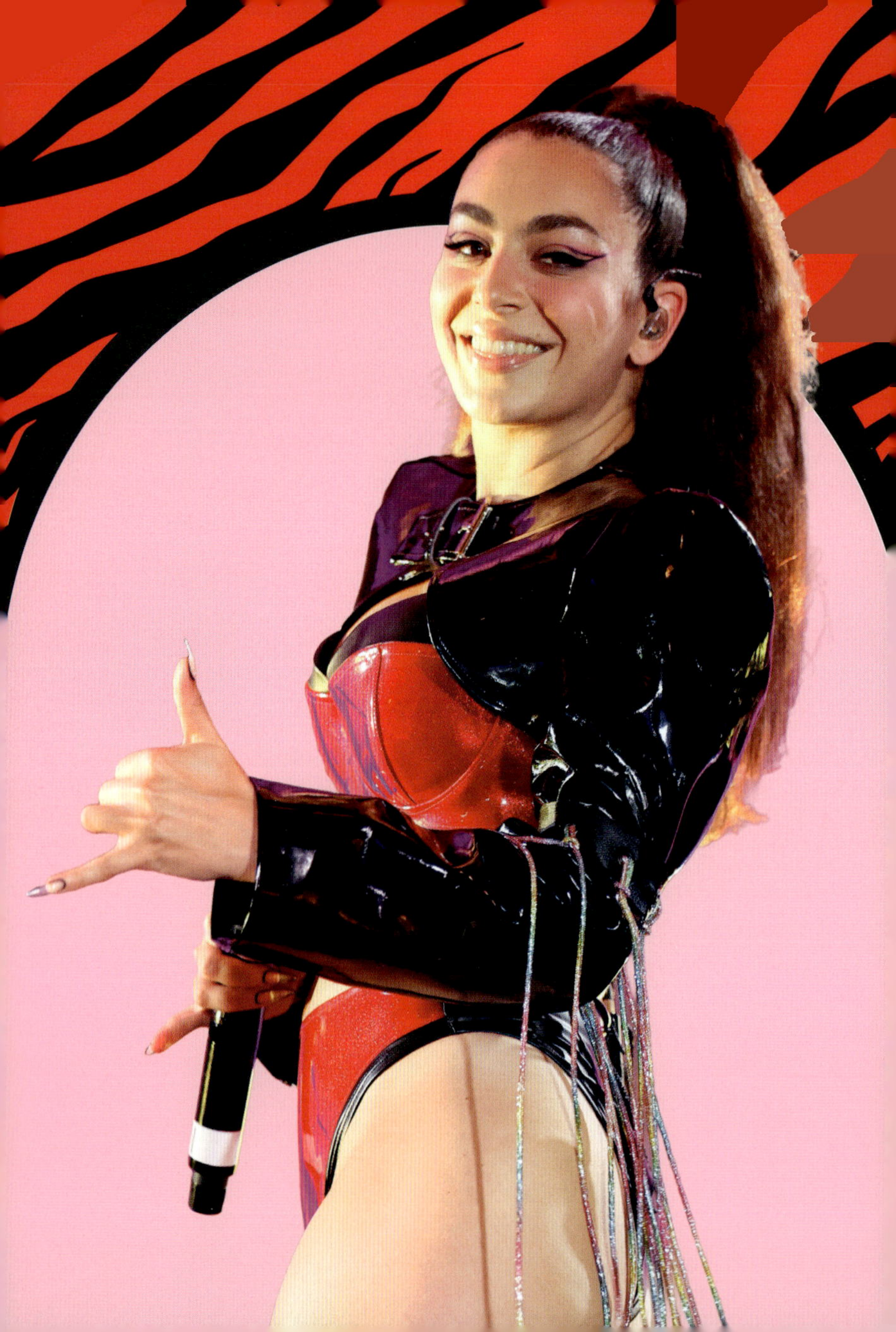

'I feel like all my previous bodies of work encapsulate all the different things I think pop music could be,' she told Apple Music Radio's Zane Lowe. 'From "Boom Clap" and big, classic shouty pop songs to the more avant-garde world of *Pop 2* or rave tracks like "Visions". All of those things feel like the little puzzle pieces of what I think pop music could be and on this record, I've put them all together.'

Yet the response to *Crash* was complex. Long-time fans, accustomed to the jagged, boundary-pushing world of *Pop 2* and *How I'm Feeling Now*, wrestled with an album that felt more polished and deliberately structured. Some praised it as a masterstroke – an artist playing with the industry's rules and still winning – while others questioned whether it sacrificed the rawness that made her so magnetic in the first place. Charli herself seemed aware of this push and pull. In interviews, she spoke candidly about feeling misunderstood – about the expectations placed upon her as an artist constantly labelled 'alternative' despite her pop instincts. She insisted her move towards radio-friendly pop was an artistic statement, that it was all very meta. Fans weren't so sure, believing Charli had bowed to label pressure and tried to reverse-engineer an engaging narrative to back it up.

Still, the *Crash* era was undeniably her most expansive yet. The visuals – sleek, hyper-sexual, inspired by everything from David Cronenberg's film of the same name to Y2K futurism – painted Charli as the 'final girl' in her own pop-music horror movie. The 2022–23 tour, spanning 76 dates and five continents, was a next-level production, filled with high-energy performances and the kind of choreography-driven stage presence that she had previously avoided. Charli's explosive pop show featured scantily-clad male dancers, in-sync choreo, multiple outfit changes and futuristic visuals. Gone were the day-glo outfits of her early years, replaced instead with black leather leotards, knee-high boots and slicked-back hair. At the risk of sounding like a tabloid headline, it oozed sex.

Caroline Polachek, Chris, Troye Sivan and Kim Petras joined Charli at stops along the way, with dates at London's Alexandra Palace, Los Angeles's Greek Theatre, Glastonbury and Coachella. Charli, for all intents and purposes, had become the pop star she had always threatened to be.

Onstage at the Thrive With Pride concert, Los Angeles, June 2021

CREATIVE DILEMMAS

But, as always with Charli XCX, nothing was static. Even as *Crash* was still unfolding, she was feeling panicked about what would come next. For the first time ever, she couldn't see it clearly. As she approached her 30th birthday, her brain stopped whirring. She'd had moments of creative block before, but they'd passed. This time it wasn't lifting.

Crash also marked the end of her five-album deal with Atlantic. Would she go independent, allowing herself freedom from the major-label machine she'd been bound to since she was 18? Or had she finally found a way to make it work for her?

If *How I'm Feeling Now* was Charli at her most immediate, and *Crash* was Charli at her most strategic, the aftermath left one question hanging in the air: what happens when she no longer has anything to prove? The answer would come soon enough. But, for now, Charli had done what she set out to do. She had played the game. And won.

By February 2023, as the *Crash* tour was close to wrapping up, it was crunch time for Charli: would she sign a new record deal with Atlantic, go it alone or team up with another major? She decided it was 'better the devil you know' and signed on for two more albums with Atlantic. Having proven she could top the charts, she'd finally earned the label's trust. They recognized her as a generational artist with underground credibility and chart-topping power. It was win-win.

Performing on the John Peel Stage, Glastonbury Festival, June 2022

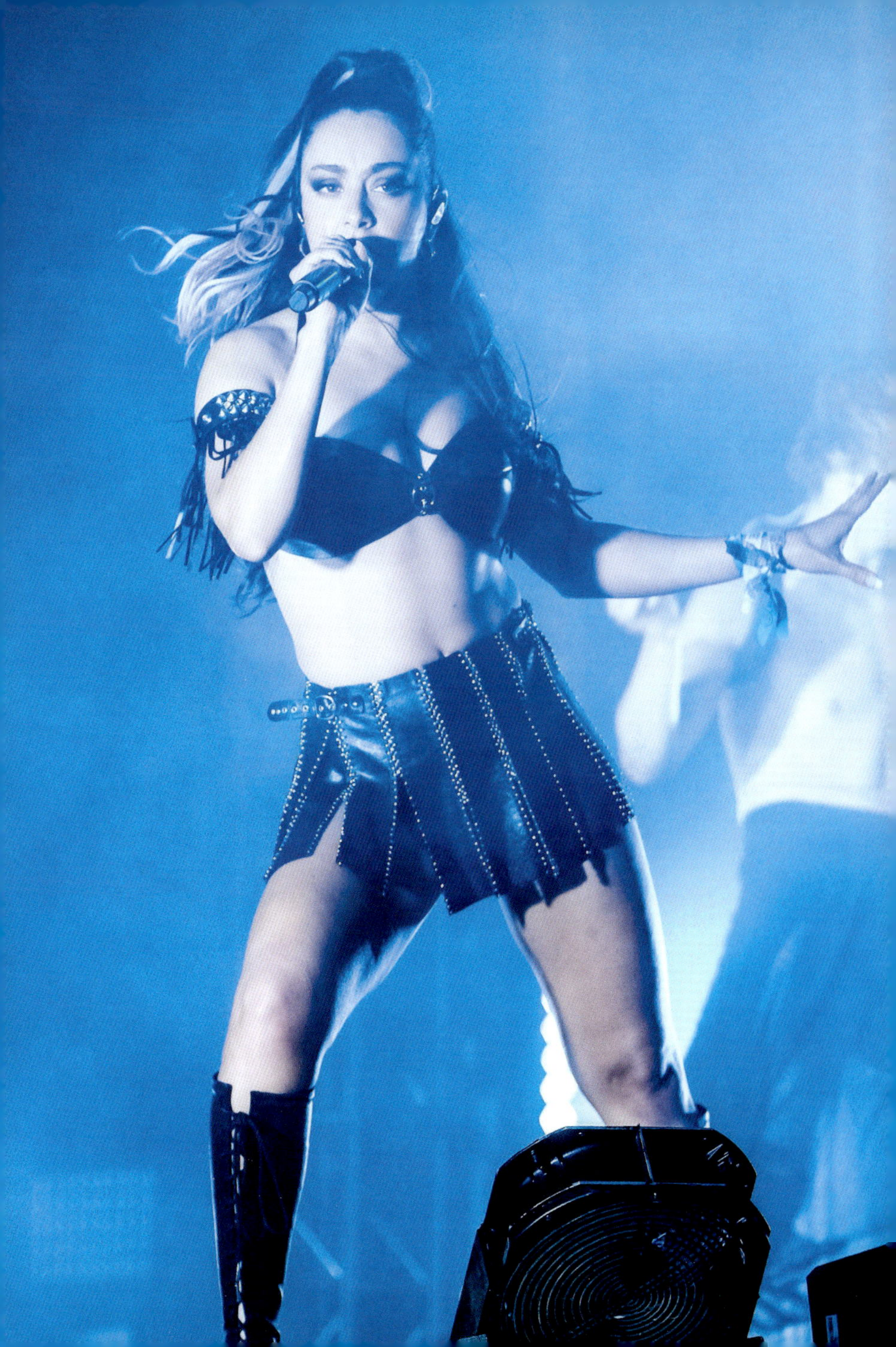

Gone were the day-glo outfits of her early years, replaced instead with ***black leather leotards, knee-high boots*** *and* ***slicked-back hair.***

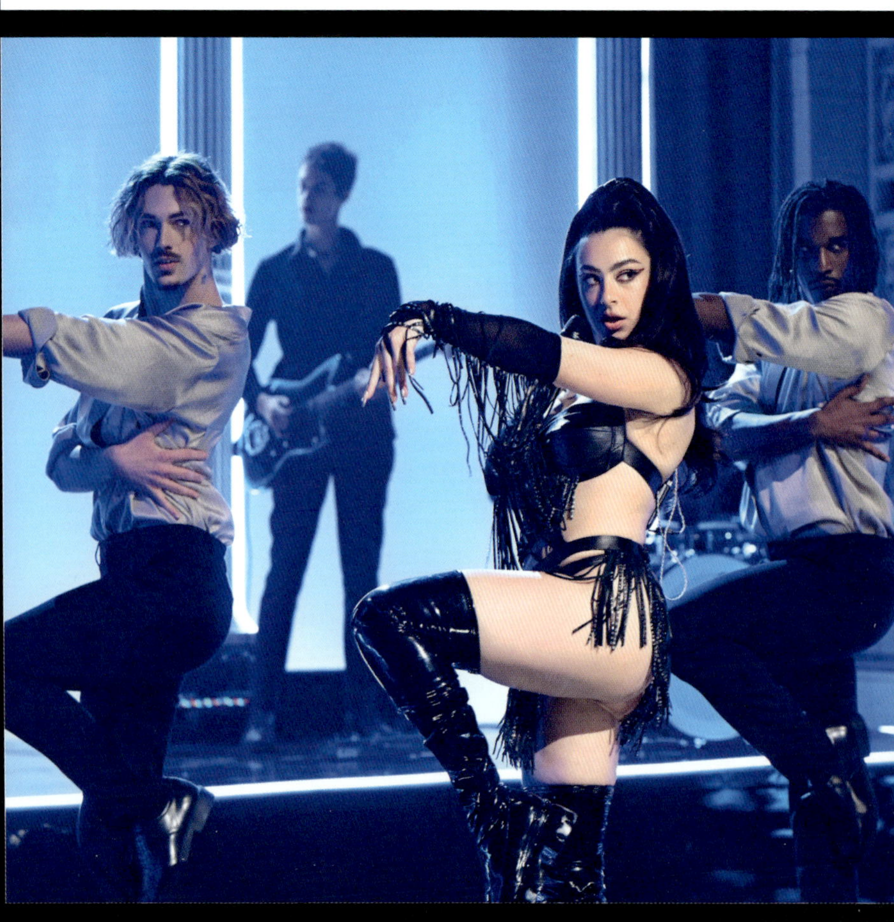

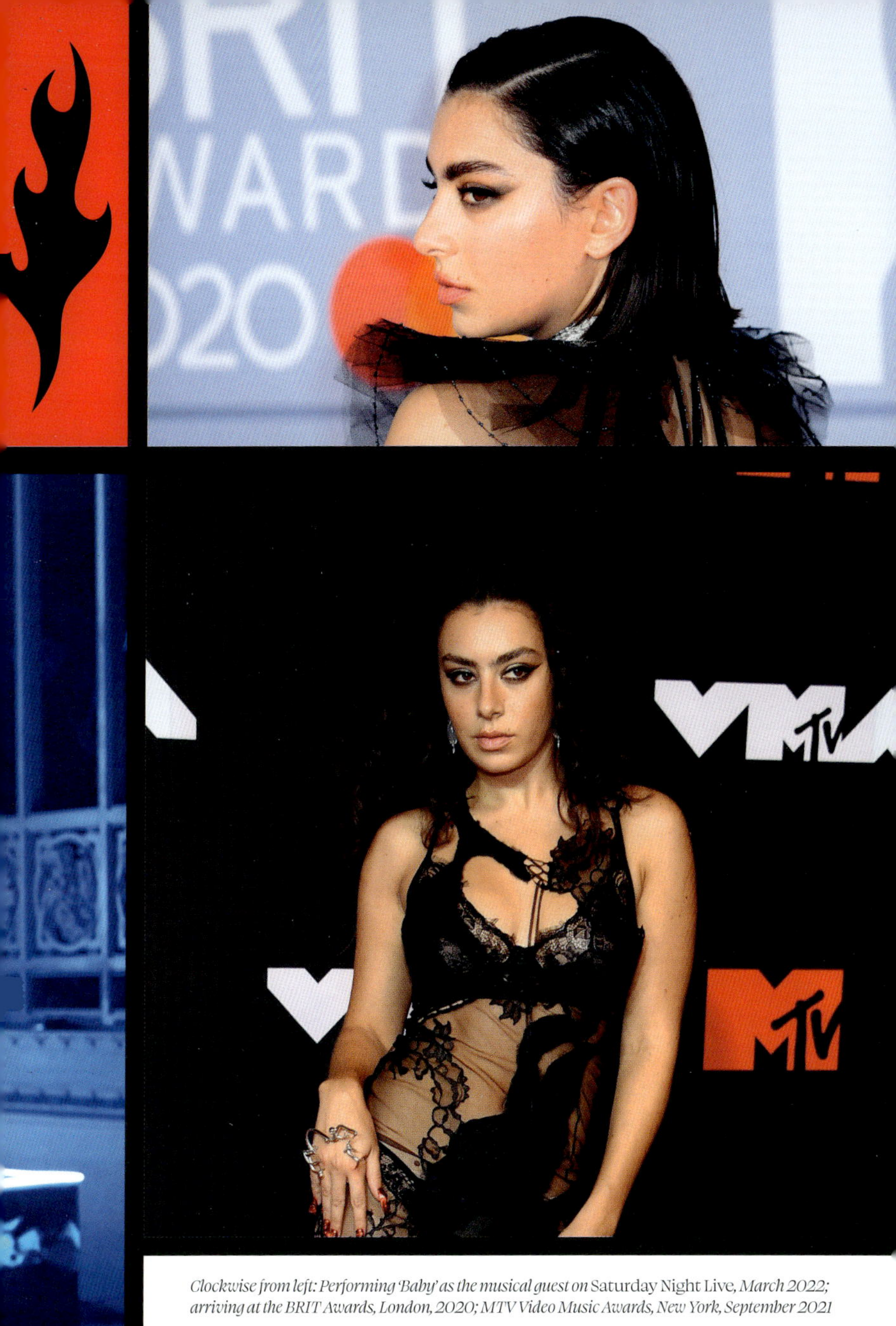

Clockwise from left: Performing 'Baby' as the musical guest on Saturday Night Live, *March 2022; arriving at the BRIT Awards, London, 2020; MTV Video Music Awards, New York, September 2021*

BRAT FOREVER

The Album that Changed Everything

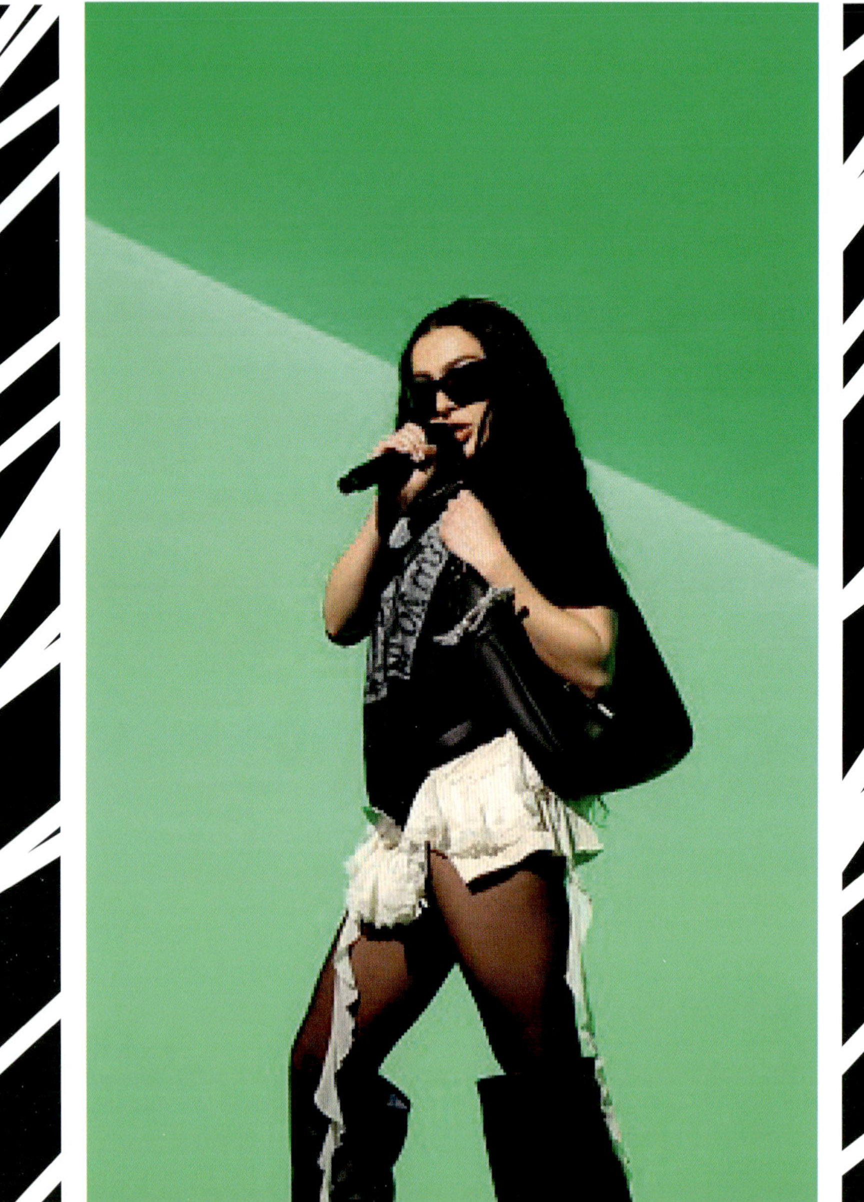

'I need an artist to create the world. A great artist to me is more than the songs, it's the entire culture and space that they inhabit.'

The idea for XCX6 had been bubbling for a while. 'On March 16, 2022, I texted my friends, "I think it should just be one word on the album cover ... Maybe it should be called *brat*",' she told *Billboard* in 2024. And though in many ways that one word summed up so much of the album that was to come, it needed more. It needed a manifesto.

'The artwork for "Brat" will be obnoxious, arrogant and bold. Some people will hate it. It will be heavily text based, either font on a plain background or some kind of painting on a wall or disregarded object,' read the credo, which Charli later shared to social media:

> *There is no explanation for what I do. The answer is always 'No Comment'.* [...] *I will throw a rave probably long before the album is out to tease new music. This should be the first thing I announce. I will play unfinished demos for the first time and have other collaborators who are working on the album DJ too.* [...] *Eventually these DJ sets will be referenced and looked back upon. You need to understand my vision. This is global. I will provide momentum and tell the story in a laser-focused way. We must execute everything with power and confidence. The angels are ready and waiting. This is the time.*

'Laser-focused' was right. From day one, every minute *Brat*-related moment had purpose. Charli had it all mapped out, and, for once, everything was about to go exactly to plan.

Performing '360' as musical guest on Saturday Night Live, *November 2024*

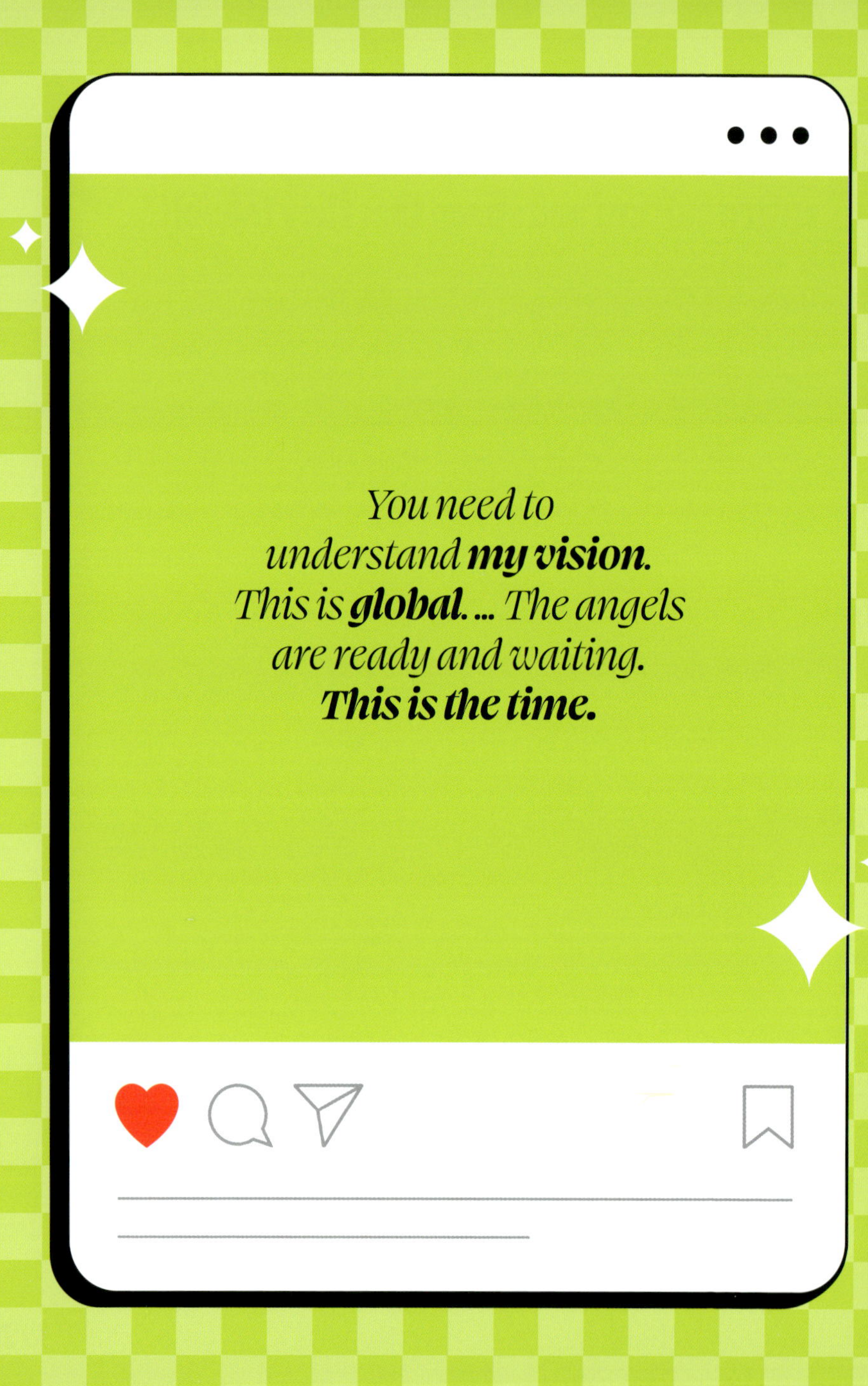
You need to understand ***my vision.*** *This is* ***global.*** *... The angels are ready and waiting.* ***This is the time.***

A long-time cinephile, Charli had been busying herself writing songs for movies. She penned the score to Rachel Sennott's queer teen comedy *Bottoms* (2023) and soundtracked the car chase in 2023's *Barbie* with epic hyperpop anthem 'Speed Drive'. But now she had a plan, it was time to knuckle down and focus on become the album that would define the next phase of her career. Inspired by the high-energy chaos of her recent soundtrack work and a renewed sense of creative purpose, she set out to craft a record that felt as bold and exhilarating as the worlds she had been scoring. It would be fast, futuristic and unrelenting – an album that blurred the lines between pop, club music and the everyday anxieties occupying her mind, taking her sound back to the underground raves from whence it came.

Much of *Brat* was written in Mexico City with a multitude of collaborators, including A.G. Cook, British producer Finn Keane (aka EasyFun), Scottish DJ Hudson Mohawke, French producer Gesaffelstein, Max Martin-collaborator Cirkut and fiancé George Daniel.

The writing style was different. Charli's process typically involved making sounds over a beat until words started to form. This time, she took a narrative approach to the songwriting, with a blunt, conversational style devoid of metaphor or insinuation. *Brat* needed to feel like she was talking to her mates over text or in the kitchen at the afters – a series of snatched conversations, like the selfies, WhatsApp threads and 10-second videos we use as hints to piece together every hazy big night out.

The first hint that a new album was incoming came by way of a genius – if accidental – spot of viral marketing. An outside social media agency had been tasked by Atlantic to come up with a list of campaign ideas for Charli's new album. The list's absurdity gave Charli another idea: instead, she would get her cohort of internet-famous friends to sarcastically read them out. 'Charli leaks a sex tape. "Von Dutch" is playing softly in the background,' deadpans Rachel Sennott with a glint in her eye. 'Charli XCX runs for President,' beams TikTok comedian Benny Drama. The video was a *Mean Girls*-coded smash, setting up Charli's new era as a gang you wanted in on, as a party you were desperate for an invite to. God knows, you didn't want to be on the outside looking in.

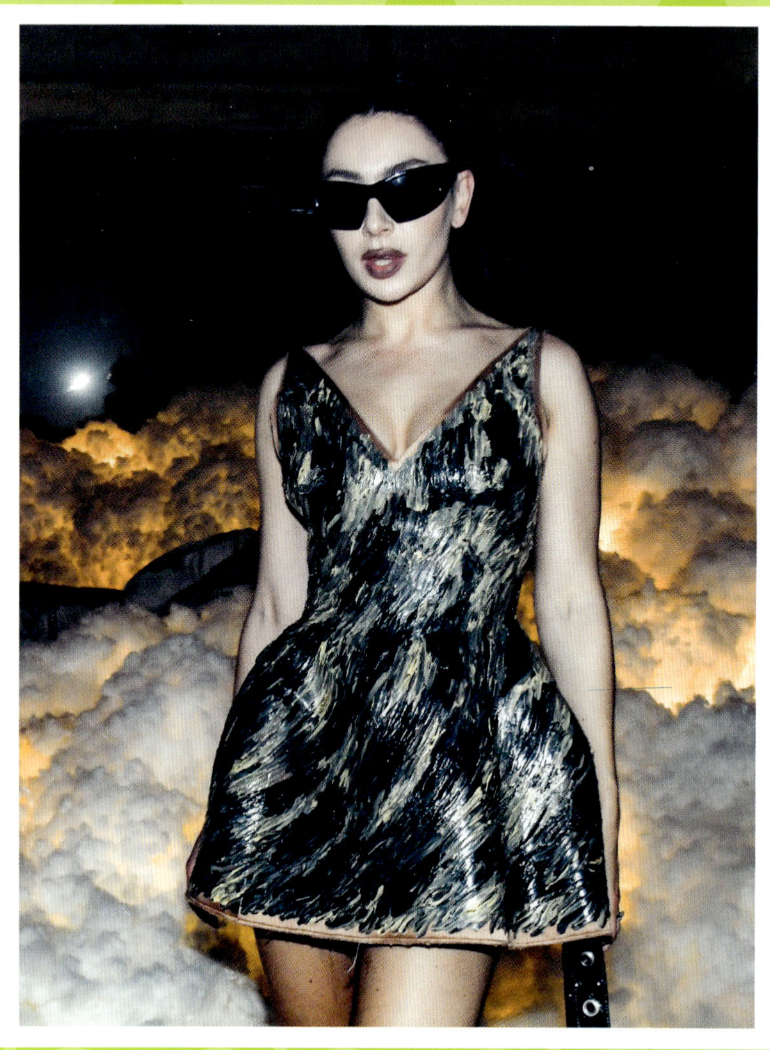

CULT CLASSIC

True to the manifesto, the next stop in the *Brat* calendar was a now-legendary Boiler Room set in Bushwick, titled 'PARTYGIRL'. Forty thousand New Yorkers RSVPed in the hope of bagging one of the 400 available tickets. It was *the* hot ticket in town and Boiler Room's most requested guest list to date. Charli arrived at 10pm in black Givenchy shades, neon-yellow face tape, an oversized blue tee, white fishnet tights and black boots. In bold typeface, her shirt read simply 'Cult Classic'.

As she filed into the venue with Daniel and A.G. in tow, Charli was nervous. Boiler Room is not your average DJ set. It's a space to show off your mixing skills, the entire, no-breaks set performed with cameras pointed at your face. DJing at this level – live-mixing songs as opposed to just selecting them – was a fairly new skill to Charli. Could she pull it off? This would also be the first time she would tease any of the *Brat* tracks, the start of her masterplan: it had to go well. But as she dropped the first beat of 'Club Classics', the crowd erupted. Charli started to relax, seamlessly blending her own music into tracks that day-one fans would know meant something to her: Mr Oizo's 'Flat Beat' and Britney's 'Everytime'.

Handing over DJ duties to A.G., Daniel and Finn Keane, our party girl let loose, jumping on stage with Addison Rae and Julia Fox and sipping drinks. The night could not have gone better. It was cool, sexy, fun and perfectly encapsulated *Brat*'s sybaritic energy.

'Historic moment in the Charli verse and broader club culture in general,' Charli posted the next day with photos and videos from the event. Fans were ravenous for more. A week later, *Brat* was announced to the world, along with lead single, 'Von Dutch'.

At the 'Après Met 2' Met Gala after-party, New York, May 2024

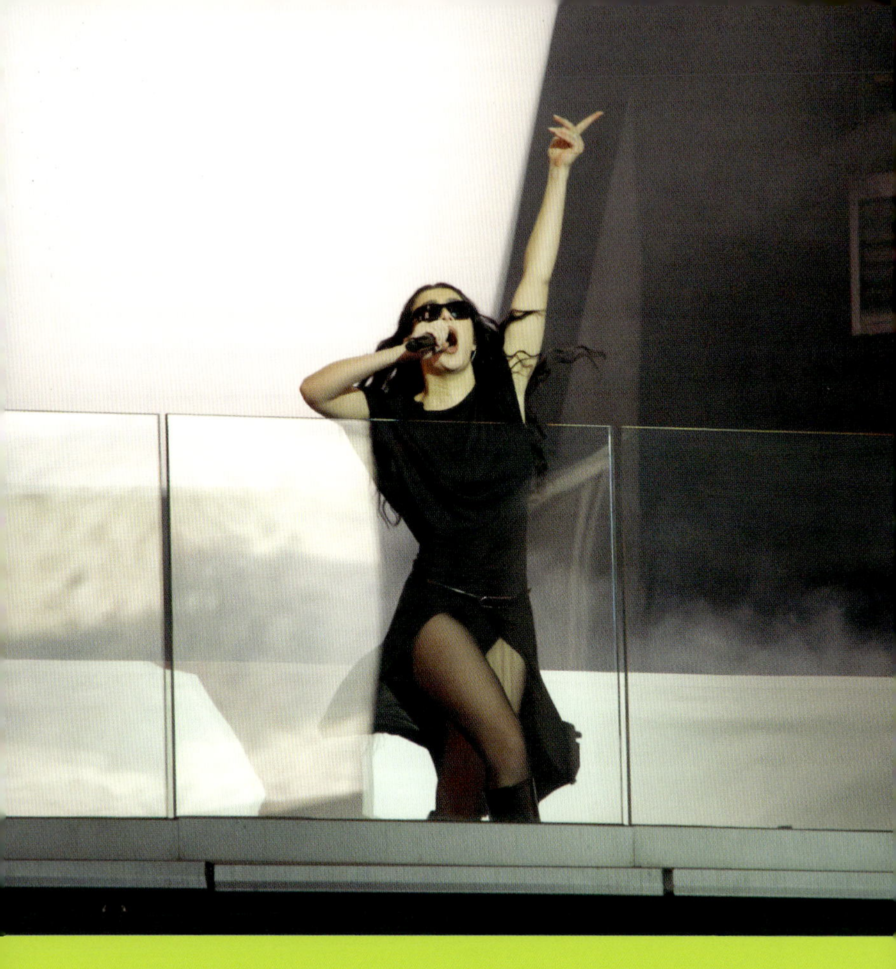

The album cover dropped the same day – its **slime green backdrop** *and pixelated* **Arial font** *instantly dividing opinion.*

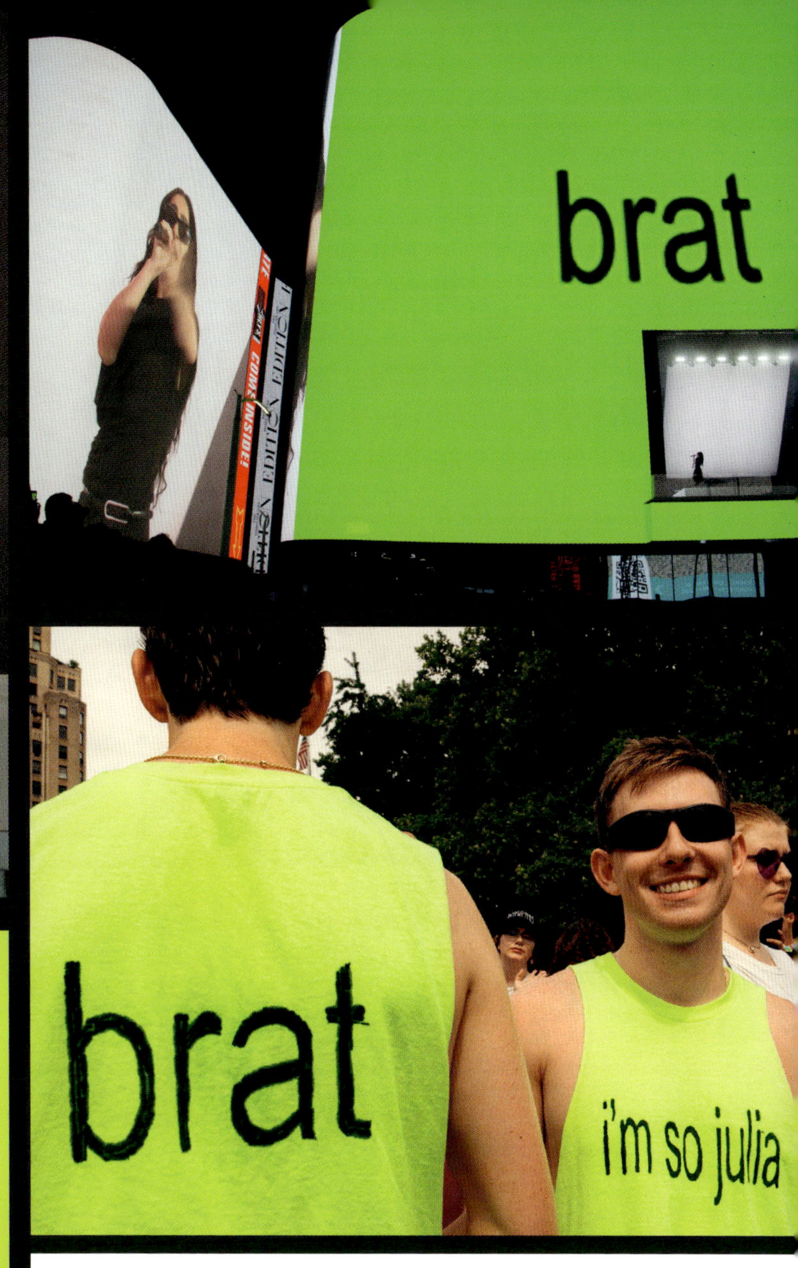

Left and top: Headlining a surprise event in Times Square, New York, November 2024
Above: 6th Annual Queer Liberation March, New York, 30 June 2024

'*Brat* promises to be an exhilarating club record built around high art references and social commentary: a new era both musically and visually,' read the press release. 'Von Dutch' was the perfect introduction to the *Brat* universe. 'It's okay to just admit that you're jealous of me,' came its braggadocious opening line. The chaotic video – directed by buzzy filmmaker Aidan Zamiri – saw Charli running through Paris Charles de Gaulle airport in a torn Uniqlo jumper and patent YSL boots, writhing around on the wings of a jumbo jet. This was worlds away from the polished aesthetic of *Crash*. Now Charli had proved she could achieve pop superstardom, she was free. This new era was about making music she wanted to listen to – music that she wanted to dance to, music for her hardcore fans.

> 'Brat *promises to be an* ***exhilarating*** *club record ... a* ***new era*** *both* ***musically*** *and* ***visually.***'

The album cover dropped the same day – its slime green backdrop and pixelated Arial font instantly dividing opinion. But far from an afterthought, hours of debate had gone into its lo-fi aesthetic. The hue of green in question was Pantone 3570C, a purposely abrasive colour that harked back to the day-glo of the early '00s, when Charli came up. The pixelation in the word 'Brat' came out of a specific process: designing the logo at 100 pixels by 100 pixels, 72 dpi – the dimensions of a MySpace avatar – and blowing it up to lose definition. The record's title, a label assigned to Charli throughout her career, was also an attitude: a singular noun that would become a descriptor – a marker of self-confidence, selfishness and an air of recalcitrant hedonism that said imperfection was OK. Not only OK, it was *brat.*

Charli later admitted that the decision to go for a typographical cover rather than a photoshoot was partly to cut costs. But if money was a motivator, this was a choice that more than paid off. Charli and team's decision not to patent the colour or the font would be key to its viral success. They launched a *Brat* album generator, allowing fans to make their own versions of the cover.

For the *Brat* era, Charli's style had once again evolved. Bringing on Chris Horan as her stylist, her look was more fashion girlie than the bombshell vibe of *Crash*. The look involved a lot of figure-hugging monochrome, mixing up-and-coming designers such as Laruicci and Dilara Findikoglu with custom Marni and Jean Paul Gaultier. It was a move that would ultimately pay off, securing Charli commercial deals with Skims, H&M and Converse, and bagging her a seat on the front row in London and Paris.

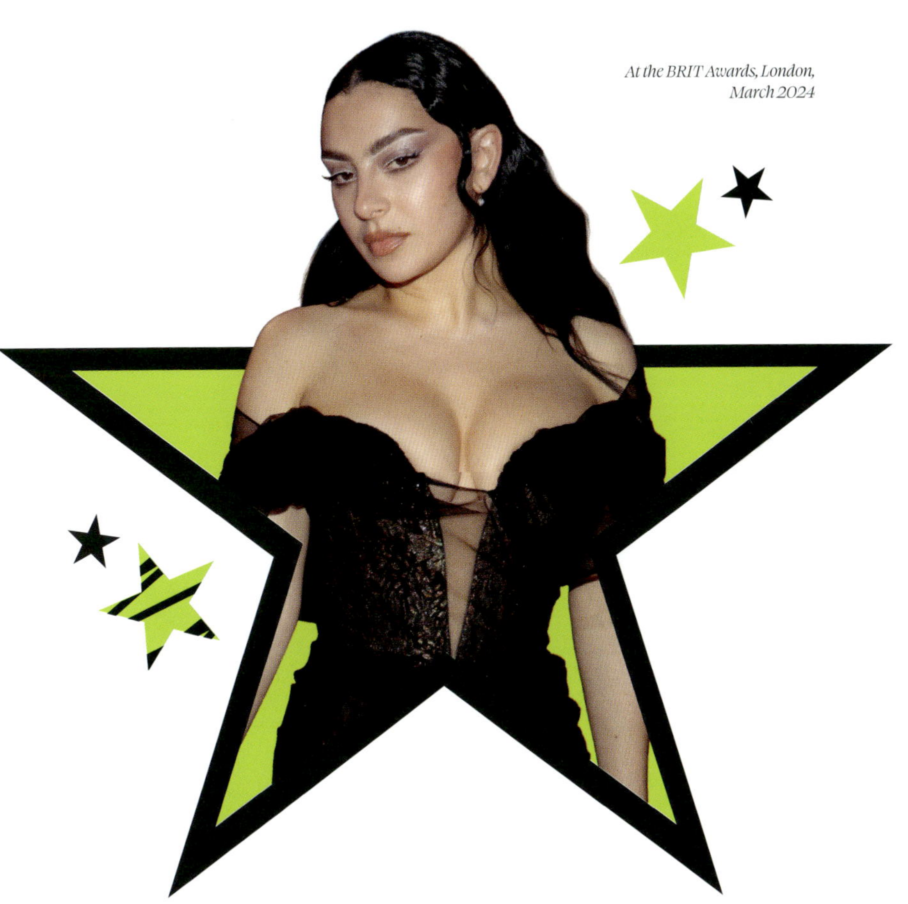

At the BRIT Awards, London, March 2024

At the Billboard Women in Music Awards in March, a nonchalant Charli, there to collect a Powerhouse prize, bemoaned the need for gender-specific awards backstage. Rather than use her performance to promote her next single, she instead debuted another *Brat* album track, 'So I'. With a tremble in her voice, she dedicated the performance to 'someone who is really really special to me who is no longer with us'. Dressed all in white to perform the sombre track, she tackled the tidal wave of emotions she had felt since SOPHIE's passing with an overwhelming rawness, celebrating her friend in a room full of industry peers, its title a direct reference to SOPHIE's track 'It's Okay To Cry'. Its vulnerability hinted that there might be more to *Brat* than meets the eye.

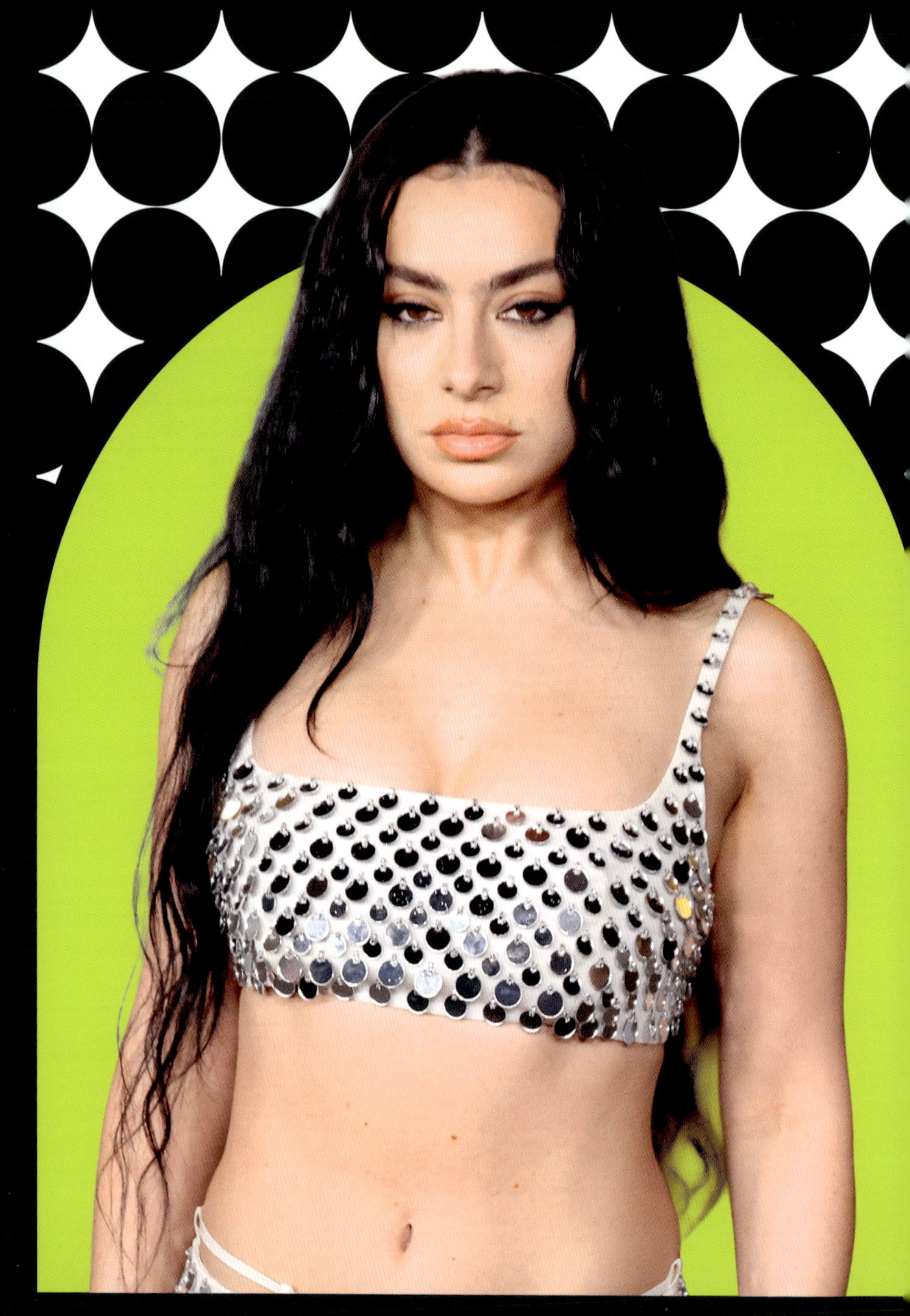

IN YOUR FEELS

On 3 April, Charli dropped her next two singles: the woozy 'B2B' and '00s-inspired party anthem 'Club Classics'. The latter was an instant hit. Harking back to her hyperpop days by namechecking friends and collaborators A.G., Daniel, Hud-Mo and SOPHIE. 'Watch this classic be played in the club in 10 years,' read a comment under the strobe-lit lyric video to 'Club Classics'. 'I had 10 seizures but it was worth it,' came another.

The song even featured a nod to king of the straight-talking club record, Mike Skinner, with Charli referencing her 'tight like Mike' flow and wanting to be 'Blinded By the Lights'. Skinner's influence can be felt across the whole record, every dance-floor high met with a moment in your feels – a combination he mastered with The Streets on their first two albums.

'*Brat* sounds bitchy and very direct and confrontational,' Charli told Jake Shane on his Therapuss podcast. She was being selective about her press appearances, prioritizing influencer-led new media, as opposed to the traditional music press. 'But it's confrontational because sometimes when you're at your most vulnerable you lash out. That's the whole thing about the name brat,' she added. 'Yes it's bitchy ... but also you act like a brat when you're feeling insecure.' Charli was making it clear there was a duality to *Brat* that people might overlook – this was deeper than just a party record.

*'It's **confrontational** because sometimes when you're at your **most vulnerable** you lash out.'*

As a further cog in the *Brat* promo machine, Charli's team painted a wall in Brooklyn bright green. Charli livestreamed the painting process as the lyrics 'I'm ur favourite reference' – taken from Charli's next single – appeared in the pixelated *Brat* font. Throughout the *Brat* rollout, the wall would be repainted every time there was a major announcement. Fans made pilgrimages to the wall and were glued to their phones, watching livestreams of it being replastered with new teasers.

Attending the 2024 LACMA Art Film Gala, Los Angeles, November 2024

Next to drop was '360' – another masterstroke in marketing. Not only did the song feature the 'bumpin' that' and 'I'm so Julia' lyrics that would come to define the era, the video boasted a who's who of viral stars on the hunt for a new 'hot internet girl'.

The video's self-deprecating tone and strong narrative arc – again, the work of Zamiri – saw Charli and her gang of confident hotties strutting around, causing havoc with their 'unknowable' vibe. Charli even managed to bag a cameo by OG It girl Chloë Sevigny, who steps out of a car in a literal puff of cigarette smoke.

BRAT SUMMER

In early June Charli headed to Spain to perform at Barcelona's Primavera festival. It would be the first live presentation of the *Brat* songs outside of the snippets of tracks and remixes heard in the Boiler Room.

At Primavera, punters party well into the night to avoid the heat of the midday sun. Charli was due to perform at 2:30am. After a 'chaotic' three-hour dinner she took to the stage. Industrial noise filled the site's concrete amphitheatre. Beams of white light shone out across the crowd; a green curtain descended featuring just one word: 'brat'. 'Shall we do a little key, shall we have a little line,' blasted the opening of '365' as she appeared, solo, on stage, in a Dilara Findikoglu corset

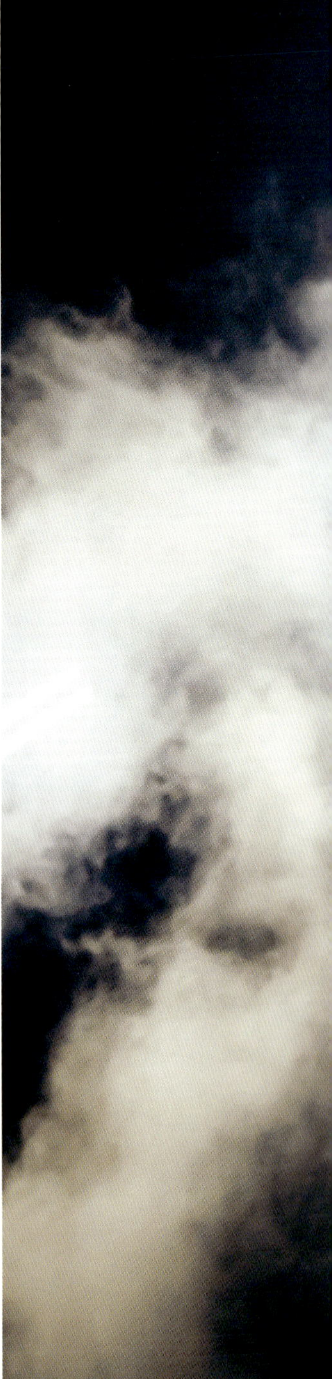

Performing on the Sweat tour, New York, September 2024

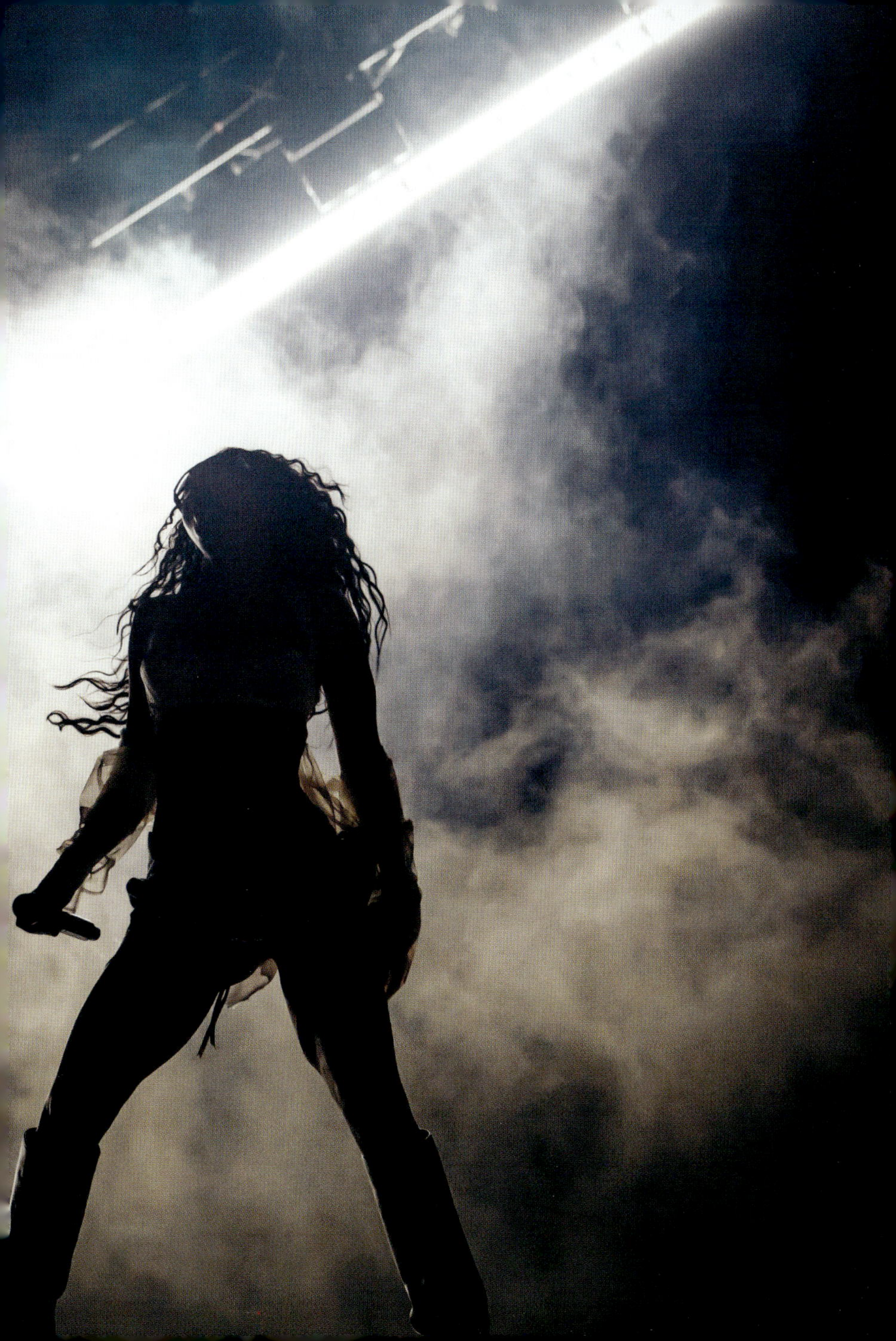

and with chartreuse streaks woven into her wild curls. Brat summer had officially arrived.

If there was to be a hint of the scale of *Brat*, the Primavera set was it. The singles had been performing well and creating online buzz, but seeing thousands of fans bounce up and down to Charli's blend of bold, brash club music, singing every word back to her? This was going to be big.

By the time *Brat* finally arrived the following week, the fans were beside themselves. In the run-up to release, Charli was a guest on Annie Mac and Nick Grimshaw's Sidetracked podcast, where she perfectly crystallized the mood of the album by listing her Brat summer essentials as a 'white strappy top with no bra, Bic lighter and a packet of cigs'. It was the opposite of previous summer trends aimed at women (Barbie summer, Hot Girl summer), which strived for polished perfection. This summer was about chaos, fun and worrying about the consequences later.

> *'To all the **angels** ... I think we all feel that something quite special happening rn ... **I love you all.**'*

On release day, Charli shouted out her collaborators and everyone who had laboured over the minutiae of the record via Instagram. 'Even when I'm being an absolute nightmare you still stand by me and make me feel comfortable to be myself,' she told management. 'And at the end of the day, that's exactly what *brat* is all about: me, my flaws, my fuck ups, my ego all rolled into one ... To all the angels ... I think we all feel that something quite special happening rn ... I love you all.'

Something special was indeed happening. The album dropped to rave reviews. The *Guardian* called it a 'masterpiece'. 'This is an album that walks a tightrope between hedonistic escapism and facing up to the cold realities that can plague you,' said *The Forty-Five*.

Fans perhaps weren't ready for the level of vulnerability on the record. On 'Sympathy is a knife' – a track thought to be about Taylor Swift – Charli talks about a relationship with a female artist who 'taps her insecurities'. Instead of being a straight-up diss track, it gazed inward, sharing Charli's own feelings of inadequacy. It was an important track that, along with 'Girl, so confusing', shared the complexity of emotions born of being a woman in the public eye. Later on, at a show in Brazil, she would shut down fans chanting 'Taylor Swift is dead'. 'Can the people who do this please stop. Online or at my shows. It is the opposite of what I want and it disturbs me that anyone would think there is room for this in this community.'

On 'I think about it all the time', Charli wrestles with her biological clock. Now in her thirties, she considers if and when she might be ready to hang up her party shoes and start a family with 'her baby' Daniel. These moments felt like unvarnished conversations shared with girlfriends at the afters, and while *Brat*'s club-ready bangers were carefree Gen-Z content, tracks like 'I think about it all the time' spoke to millennial concerns. The track also lines up the best song segue of the record: from debating whether to procreate straight into the 'shall we do a little key, shall we have a little line' of '365'. For the moment at least, the pull of the party was still winning that war.

The album peaked at number 2, getting pipped to the top spot by a UK-specific re-release of Taylor Swift's *The Tortured Poets Department*, which some saw as a tactical move by Swift in retaliation to the barbed lyrics of 'Sympathy is a knife'. In the US, *Brat* reached number 3, making it Charli's highest-charting album to date.

Just three days later came the deluxe version of the album: *Brat and it's the same but there's three more songs so it's not*, which saw the addition of 'Hello goodbye', 'Spring breakers' and 'Guess' – the latter would become one of the most important tracks in the *Brat* universe.

Charli was thrown into a whirlwind of press and promotion. And while the trad media slowly caught on to *Brat*'s cultural sway, the internet was doing its thing. On 14 June, a little-known TikToker named Kelley Heyer took one of the record's more underrated songs, 'Apple', and crafted a dance to it in her bedroom. It exploded, with everyone from Dave Grohl to the cast of *Twisters* jumping on the trend. Who knew that a track about generational trauma would fuel the dance craze of the summer?

Whispers of *Brat* summer were starting to spread. Stores rushed to fill their shelves with lime-green clothes. Nail salons were dusting off hues of polish that hadn't been requested since the days of nu rave and there was something in the air – a desire to rebel, stay up late, find your people and party. Where better place to do that than the Glastonbury Festival?

Just a couple of days before the UK's grande dame of music festivals kicked off, there was another surprise in store. Another remix was on the way and this one would send the internet into a full-blown meltdown. Fans had been speculating that the lyrics of 'Girl, so confusing' – a song about the uncertainty of a female friendship – might be about Lorde. The pair had long been compared, both first seeing success in the mid-'00s, and Charli had

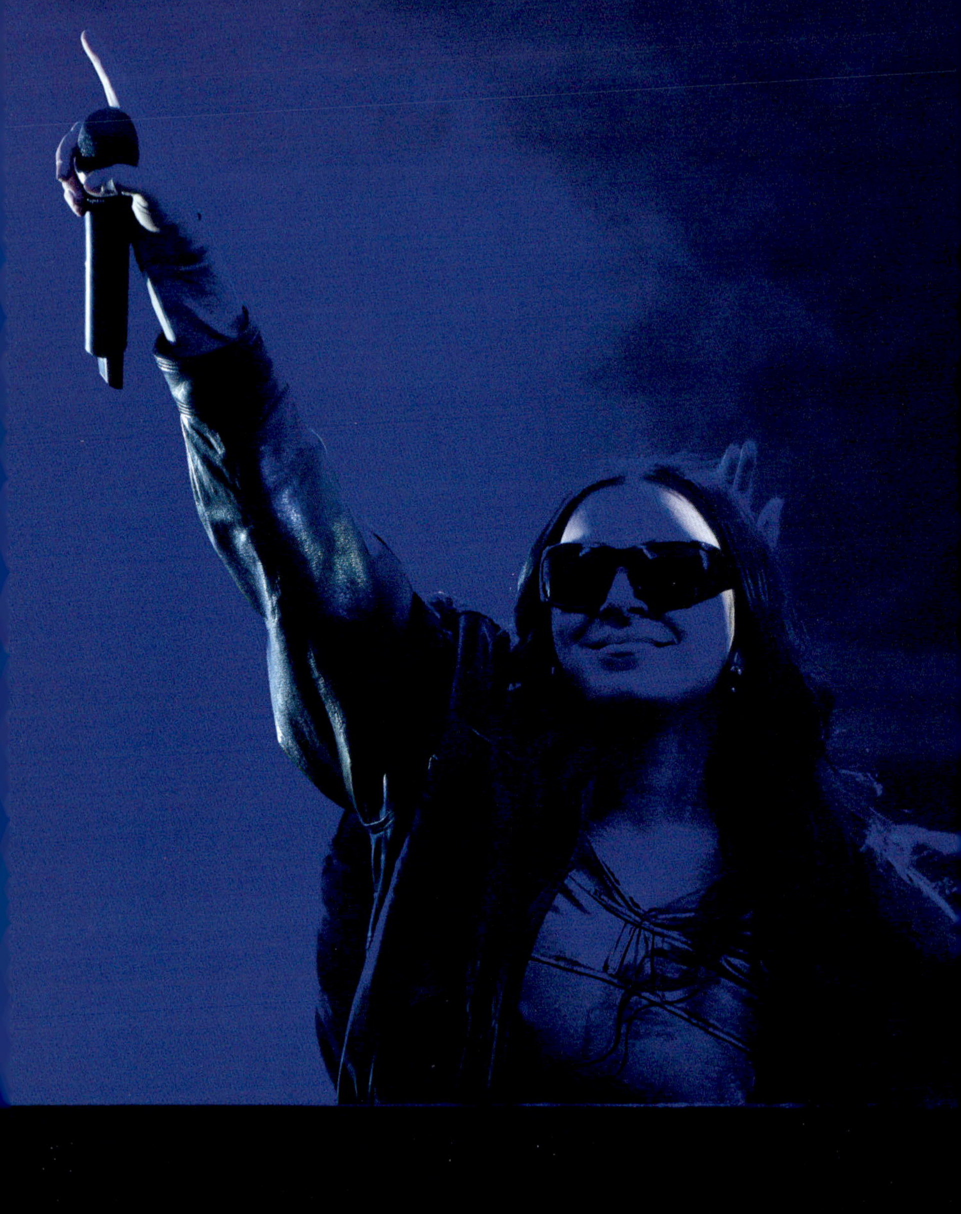

once famously been confused for Lorde in an interview (and went on to answer questions as her). On 21 June, the pair did the unthinkable – whatever tension may have existed between them, they worked it out on the remix.

Charli called Lorde on *Brat* release day to give her a heads up about the track; Lorde then offered to write Charli a verse in response to be used on the remix. The result was a weep-worthy confessional that, with startling honesty, put to bed the idea that being a main pop girl had to be a solo sport. In a world of petty chart battles, online feuds and sly digs, the pair chose to be vulnerable, linking arms to celebrate their flawed humanity and raise each other up instead of pushing each other down. To call this song one of the most important tracks of the last decade might sound hyperbolic, but in under four minutes Charli and Lorde managed to crush patriarchal constructs that pit women against each other. It was a class act.

Charli's Glastonbury booking was a Friday night PARTYGIRL DJ slot at one of the festival's smaller dance stages. As Dua Lipa topped the Pyramid stage for the first time, die-hard Charli fans flocked to Silver Hayes to catch her set. Over an hour before Charli was due to perform, admission to the stage was closed for fear of overcrowding. Those that made it in were gifted one of the highlights of the weekend; as green light and dry ice engulfed the stage, Charli's distinctive drawl arrived over the speakers. 'Is anyone having a Brat summer?' For those who had been waiting for hours to experience *Brat* in the flesh, it was everything they wanted. Much like Boiler Room, the set was a revolving door of friends on the decks, from Robyn to Romy, George to A.G. Charli had come to Worthy Farm to party, and what's a party without your nearest and dearest? It was a triumph.

Back on planet Earth the following week, word of 'Brat Summer' was starting to spread beyond the Angels and into the mainstream. News broadcasters dissected *Brat* as a construct, while magazines like *Glamour* and *Cosmo* published guides on 'how to have a *Brat* summer'. This was no longer just about being a Charli fan – it had become a full-fledged cultural behemoth that showed no signs of slowing down. But even with all the momentum – few, including Charli herself, could have predicted it would spread to the White House.

Performing at Glastonbury Festival, Worthy Farm, June 2024

On 14 July, as Joe Biden announced he was stepping down from the 2025 presidential race, instead naming Kamala Harris as the Democratic candidate, Charli tweeted, 'Kamala IS Brat'. Kamala HQ ran with the tweet, changing their social media profiles to *Brat* green, replicating the campaign's pixelated font. It was a shrewd move that resonated with young voters and saw Charli being debated on Fox News, who replayed her 'white strappy top, packet of cigs' definition and questioned if she should really be a role model. Charli found the whole thing surreal and brilliant. It was a moment in the meticulously planned *Brat* campaign that nobody could have predicted, but which served to amplify the album even more. And believe it or not, there was more to come.

GUESS

Back in the spring of 2024, Billie Eilish had dropped her critically acclaimed third album, *Hit Me Hard and Soft*. In interviews, Billie talked about a new-found appreciation of women, releasing openly queer, thirsty banger 'Lunch', as the record's opening single. When Charli teased a 'Guess' remix at the end of July, with a photo of her 'lower back tattoo' next to a person in baggy jeans and boxers, some eagle-eyed fans were quick to guess that it wasn't going to be a random dude guessing the colour of her underwear.

They would only need to wait another 24 hours before the internet would combust once more with the release of the Billie Eilish-featuring remix of 'Guess', and the line that spawned a thousand memes: 'Charli likes boys but she knows I'd hit it.' It was a sexy, sapphic bop and an incredible get – Billie seldom collaborates with anyone aside from brother Finneas. Another Aidan Zamiri-directed video, filmed just days before release, dropped the same day. Charli and producer The Dare get down at an underwear-flinging house party before being quite literally bulldozed by Billie's killer verse. The climax sees Charli and Billie climb an underwear mountain which, in another class move, was donated to a domestic violence charity after the video shoot was over.

We're deep into Leo season now and that can mean only one thing – a Charli XCX birthday party. Everyone wanted an invite to the LA bash, held at Tenants of the Trees in Silver Lake. And the A-listers – including Glen Powell, Anya Taylor-Joy, Sabrina Carpenter, Alexa Demie and Nelly Furtado – arrived in droves. Rosalía won best gift-giver for her bouquet full of Parliament Light cigarettes, Lorde and Billie joined Charli on top of a table to sing their remix verses, and every *Brat*-addled moment was captured by indie sleaze photographer extraordinaire, The Cobrasnake.

On the Billie Eilish Hit Me Hard and Soft *tour, Inglewood, California, December 2024*

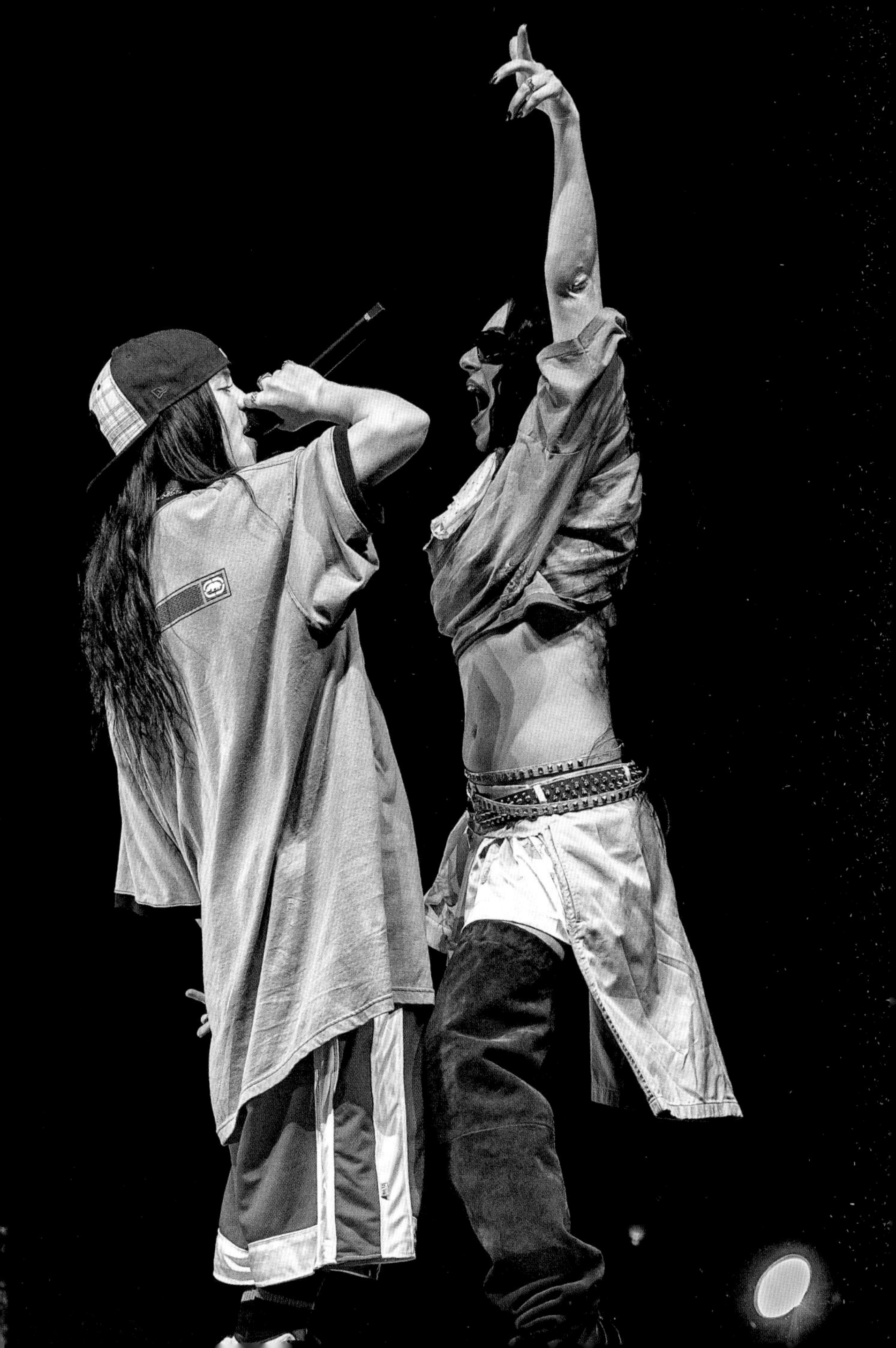

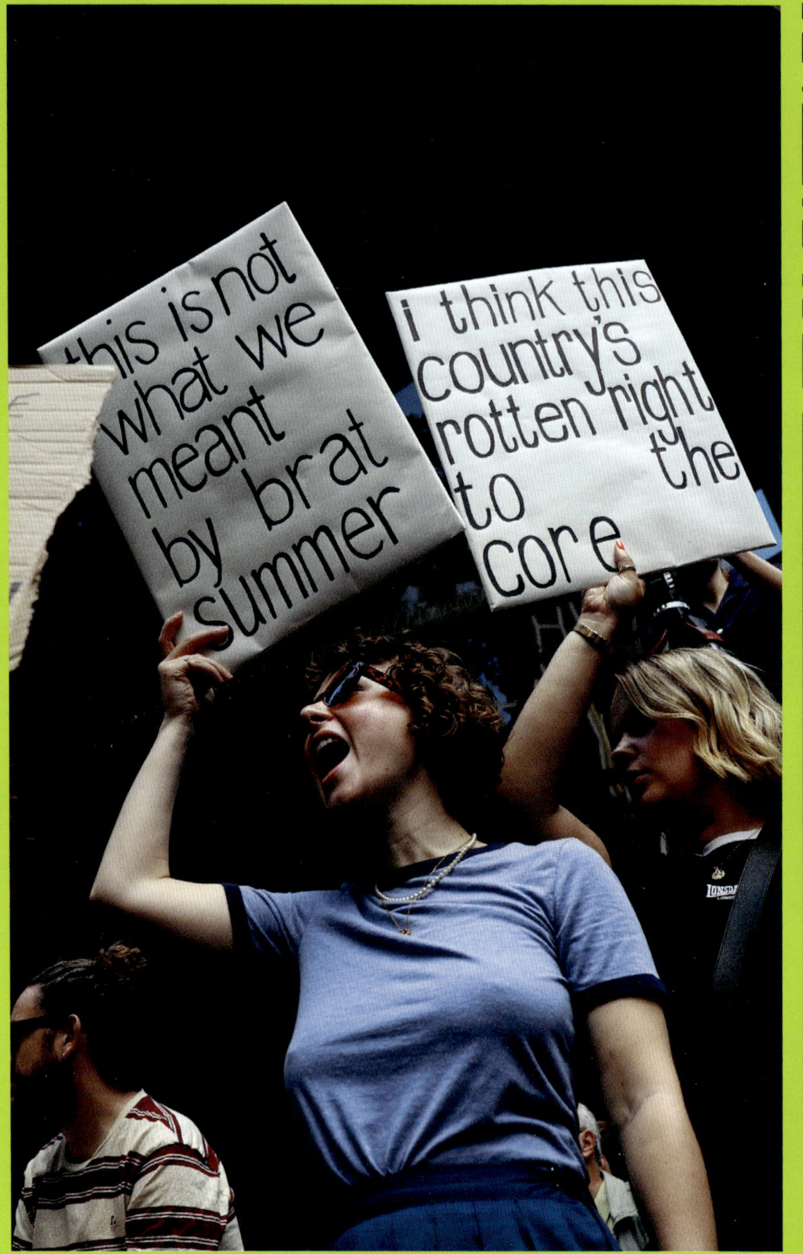

'Stop the Far-right' demonstration, outside the headquarters of the Reform UK political party, London, August 2024; right; A Kamala Harris supporter at the Democratic National Convention, Chicago, August 2024

'Kamala IS ***Brat'***

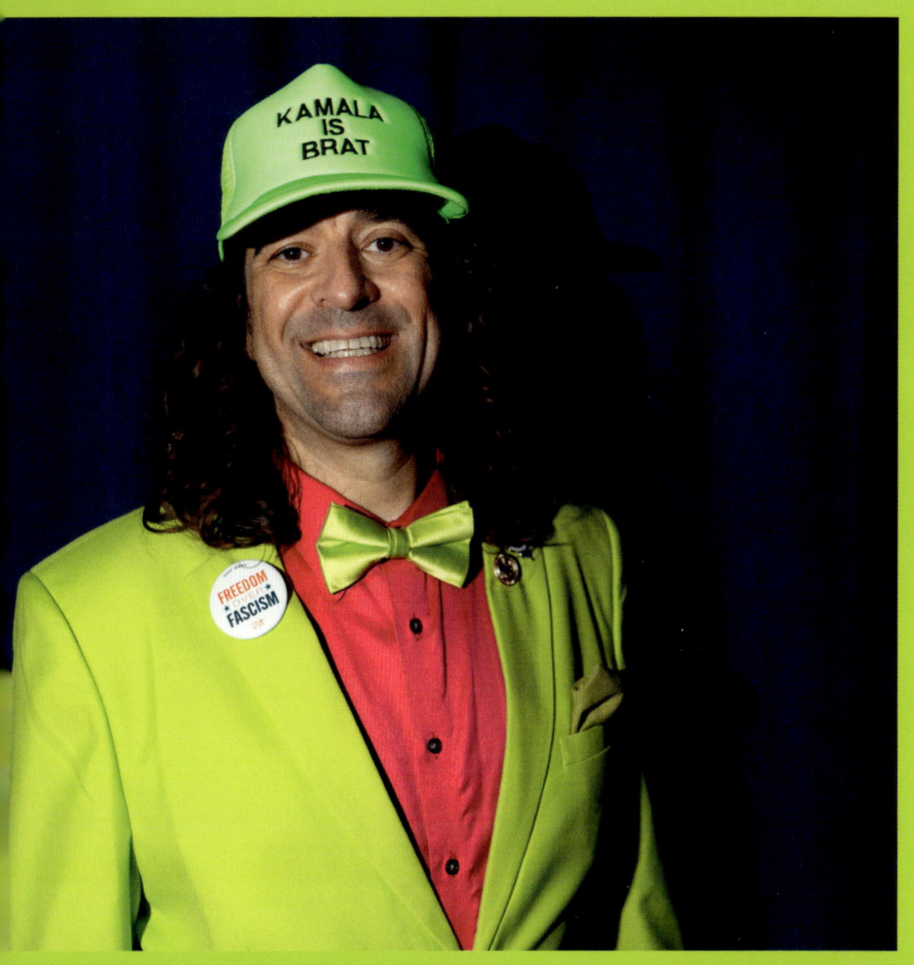

SWEAT IT OUT

Declarations that Brat summer was over had been bandied around since the Kamala endorsement, but each time Charli brushed them off, laughing as she served yet another viral moment. But aside from Primavera and the PARTYGIRL DJ sets, fans were yet to experience *Brat* live. If Atlantic Records had had any idea of how big *Brat* was going to get, you can't help but wonder if Troye Sivan might have been left in the dust, but earlier in the year the decision was made that the pair would team up for a North American joint tour to promote both their records. It was a way to ensure ticket sales – not that Charli would have needed it. By autumn, it was time to sweat.

The Sweat tour kicked off in Detroit in September, drawing a curious mix of queer club kids – as expected – and a newer wave of fans eager to ride the *Brat* trend. Still, it worked. Charli and Troye leaned into the clubbier side of their catalogues, each taking three songs at a time, and managing to transform sterile arenas into euphoric dance floors. Charli was the star, but Troye was a fitting complement.

But it was at Madison Square Garden in New York that things truly took a turn for the *Brat*. Charli played her trump card: bringing out Lorde to perform 'Girl, so confusing'. No words could fully capture the deafening roar that followed. Watching the two wavy-haired frenemies, draped in 'fur' coats and boots, strut in unison across the stage was a pop culture moment for the ages. Troye could only look on and smile.

Knowing there was an appetite for even more gigs, Charli announced four solo UK arena shows in November 2024. The tour announcement poster showed the dates printed atop a little plastic baggy, but the British Online Advertising Association wasn't pleased, saying it was promoting illicit activity, and insisted Charli change the poster. Charli had the best retort: 'It's obviously a sandwich bag, so I've just made it really obvious by putting a sandwich in there,' she said on TikTok in front of a modified poster, which indeed now contained a ham sandwich. 'So bring your sandwiches to the *Brat* tour!'

On the Troye Sivan Something to Give Each Other *tour, London, June 2024*

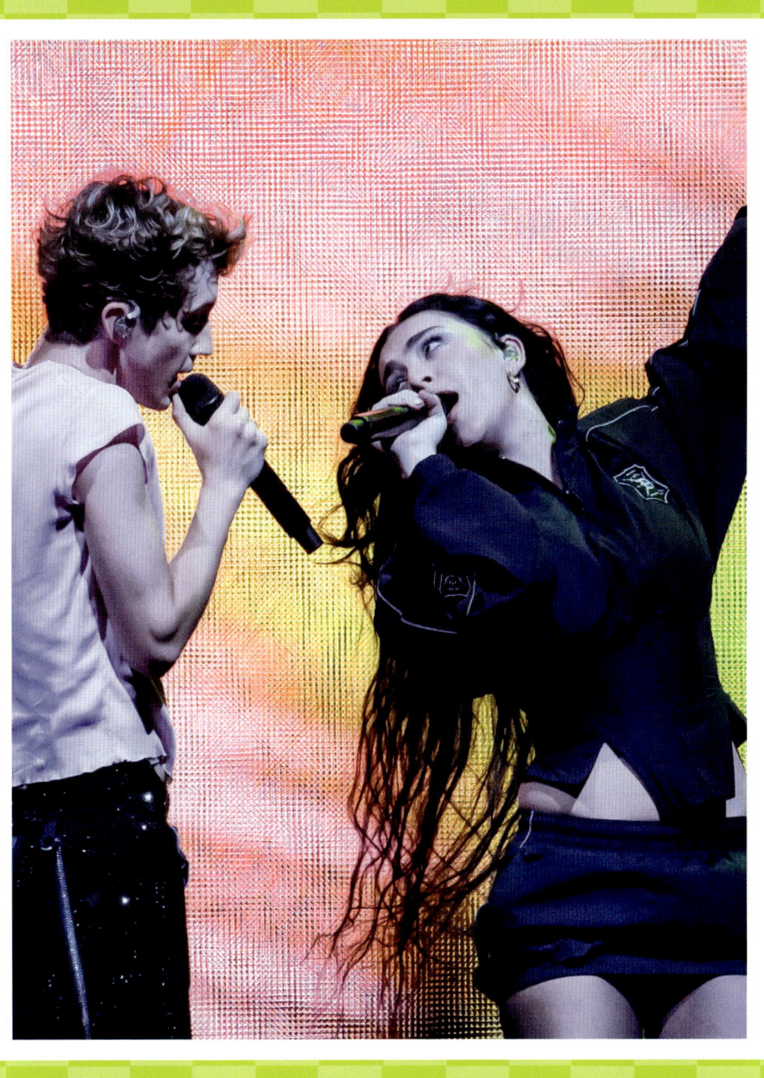

The UK dates were the perfect way to top off a truly monumental year. At the O2 show in London, Charli was joined by Robyn, Caroline Polachek and Yung Lean on stage, generously handing over the mic to Robyn to sing the impossibly perfect 'Dancing On My Own' in full. In a viral moment, the camera swung to a reluctant Daniel, debuting his 'Apple' dance skills after months of TikTok persuasion from Charli to jump on the trend. These arena shows felt like a victory lap, the culmination of over 15 years of hard work and cold, hard proof that choosing authenticity over artifice is always the best idea.

The icing on the cake came in early 2025 when, finally, Charli got the industry recognition she deserved, taking home three Grammy Awards and five Brits. At the UK award show, in a hooded Dilara Findikoglu dress, she thanked those who had inspired her along the way.

> *'This genre of music, for me, is **euphoric**. It allows me to **escape**.'*

'I feel like dance music, electronic music, gets a really bad rep,' she said, while collecting the last of her awards. 'Because everybody's like, "Oh well, it's not really that deep, is it?" And I kind of feel like it is. This genre of music, for me, is euphoric. It allows me to escape; it allows me to feel on such a deep level. And so I would like to thank some legends in the field who inspire me to make the music that I've made – Finn, A.G., George – and also someone who none of us would be here without, SOPHIE.'

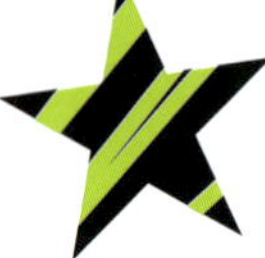

At the BRIT Awards, London, March 2025

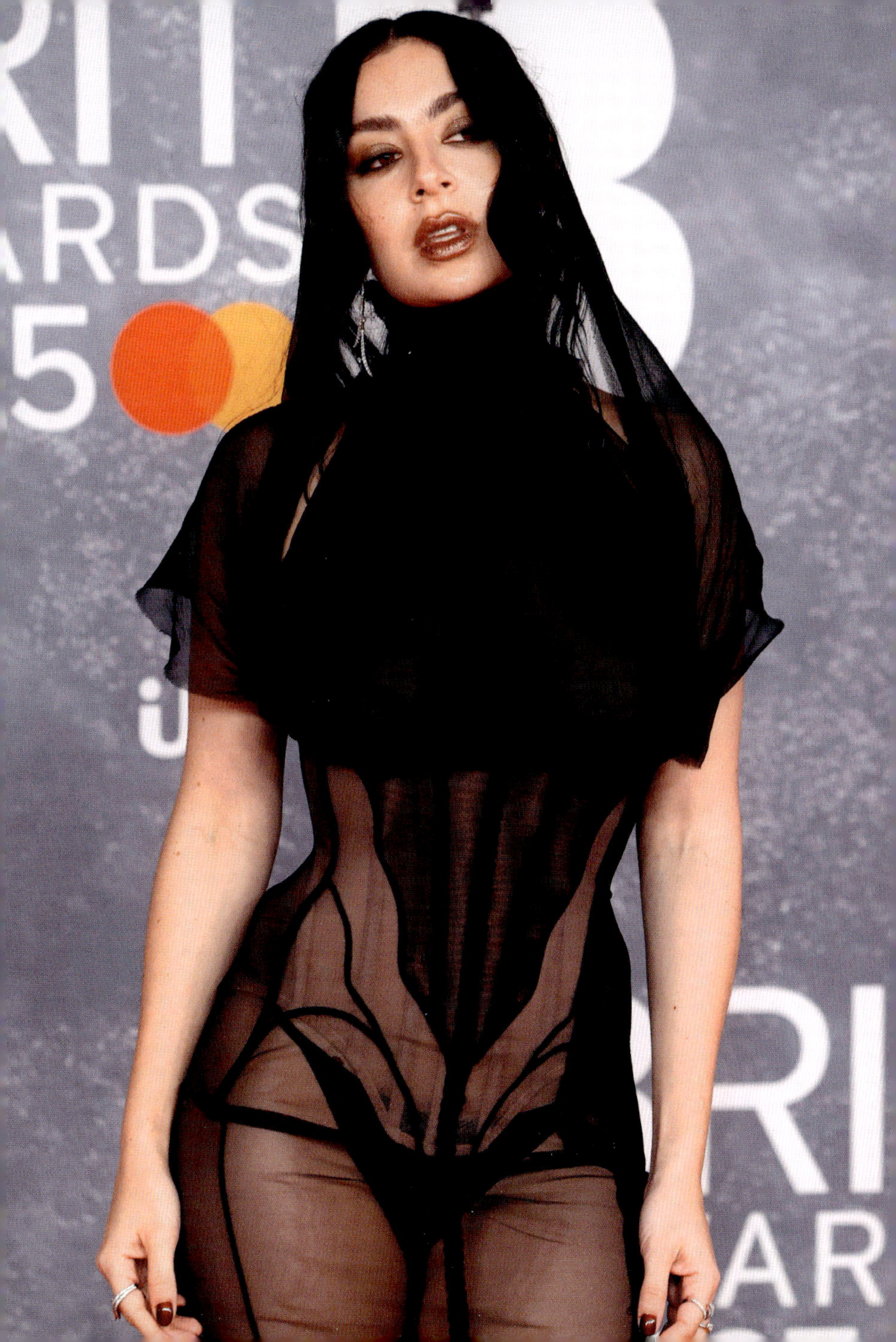

BRAT

By spring, Charli's attention had turned to Coachella. Ever self-aware, she was seemingly concerned about *Brat*'s longevity – would she be seen to be milking it, with another summer of *Brat* shows on the horizon? On the long desert road that leads to the Californian festival ground, fans spotted a *Brat* billboard with its title scribbled out. What could it mean?

On stage – after an electric set with the holy trinity of guests, Sivan, Eilish and Lorde – Charli prompted further conversation around whether the *Brat* era was over. After the final song, she lingered on stage, in front of images that read: 'Does this mean that *Brat* summer is finally over? Idk? Maybe? Wait was it? No?? Yeah cuz duh it was already over like last year. Wait. Was it? NO??? I don't know who I am if it's over??? F–KKKKKKKK.'

The set ended with the *Brat* backdrop going up in flames. At weekend two, similar typographical messages on screen saw Charli handing over the 'summer' baton to 'Haim, Turnstile, Pulp, Lorde' and a host of other artists soon to release new music. Posting a video to social media, she lingered on the same themes: worries over staying too long versus not wanting the moment to end.

In May, *Brat*'s album cover changed again, to a singed image with 'Brat' crossed out. And at her Glastonbury festival Other Stage headline set, she opened the show by burning the Brat flag, but closed it with a statement that says 'Brat is Forever'.

Performing at the 67th Annual Grammy Awards, Los Angeles, February 2025

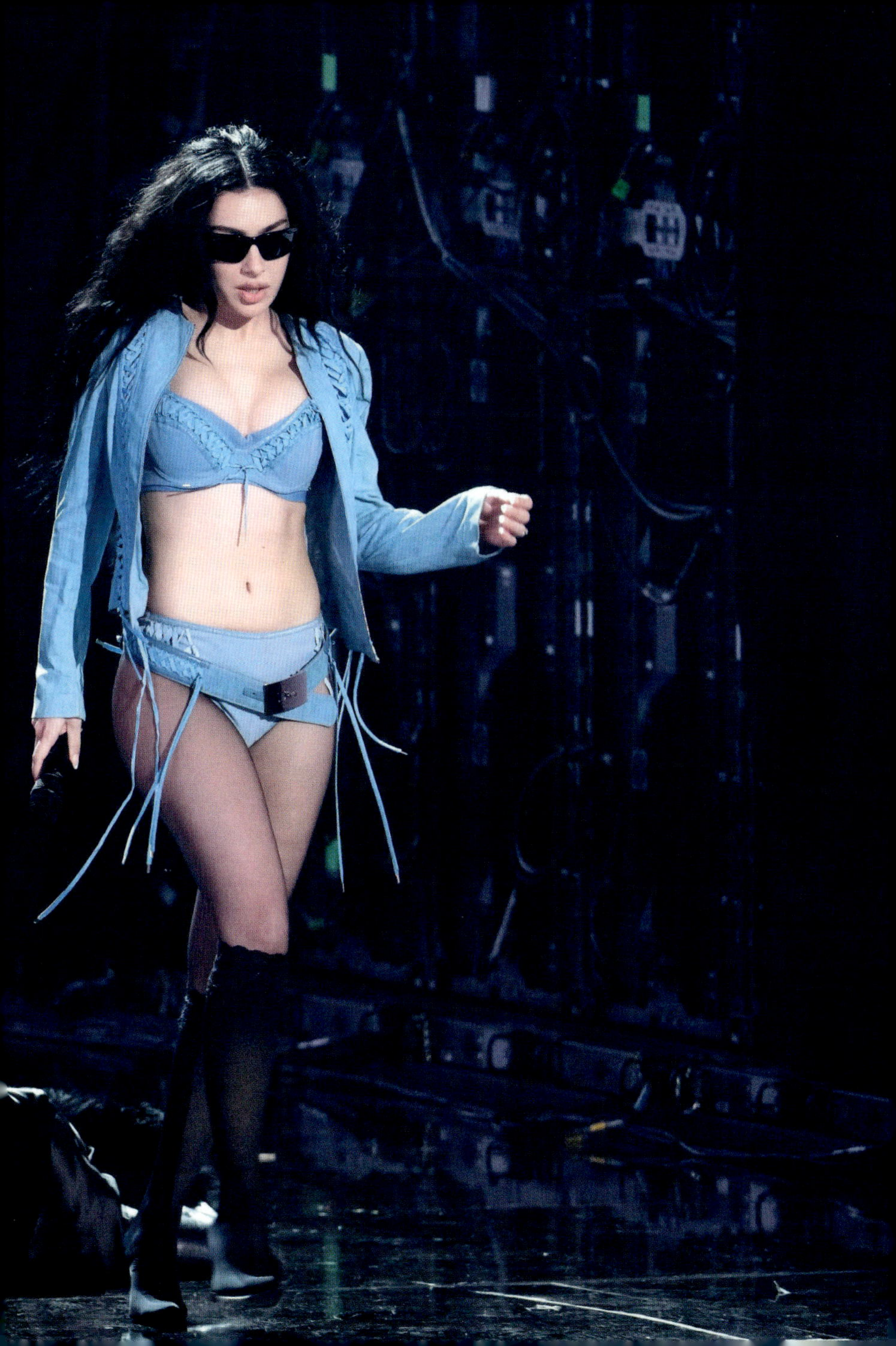

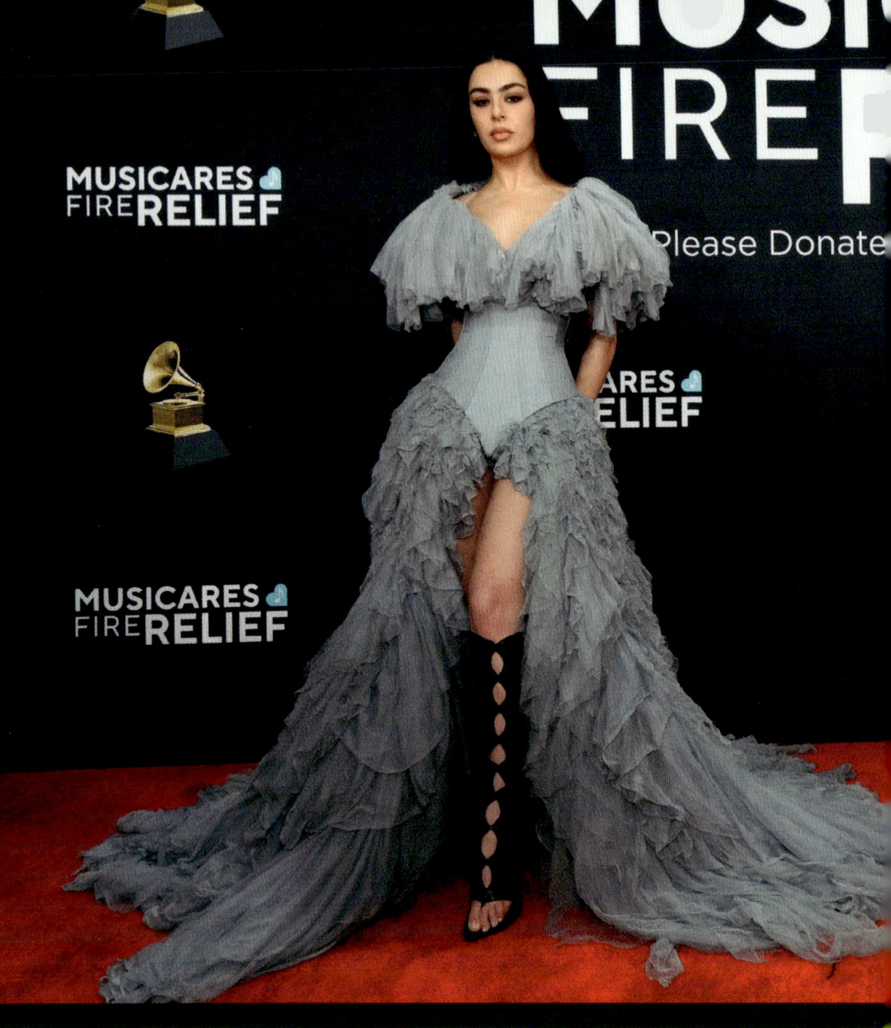

*Charli got the industry recognition she deserved, taking home **three Grammy Awards** and **five Brits**.*

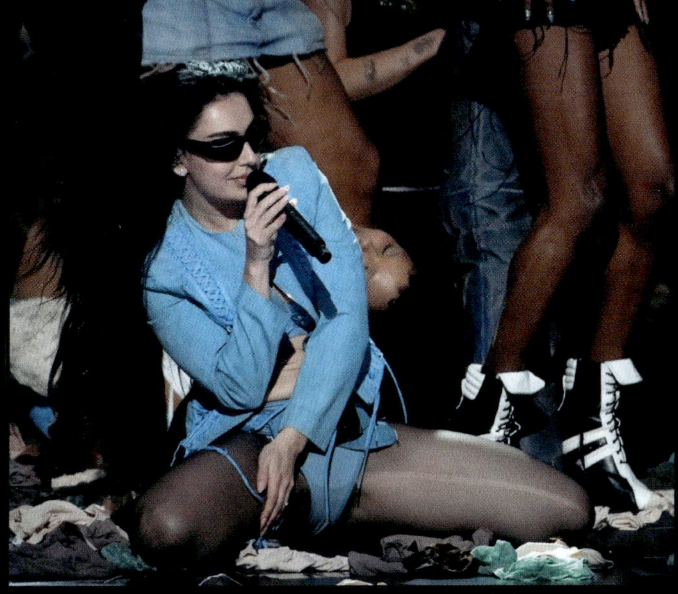

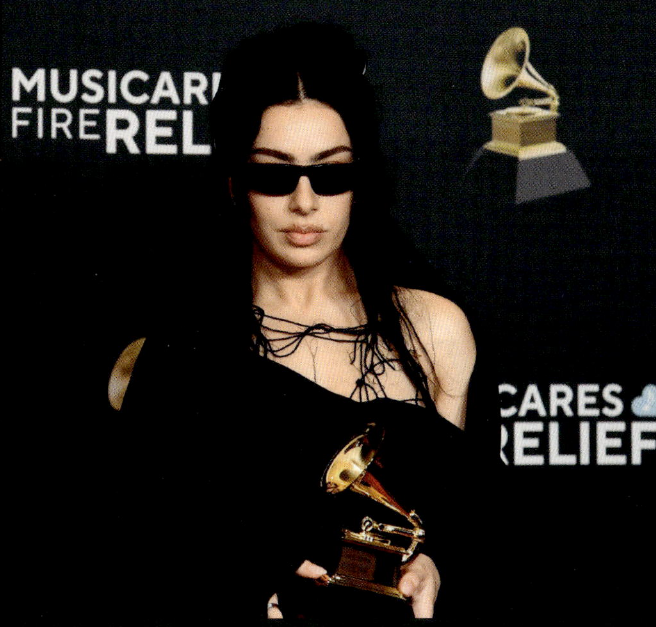

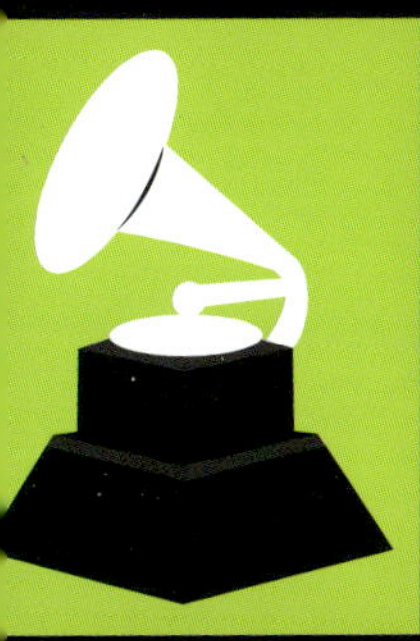

Clockwise from left: At the 67th Annual Grammy Awards, Los Angeles, February 2025

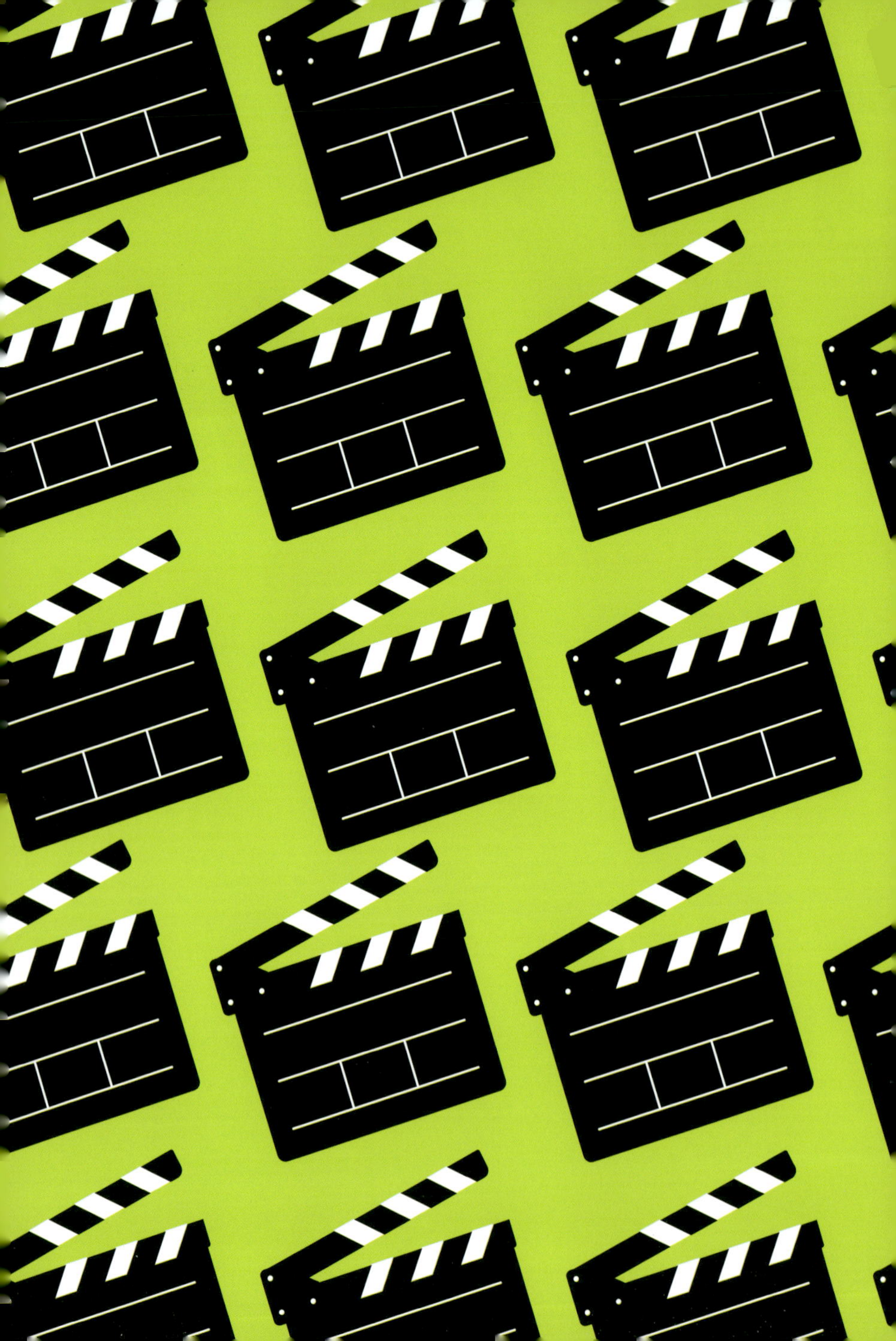

LIGHTS CAMERA *Charli*

What's Next for the Party Girl?

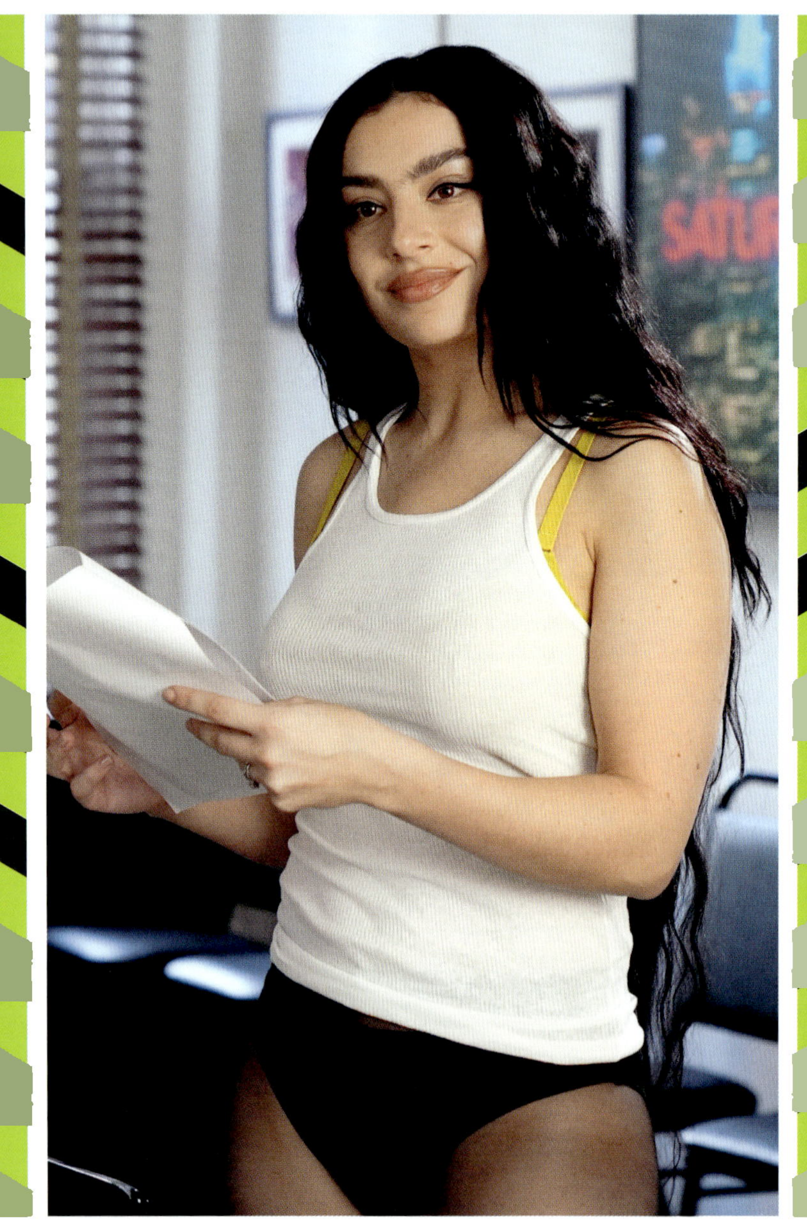

'I think what I'd like to do is achieve a really successful 180 in ten years, like, "I'm a musician, I'm a musician" and then BAM!'

How do you top a cultural reset like *Brat*? Perhaps the best answer is not to try. As summer 2025 approached, Charli was honest about her reluctance to let *Brat* go, her love for the project at odds with the knowledge that all good things must come to an end. With the Sweat tour behind her and just a few more festival dates left in the calendar, the *Brat* era did appear to be coming to a close. On-stage visuals suggested a passing of the baton – to Lorde, Haim or even Turnstile – as guardians of the summer.

But what's really left to accomplish for our 365 Party Girl? 'I think maybe it's going to be no music for a while,' she told Zane Lowe in an interview at the end of 2024, a statement that sent Angels everywhere into a tailspin.

THE MOMENT

So what do we know about the potential for XCX7 and beyond? Charli is contracted to make two records with Atlantic – *Brat* being the first – so there will be at least one more LP in the future, we're just not sure when. For an artist at the peak of her powers, the lure of capitalizing on success with a rapid follow-up release would be hard to resist. Yet, for perhaps the first time ever, Charli seems musically fulfilled, with *Brat*'s God-tier status recognized by both fans and the industry alike.

But the self-confessed workaholic won't be twiddling her thumbs; she's focused on adding even more creative strings to her bow. The long-term cinephile is attached to a whopping nine film and TV projects, flexing her acting and production chops in a big way in 2025 and beyond. If her *Saturday Night Live* hosting debut was any indication, she's got the skills. But whether these will be fully fledged roles or cameos is yet to be seen.

The Moment is one project that's certainly piqued Angels' interest. The upcoming A24 movie is set to be a music industry mockumentary, based on an original idea by Charli herself. 'A rising star navigates the

Guest starring on Saturday Night Live, *November 2024*

complexities of fame and pressure while preparing for her arena tour debut, revealing the transformation of underground culture into mainstream success,' reads the IMDB listing. Sound familiar? Charli will star in the film alongside Alexander Skarsgård, Jamie Demetriou, Rosanna Arquette, Rish Shah and Kate Berlant. It will be directed by Aidan Zamiri – his movie debut – and produced by Charli's brand new production company, Studio365.

Charli has also landed a role in Gregg Araki's upcoming film, I *Want Your Sex* – a major moment for her as a long-time fan of the director. Her admiration dates back to her *True Romanc*e era, when she first fell for his film *The Doom Generation*, and extends to *Smiley Face* (2007), a movie she cites as a key influence on *Brat*'s aesthetic.

In the midst of Brat summer, Charli also found time to sneak off to Poland to film her part in Pete Ohs's feature film, *Erupcja*, which is in post-production at the time of writing. There's also a rumoured part in *Sacrifice*, a re-interpretation of the Joan of Arc story starring Anya Taylor-Joy and Yung Lean, and Cathy Yan's *The Gallerist*, with Jenna Ortega and Natalie Portman.

XCX7

While all these projects feel like more than just a toe-dip into Tinseltown, there have been hints she has not completely abandoned music. After performing 'Sofia' on stage with Clairo at Laneway festival in Melbourne, Charli jumped on TikTok to say how much she'd enjoyed herself. 'And it got me thinking,' she continued, 'What if I made an album with guitars or strings or both? Lou Reed era maybe?'

While she flirted with guitars on *Sucker* – a record she now admits was aiming for what Olivia Rodrigo has since mastered but didn't quite nail – we've never seen an indie-girl version of Charli. Could her next evolution be a boygenius-meets-beabadoobee era of bedroom pop bops?

Charli has mentioned Lou Reed a couple of times in interviews over the last 12 months and even sported a Lou Reed tee at Coachella. Talking to Howard Stern, she shouted out Reed's conversational lyrical style. 'He paints a really specific picture, referencing "Candy" and "Jackie" or "Max's Kansas City",' she said, 'Maybe the listener doesn't always know who he's talking about but you can go and read. That was something inspiring to me on *Brat* – to paint a specific picture about people in my life and places that I go.'

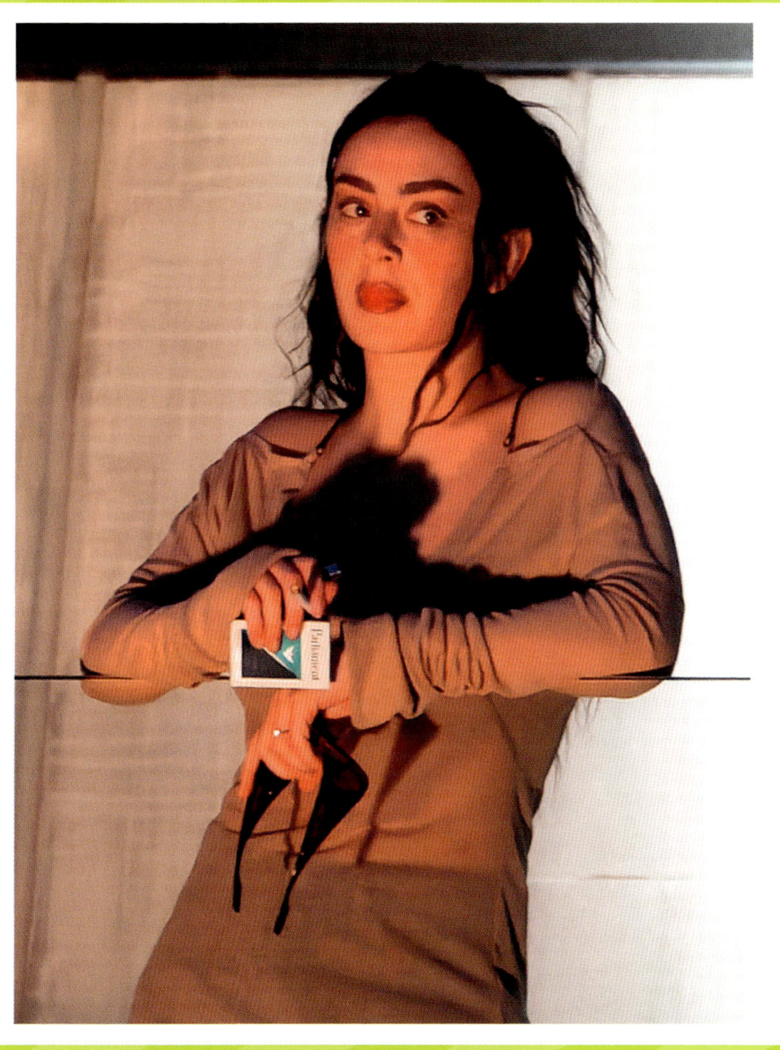

In a conversation with *W* magazine, Charli also shared an appreciation for The Velvet Underground's ability to write songs that are both 'brutal and elegant', qualities that often brush up against each other on *Brat*. But has Reed's influence always been simmering beneath the surface, or should Angels get prepped to take a Walk on the Wild Side for XCX7? Given the intentionality behind everything Charli does, it seems like she's sending a message.

Another hint that the puzzle isn't yet complete might lie in her album artwork. In the *Brat* era, she changed the covers of her past albums to match the *Brat* aesthetic. Fans have been begging her to change them back for some time, but in March 2025 she finally responded via TikTok:

> *I see that you want this and I love that you want this but all I'll say is that on this record, every single thing that I've done, even the tiniest thing, has been for a reason. So all I'm saying is, everything has a purpose and so WHEN this happens, it will be for a reason.*

Could this mean that the *Brat* era has more to give? Or that she's secretly working on XCX7 and the switcheroo will come when the new record drops?

Whatever direction Charli takes next, it's unlikely she'll be treading familiar ground. Whether diving headfirst into Hollywood, working on a musical 180, or disappearing entirely before her next move, her thrill has always been in her unpredictability. *Brat* may have been the culmination of everything she's worked towards, but it's not the final word. If history has taught us anything, it's that Charli is always ten steps ahead – plotting, scheming and laughing at us all in the rearview.

On the steps of the Metropolitan Museum of Art Costume Institute Benefit Gala, New York, May 2025
Overleaf: At Dcode Music Festival, Madrid, September 2017

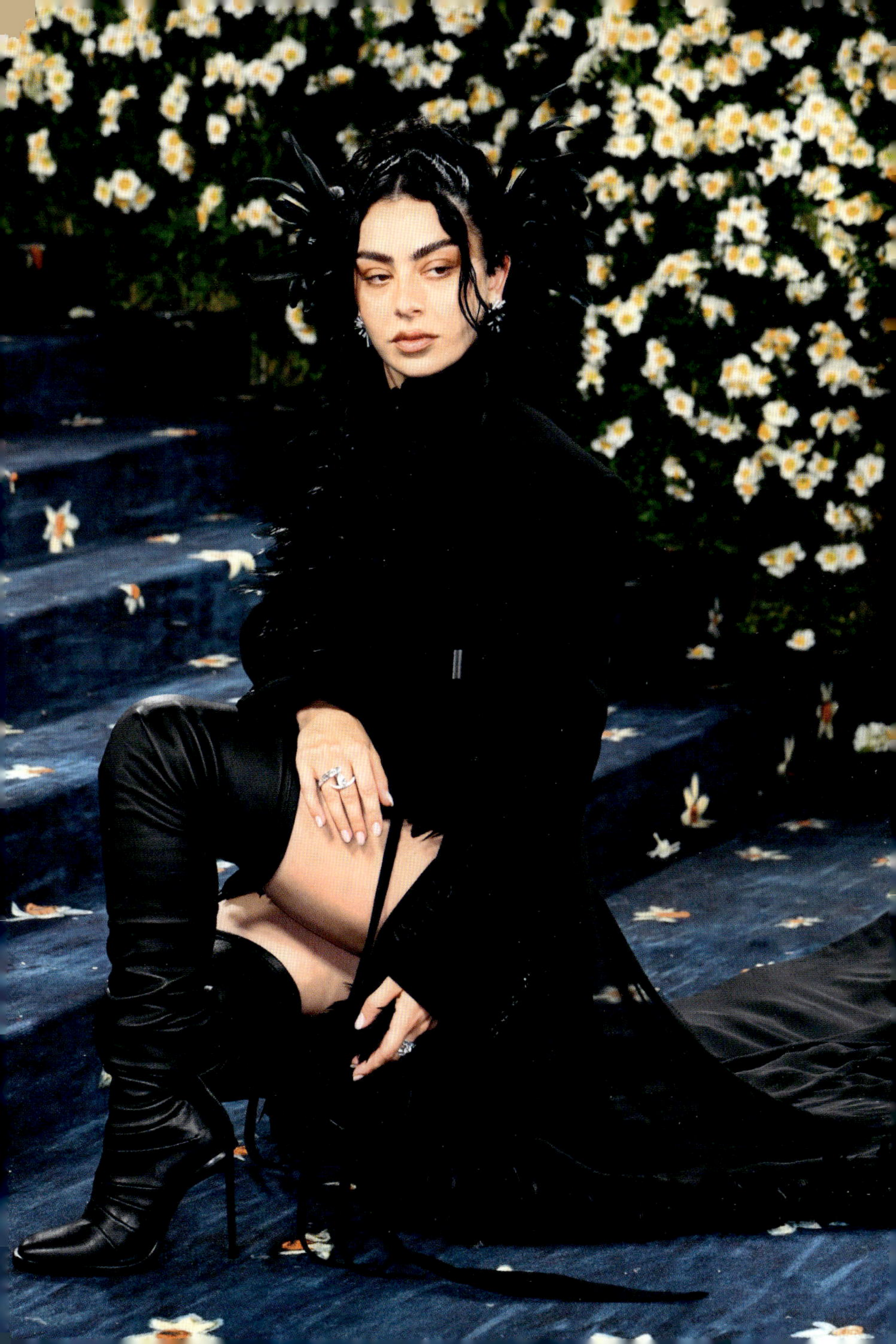

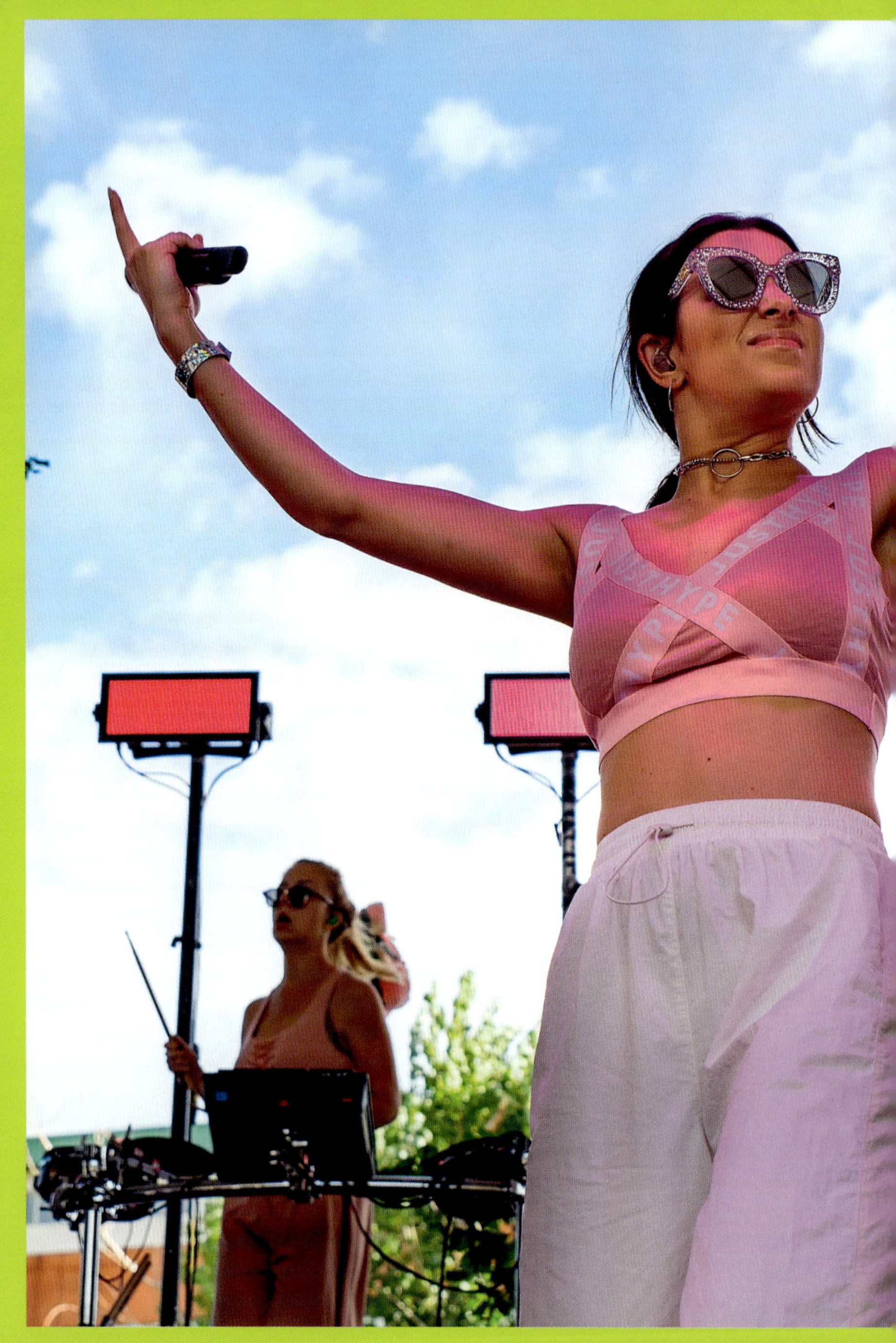
JUSTHYPE

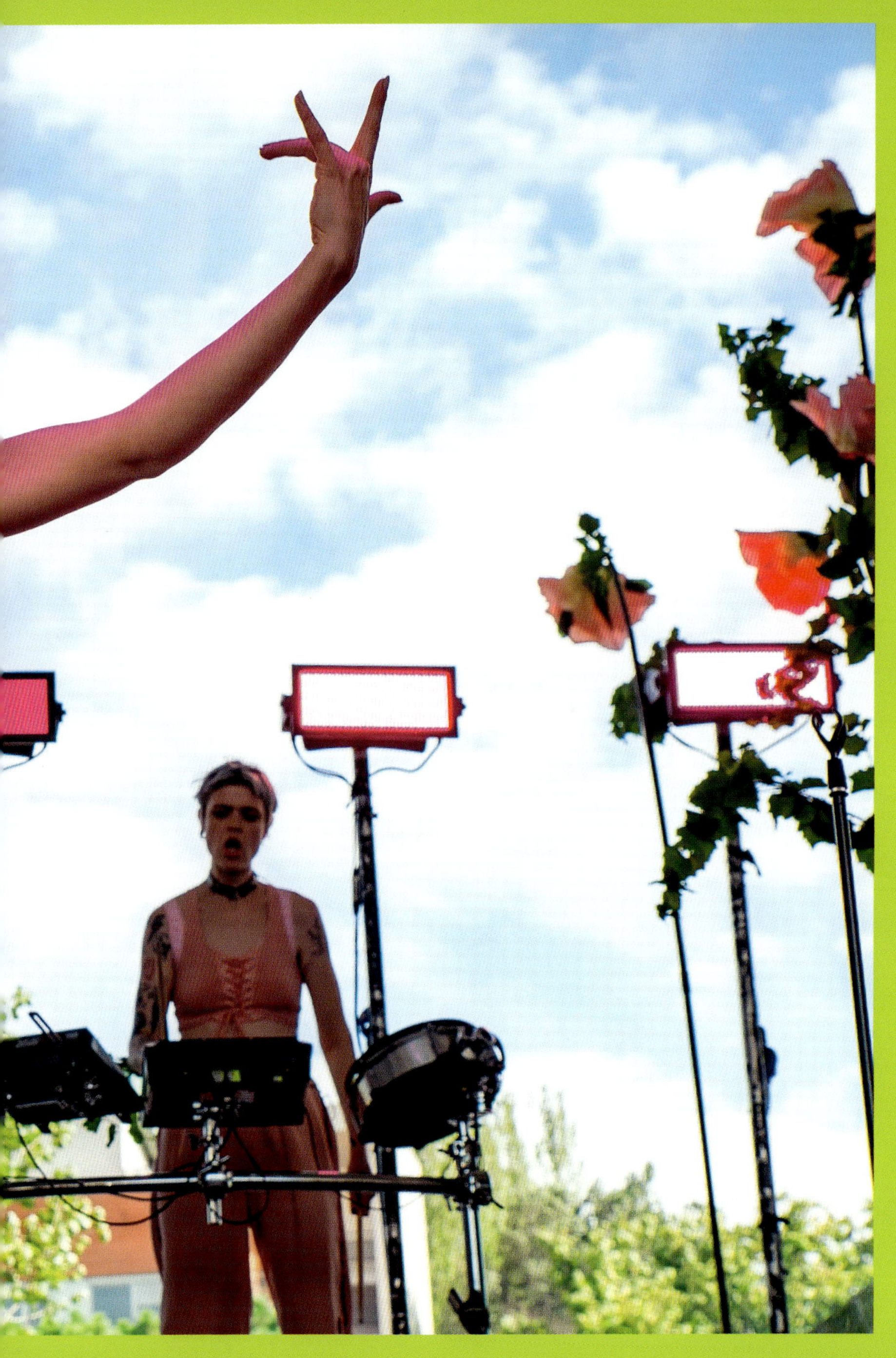

SONG CREDITS

A Young Girl from Essex

Girl, so confusing, featuring Lorde
Written by: A.G. Cook, Charli XCX, Jim-E Stack, Lorde
Year of release: 2024
Record label: Atlantic Records

Feel It
Written by: Jackie Jackson, Jim Dyke, Michael Jackson and Steve Gittelman
Year of release: 1998
Record label: VC Recordings (UK)

Rebel without a Pause

Sucker
Written by: SADPONY, Charli XCX, Justin Raisen
Year of release: 2014
Record label: Atlantic Records

Shifting Gears

Club Classics
Written by: Charli XCX and George Daniel
Year of release: 2024
Record label: Atlantic Records

Trophy
Written by: MNDR, Noonie Bao, Patrik Berger, Charli XCX and SOPHIE
Year of release: 2016
Record label: Vroom Vroom Recordings

Boys
Written by: Ari Leff, Cass Lowe, Emily Warren, Ingrid Andress, Jerker Hansson and Michael Pollack
Year of release: 2017
Record label: Atlantic Records

Next-Level Charli

Gone
Written by: A.G. Cook, Charli XCX, Nömak, Noonie Bao, Lotus IV and Christine and the Queens
Year of release: 2019
Record label: Atlantic Records

Brat Forever

Von Dutch
Written by: Charli XCX and Finn Keane
Year of release: 2024
Record label: Atlantic Records

Club Classics
Written by: Charli XCX and George Daniel
Year of release: 2024
Record label: Atlantic Records

360
Written by: Charli XCX, A.G. Cook, Finn Keane, Cirkut, Blake Slatkin and Omer Fedi
Year of release: 2024
Record label: Atlantic Records

365
Written by: Charli XCX, A.G. Cook, Cirkut, Omer Fedi and Blake Slatkin
Year of release: 2024
Record label: Atlantic Records

Sympathy is a Knife
Written by: Charli XCX, Finn Keane and Jon Shave
Year of release: 2024
Record label: Atlantic Records

Guess, featuring Billie Eilish
Written by: Charli XCX, Dylan Brady, Billie Eilish, FINNEAS and The Dare
Year of release: 2024
Record label: Atlantic Records

REFERENCES

All quotes from social media platforms are accurate, come from official, verified accounts, and are visible online at the time of publication.

A Young Girl from Essex

pp.13, 19, 'I was this half-Indian girl...': Jeff Weiss, 'Charli XCX is too real', *GQ*, 31 May 2024, https://www.gq-magazine.co.uk/article/charli-xcx-interview-2024

p.13, 'When I would go and visit...': Chandreyee Ray, '"I wouldn't have a career without the LGBTQ+ community": Charli XCX on pop culture, heritage and using her voice for good', *Vogue Singapore*, 1 April 2024

p.14, My parents really didn't want me...': Jenn Selby, 'MUSIC: Introducing ... Charli XCX', *Glamour*, 25 April 2013, https://www.glamourmagazine.co.uk/article/charlie-xcx-true-romance-pop-music-interview

p.19, 'geeky', 'kind of a nerd': Dylan Morris, 'Teenage Takeover: Kickin' it With Charli XCX', *Dazed*, 9 January 2009, https://www.dazeddigital.com/music/article/1629/1/teenage-takeover-kickin-it-with-charli-xcx

p.19, 'Whenever I would listen to their music ... Even still...': El Hunt, 'Charli XCX: "I like playing games with pop music. I enjoy poking fun at it"', *NME*, 28 October 2022, https://www.nme.com/big-reads/charli-xcx-cover-interview-2022-crash-3337132

p.21, 'My parents refused to let me go alone...': 'Charli XCX on the making of Boom Clap and Boys: "I wanted to flip the male gaze on its head"', *The Telegraph* on YouTube, 28 September 2017, https://www.youtube.com/watch?v=yVZ1P1r5MAM&t=133s

p.22, 'I like to really involve myself...': Dylan Morris, 'Teenage Takeover: Kickin' it With Charli XCX', *Dazed*, 9 January 2009, https://www.dazeddigital.com/music/article/1629/1/teenage-takeover-kickin-it-with-charli-xcx

p.22, 'When you're 16 and you sign...': Duncan Cooper, 'Shame Less', *Fader*, no.105, August/September 2016, https://www.thefader.com/2016/08/16/charli-xcx-cover-story-interview

p.22, 'I left because I'm not good...': 'Music tip for 2013: Charli XCX interview', *The Guardian* on YouTube, 4 January 2013, https://www.youtube.com/watch?v=FodxZXNY0Fo

p.24, 'I feel like the mixtapes...': Music tip for 2013: Charli XCX interview', *The Guardian* on YouTube, 4 January 2013, https://www.youtube.com/watch?v=FodxZXNY0Fo

p.24, 'a candy-coated hit of molly...': 'Album Review: Charli XCX – Super Ultra Mixtape', *Consequence*, 15 November 2012, https://consequence.net/2012/11/album-review-charli-xcx-super-ultra-mixtape/

The Pop Debut

p.29, 'We only had two hours...': Kate Hutchinson, 'How Charli XCX grafted her way to the cusp of pop stardom', *Guardian*, 30 November 2013, https://www.theguardian.com/music/2013/nov/30/charli-xcx-true-romance

p.29, 'When "I Love It" happened...': Lauretta Charlton, 'Listening Booth: Charli XCX and the "Boys"', *New Yorker*, 3 August 2017, https://www.newyorker.com/culture/listening-booth/charli-xcx-and-the-boys

p.30, 'emotionally direct, bubblegum-catchy...': Marc Hogan, 'True Romance: Charli XCX', *Pitchfork*, https://pitchfork.com/reviews/albums/17880-charli-xcx-true-romance/

p.30, 'surprisingly oddball': Rebecca Nicholson, 'Review: Charli XCX: True Romance', *Guardian*, 11 April 2013, https://www.theguardian.com/music/2013/apr/11/charli-xcx-true-romance-review

p.30, 'I never wanted to be cool...': Lauren Nostro, 'Interview: Charli XCX Talks Debut Album, Internet Haters, and Writing Icona Pop's "I Love It"', *Complex*, 6 March 2013, https://www.complex.com/music/a/lauren-nostro/interview-charli-xcx-talks-debut-album-internet-haters-icona-pop

p.30, 'What was different about me...': Jill Mapes, 'Interview: Charli XCX', *Pitchfork*, 12 November 2014, https://pitchfork.com/features/interview/9542-charli-xcx/

p.33, 'Catchier than the Clap': 'This Week's Fresh Music Top 20', 4Music, 10 August 2014

p.34, 'I'd just had a break-up...': Nick Levine, 'Charli XCX on the formula for twenty-first century popstardom', The Line of Best Fit, 16 February 2015, https://www.thelineofbestfit.com/features/longread/charli-xcx-sucker-interview

Rebel without a Pause

p.43, 'It's not a synth-pop record ... After "I Love It"...': David Renshaw, 'Charli XCX: "Some people are going to hate my new album"', *NME*, 24 May 2014, https://www.nme.com/news/music/charli-xcx-53-1237447

p.44, '*Sucker* isn't an endpoint for Charli...': Jamieson Cox, 'Albums: Sucker', *Pitchfork*, 2014, https://pitchfork.com/reviews/albums/20066-sucker/

p.44, 'For all its failings...': Alexis Petridis, 'Review: Charli XCX: Sucker – Hype and Glory', *Guardian*, 12 February 2015, https://www.theguardian.com/music/2015/feb/12/charli-xcx-sucker-review

p.44, 'It was so interesting working with him...': 'Charli XCX on Her Album Sucker, Rivers Cuomo, Michelle Obama', Audacy on YouTube, 21 November 2014, https://youtu.be/TC_OWipkeR0

p.46, 'I still struggle with my place...': Nick Levine, 'Charli XCX on the formula for twenty-first century popstardom', The Line of Best Fit, 16 February 2015, https://www.thelineofbestfit.com/features/longread/charli-xcx-sucker-interview

p.48, 'I've never opened for a superpop-tastic artist before...': Jack Antonoff, 'Charli XCX Talks to Jack Antonoff about Taking Risks, Katy Perry, and Rising Above the Haters', *Teen Vogue*,

22 May 2015, https://www.teenvogue.com/gallery/charli-xcx-jack-antonoff-interview

p.48, 'It really depends on how I'm feeling...': Jen Ortiz, 'Inside the Life of Charli XCX: Our Branché Cover Star Talks Seeing Music in Color and How She Got That Stage Name', *Marie Claire*, 18 March 2015, https://www.marieclaire.com/celebrity/news/a13738/charli-xcx-branche-spring/

p.52, 'I'm a creative person ...': 'Charli XCX On Her Cancelled US Tour: "I Was In A Really Bad Place"', *NME* on YouTube, 30 August 2015, https://www.youtube.com/watch?v=j1To4XNlr_k

Shifting Gears

p.57, 'It took some people...': Kate Mossman, 'Charli XCX: "Labels are desperate for artists to be liked, otherwise you're bad, evil and wrong"', *Guardian*, 2 June 2024, https://www.theguardian.com/music/article/2024/jun/02/charli-xcx-interview-brat-360-b2b-club-classics-dutch

p.57, 'I couldn't believe that... it was satisfying to finally be...': https://agcook.com/msmsmsm/

p.60, 'Vroom Vroom Recordings is my new... I've worked with SOPHIE on the new EP...': Owen Myers, 'Charli XCX Announces New Label, Previews "Vroom Vroom" Prod. SOPHIE', Fader, 23 February 2016, https://www.thefader.com/2016/02/23/charli-xcx-announces-new-label-previews-vroom-vroom-feat-sophie

p.60, 'few things are as wearying as pop culture...': Laura Snapes, 'Albums: Vroom Vroom EP', *Pitchfork*, 2016, https://pitchfork.com/reviews/albums/21683-vroom-vroom-ep/

p.61, 'XCX Towers, a Vroom Vroom car workshop...': The manifesto is replicated on the following fan blog: https://xcx-world.fandom.com/wiki/Scrapped_third_major-label_album?file=XCXManifesto.webp

p.62, 'you have no idea how...': Charli on X, 24 February 2017, https://x.com/charli_xcx/status/835097831534964737?lang=en

p.62, 'It's just songs that me and AG Cook...': Rhian Daly, 'Charli XCX's "Number 1 Angel" mixtape is more than just a stopgap between records', *NME* (blog), 10 March 2017, https://www.nme.com/blogs/nme-blogs/charli-xcx-number-1-angel-2011045

p.65, 'Partying is sometimes a really important...': Owen Myers, 'Charli XCX Gets Extremely Real About Her Mixtape And New Music', Fader, 12 May 2017, https://www.thefader.com/2017/05/12/charli-xcx-interview-number-1-angel-new-album

p.66, 'It felt like an invasion...': Lizzie Edmonds, 'Charli XCX: When my songs were leaked it felt like my life had been invaded', *Standard*, 27 November 2019, https://www.standard.co.uk/showbiz/celebrity-news/charli-xcx-when-my-songs-were-leaked-it-felt-like-my-life-was-invaded-a4298226.html

p.68, 'Pop 2 does an impressive job...': Alexis Petridis, 'Review: Charli XCX: Pop 2 – kick-ass hits from a parallel universe', *Guardian*, 4 January 2018, https://www.theguardian.com/music/2018/jan/04/charli-xcx-pop-2-review

Next-Level Charli

p.73, 'They've made me more confident...': Nate Jones, The Chorus Girl, Vulture, August 2018, https://www.vulture.com/2018/08/charli-xcxs-path-to-becoming-pops-preeminent-hook-maker.html

p.75, 'angels, my new album...': Charli on X, https://x.com/charli_xcx/status/1139205297707388928?lang=en

p.79, 'It's an unoriginal statement...', 'I didn't set out to make a record...': Salvatore Maicki, 'Charli XCX is making space for the pop music we deserve', Fader, 19 September 2019, https://www.thefader.com/2019/09/19/charli-xcx-album-interview-2019-sky-ferreira-christine-queens

From Lockdown to Lift-Off

p.97, 'I feel true anxiety...': Ben Homewood, 'Sound of lockdown: Charli XCX tells the story of her isolation album', *Music Week*, 23 July 2020, https://www.musicweek.com/interviews/read/sound-of-lockdown-charli-xcx-tells-the-story-of-her-isolation-album/079827

p.98, 'I'm going to be sharing...', 'I'm going to be sharing demos...': These Zoom calls are part of the BBC documentary 'Alone Together', which is available online on BBC iPlayer, https://www.bbc.co.uk/programmes/m0018m7h

p.103, 'I can't believe *How I'm Feeling Now*...': Ben Homewood, 'Sound of lockdown: Charli XCX tells the story of her isolation album', *Music Week*, 23 July 2020, https://www.musicweek.com/interviews/read/sound-of-lockdown-charli-xcx-tells-the-story-of-her-isolation-album/079827

p.104, 'to watch the full moon': transgressivehq on Instagram, https://www.instagram.com/p/CKqxg2AnyLY/

p.104, 'It's really hard for me to sum up...': Charli on X, https://x.com/charli_xcx/status/1356643095903752193

p.109, 'I feel like all my previous...': 'Charli XCX: "CRASH," Legacy of SOPHIE, and Major Label Record Decisions', Apple Music on YouTube, 17 March 2022, https://www.youtube.com/watch?v=61409OxvOEg

Brat Forever

p.117, 'I need an artist to create...': subwaytakes on Instagram, https://www.instagram.com/subwaytakes/reel/C3-iCCDuo6K/?hl=en-gb

p.117, 'On March 16, 2022, I texted...': Kristin Robinson, '"BRAT" UNFILTERED: CHARLI XCX ON HOW SHE STOLE THE SUMMER (AND WORKED IT OUT WITH LORDE ON THE REMIX)', *Billboard*, 17 July 2024, https://www.billboard.com/music/pop/charli-xcx-brat-billboard-cover-story-interview-1235732025/

p.117, 'The artwork for "Brat" will be... There is no explanation...': Pop Crave on X, https://x.com/PopCrave/status/1873507707417968876?ref_src=twsrc%5Etfw%7Ctwcamp%5Etweetembed%7Ctwterm%5E1873507707417968876%7Ctwgr%5Eaf316d951235b01be42001a7d216b957c9eeba73%7Ctwcon%5Es1_&ref_url=https%3A%2F%2Fwww.nme.com%2Fnews%2Fmusic%2Fcharli-xcx-shares-brat-manifesto-from-2023-we-must-cultivate-chaos-desire-and-destruction-3825246

p.121, 'Historic moment in the Charli verse...': charli_xcx on Instagram, https://www.instagram.com/p/C3tcGMzO8vS/

p.125, 'someone who is really really special to me...': 'Charli XCX Performs "So I" | *Billboard* Women In Music 2024', Billboard on YouTube, 8 March 2024, https://www.youtube.com/watch?v=UdZRDY3AT74

p.127, '*Brat* sounds bitchy...': 'Session 21: Charli XCX | Therapuss with Jake Shane', Jake Shane on YouTube, 16 May 2024, https://www.youtube.com/watch?v=5AAS7Ok9EiQ&pp=0gcJCdgAo7VqN5tD

p.130, 'Even when I'm being an absolute nightmare...': charli_xcx on Instagram, https://www.instagram.com/charli_xcx/p/C77frc7gy_y/?hl=en

p.130, 'a masterpiece': Laura Snapes, 'Review: Charli XCX: Brat – insecurity-obliterating anthems by pop's most human superstar', *Guardian*, 6 June 2024, https://www.theguardian.com/music/article/2024/jun/06/charli-xcx-brat-review-insecurity-obliterating-anthems-by-pops-most-human-superstar

p.130, 'This is an album that walks...': Rhian Daly, 'Charli XCX – 'Brat' review: her most introspective work yet', *The Forty-Five*, 6 June 2024, https://thefortyfive.com/opinion/reviews/charli-xcx-brat-review-her-most-introspective-work-yet/

p.133, 'how to have a Brat summer': Alexandria Dale, 'Everything you need to know – and shop – for a brat girl summer', *Cosmopolitan*, 27 June 2024, https://www.cosmopolitan.com/uk/fashion/celebrity/a61434266/brat-girl-summer/

p.134, 'Kamala IS Brat': Charli on X, https://x.com/charli_xcx/status/1815182384066707861?lang=en

p.138, 'It's obviously a sandwich bag...': charlixcx on TikTok, https://www.tiktok.com/@charlixcx/video/7372651999159930144?lang=en

p.140, 'I feel like dance music, electronic music...': 'Charli XCX Wins Dance Act | The BRIT Awards 2025', BRITs on YouTube, 1 March 2025, https://www.youtube.com/watch?v=1Ua-YX-Q7Ru0

Lights, Camera, Charli

p.149, 'I think what I'd like to do...': Hannah Mylrea, 'The Big Read – Charli XCX: "People think I'm this person who parties every single day – but I'm a business woman"', *NME*, 15 November 2019, https://www.nme.com/big-reads/big-read-charli-xcx-interview-2019-nme-cover-nasty-cherry-netflix-2575260

p.149, 'I think maybe it's going to be no music...': 'Charli xcx: The BRAT Interview', Apple Music on YouTube, 8 October 2024, https://www.youtube.com/watch?v=LgBMFg7ZgJw

p.150, 'A rising star navigates...': 'The Moment', IMDb, https://www.imdb.com/title/tt35524793/

p.150, 'He paints a really specific picture...': 'Howard Stern Charli XCX full interview – Touring, Remix Album and being brat 10/2/24', cult classic on YouTube, 13 October 2024, https://www.youtube.com/watch?v=LuzaUO_HNjA

p.152, 'brutal and elegant': 'Charli xcx On Her First Kiss & Grammys Plans', *W Magazine* on YouTube, 31 January 2025, https://www.youtube.com/watch?v=QxLi6S-s8Og

p.152, 'I see that you want this...': charlixcx on TikTok, https://www.tiktok.com/@charlixcx/video/7478668670005267734?lang=en

First published in Great Britain in 2025
by Greenfinch
An imprint of Quercus
Part of John Murray Group

A CIP catalogue record for this book is available from the British Library

HB ISBN 978-1-52944-693-7
EBOOK ISBN 978-1-52944-694-4

10 9 8 7 6 5 4 3 2 1

Design and Illustration by Beth Free, Studio Nic + Lou
Printed and bound in Italy by L.E.G.O. S.p.A.

Papers used by Quercus are from well-managed forests and other responsible sources.

Quercus
Carmelite House
50 Victoria Embankment
London EC4Y 0DZ

John Murray Group
Part of Hodder & Stoughton Limited
An Hachette UK company

The authorised representative in the EEA is Hachette Ireland, 8 Castlecourt Centre, Dublin 15, D15 XTP3, Ireland (email: info@hbgi.ie)

THANK YOU

Thanks to my 365 party girls Jo, Lisa, Raz, Katie, El and Millie for making every Charli moment so unbelievably fun. And to Matty – the George to my Charli – for listening to me whine like a little baby brat about writing this book.

Charlotte Gunn is a British music and culture writer. Formerly the Editor of *NME*, Charlotte went on to launch *The Forty-Five* – a music publication with a focus on championing female and non-binary artists. As a journalist, Charlotte has interviewed artists such as Madonna, Haim, Phoebe Bridgers and Chappell Roan. Her writing has been published in publications including *NME*, *Rolling Stone*, *The Face*, *Consequence of Sound* and *Wallpaper**. She has reported from music and culture events across the globe, sits on the judging panel for the annual BRIT Awards and is a regular critic on *Times* and BBC Radio.

PHOTOGRAPHIC CREDITS

pp.2, 123 below Sipa US/Alamy Stock Photo; pp.4, 84 left, 88 Abaca Press/Alamy Stock Photo; pp.8–9, 31, 32, 36 below, 45, 46–7, 49, 56, 69, 142–3, 144, 145 above, 145 below Associated Press/Alamy Stock Photo; p.12 David Jensen/Alamy Stock Photo; p.15 Featureflash Photo Agency/Shutterstock; pp.16, 113 above, 153 PA Images/Alamy Stock Photo; p.17 above Pictorial Press Ltd/Alamy Stock Photo; p.17 below Cinematic/Alamy Stock Photo; p.18 commonlight/Alamy Stock Photo; p.21 left Edd Westmacott/Alamy Stock Photo; pp.21 right, 34–5, 39, 50, 51 above, 66–7 WENN Rights Ltd/Alamy Stock Photo; p.23 Andy Sheppard/Getty Images; p.25 Suzan Moore/Alamy Stock Photo; pp.28, 77, 92 ZUMA Press, Inc./Alamy Stock Photo; p.36 above Doug Peters/Alamy Stock Photo; p.37 Richard Gray/Alamy Stock Photo; p.42 Robert Stainforth/Alamy Stock Photo; p.51 below UPI/Alamy Stock Photo; pp.52–3 Mark Horton/Getty Images; pp.59, 132 Joseph Okpako/Getty Images; pp.61, 154–5 Christian Bertrand/Alamy Stock Photo; pp.63, 84 right, 87 MediaPunch Inc./Alamy Stock Photo; p.64 Randy Holmes/Getty Images; p.72 Scott Dudelson/Getty Images; pp.74–5 Gareth Cattermole/TAS18/Getty Images; p.79 John Phillips/Getty Images; pp.80–1 Joe Okpako/Alamy Stock Photo; pp.84 centre, 89 TT News Agency/Alamy Stock Photo; p.86 Joe Maher/Getty Images; p.90 Sam Oaksey/Alamy Stock Photo; p.91 Bertrand Rindoff Petroff/Getty Images; p.93 Foc Kan/Getty Images; p.96 Marc Grimwade/Getty Images; pp.99, 100, 101 above, 101 below Everett Collection Inc./Alamy Stock Photo; p.105 Matt Winkelmeyer/Getty Images; p.107 Dave Benett/Getty Images; p.108 Rich Fury/Getty Images; p.111 JEP Live Music/Alamy Stock Photo; pp.112, 116, 148 NBC/Getty Images; p.113 below AFF/Alamy Stock Photo; p.120 WWD/Getty Images; pp.122, 123 above Howard Weiss/Shutterstock; p.125 JMEnternational/Getty Images; p.126 Imagespace/Alamy Stock Photo; pp.128–9 Rich Fury/MSG/Getty Images; p.135 Christopher Polk/Getty Images; p.136 Benjamin Cremel/Getty Images; p.137 The Washington Post/Getty Images; p.139 Katja Ogrin/Getty Images; p.141 Imago/Alamy Stock Photo; p.151 Mr Pics/Alamy Stock Photo

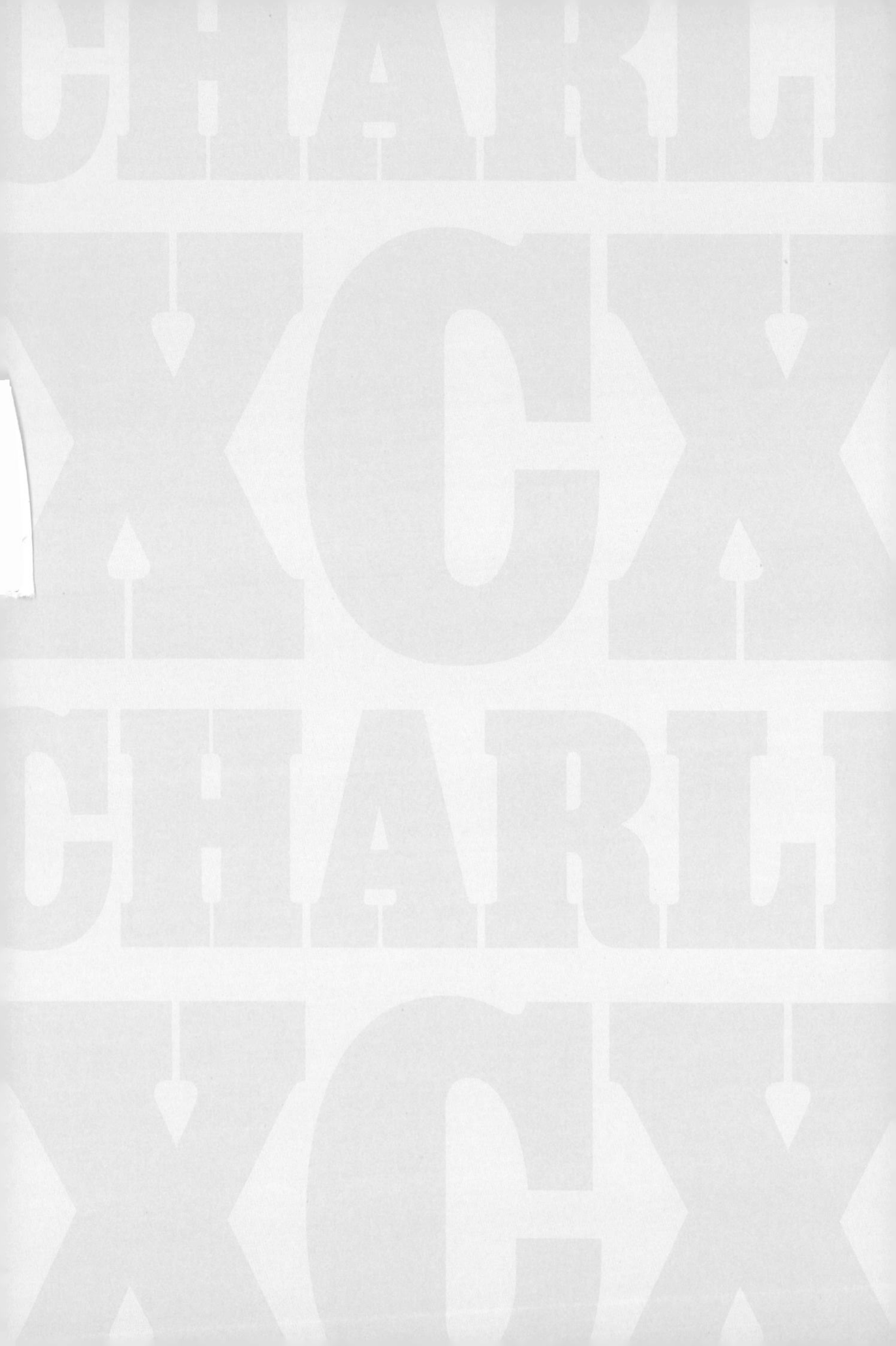